Internationalizing Teacher Education in the United States

Internationalizing Teacher Education in the United States

Edited by Beverly D. Shaklee
and Supriya Baily

ROWMAN & LITTLEFIELD PUBLISHERS, INC.
Lanham • Boulder • New York • Toronto • Plymouth, UK

Published by Rowman & Littlefield Publishers, Inc.
A wholly owned subsidiary of The Rowman & Littlefield Publishing Group, Inc.
4501 Forbes Boulevard, Suite 200, Lanham, Maryland 20706
http://www.rowmanlittlefield.com

Estover Road, Plymouth PL6 7PY, United Kingdom

Copyright © 2012 by Rowman & Littlefield Publishers, Inc.

All rights reserved. No part of this book may be reproduced in any form or by any electronic or mechanical means, including information storage and retrieval systems, without written permission from the publisher, except by a reviewer who may quote passages in a review.

British Library Cataloguing in Publication Information Available

Library of Congress Cataloging-in-Publication Data

Internationalizing teacher education in the United States / edited by Beverly D. Shaklee and Supriya Baily.
  p. cm.
  Includes index.
  Summary: "This book addresses the role of internationalization as conceptual framework for U.S. teacher education in a time of globalization. The authors especially believe that it is helpful for new teachers to have a strong foundation in order to ensure that the students that they work with will be better prepared for an increasingly interdependent world" — Provided by publisher.
  ISBN 978-1-4422-1248-0 (hardback) — ISBN 978-1-4422-1250-3 (electronic)
  1. Teachers—Training of—United States. 2. Multicultural education—United States. 3. International education—United States. 4. International education—Curricula—United States. 5. Education—Aims and objectives—United States.
  I. Shaklee, Beverly D., 1950– II. Baily, Supriya, 1973–
  LB1715.I64 2012
  370.71'10973—dc23   2011045690

∞™ The paper used in this publication meets the minimum requirements of American National Standard for Information Sciences—Permanence of Paper for Printed Library Materials, ANSI/NISO Z39.48-1992.

Printed in the United States of America

Contents

Acknowledgments   vii

Introduction. A Framework for Internationalizing Teacher Preparation   1
Beverly D. Shaklee and Supriya Baily

Section 1. Preparations for Teaching International Populations: What Are the Knowledge, Skills, and Attitudes?
15

1. A Comparison of K–12 Multicultural and International Education in the United States   17
   Natasha G. Kolar

2. Intercultural Competence for Teaching and Learning   41
   Kenneth Cushner

3. The Critical Role of Language in International Classrooms   59
   Rebecca K. Fox

4. One Size Fits All: Balancing Internationalization and Standardization of the U.S. Education System   77
   Laura C. Engel and Kate Olden

5. Global Perspectives on the Internationalization of Teacher Education: Through an Australian Lens   93
   Libby Tudball

Section 2. Areas of Complexity and Confluence: Questions Still to Be Answered in U.S. Schools and Teacher Education
113

6. Engaging Teachers in Building Relationships with International Families — 115
   Monimalika Day

7. Redefining Vulnerability in American Schools: Reaching and Teaching Students after International Crises — 139
   Supriya Baily

8. Understanding Secondary Models for Advanced Programs in the United States — 155
   Kimberley Daly

9. STEM Disciplines and World Languages: Influences from an International Teacher Exchange — 175
   Wendy M. Frazier, Rebecca K. Fox, and Margret A. Hjalmarson

10. Pedagogical Diversity and the Need for Contextually Responsive Teacher Education in the United States — 205
    Rachel Grant and Maryam Salahshoor

11. Expanding Horizons through Technology for Teachers and Students — 221
    Debra Sprague

Section 3. Concluding Thoughts: Developing Opportunities to Internationalize Teacher Education
237
Beverly D. Shaklee

Index — 253
About the Contributors — 259

Acknowledgments

We would like to acknowledge the contributions of all of our authors, both their work and their expertise. Without them this book would be just an idea rather than the reality that it is. Our thanks to our editor, Patti Belcher, and her team at Rowman & Littlefield, who contributed their expertise from the beginning, culminating with this final product. Also we would like to recognize those researchers whose work has formed the historical foundations of international education and who have continually encouraged a worldview of teacher education.

Finally to our respective families, their support, patience, and willingness to "let us write" was instrumental to the success of this effort.

Introduction

A Framework for Internationalizing Teacher Preparation

Beverly D. Shaklee and Supriya Baily

*D*uring the last ten years, there have been mounting calls to engage teacher education programs to address the needs of an increasingly interdependent and global world (Tye, 1999; Kissock & Richardson, 2009). While numerous authors have recommended that preservice teachers study abroad, embrace global perspectives (Kissock & Richardson, 2009), and apply international pedagogies to classroom practice (Reagan, 2005), only a small percentage of teacher education programs have sought to incorporate a global curriculum for new teachers (Tye, 1999). Yet globalization continues to march on, and as students in countries such as China and India are hungry to compete on a world stage, we limit the potential opportunities for U.S. teachers and subsequently students when we are not able to prepare them to understand the shifting political, economic, and social landscapes that are dominating this increasingly shrinking world.

While the focus on globalization has gained ground in education circles, the emphasis on teacher preparation as a way to address it has been a more recent development. Increasingly, critiques suggest that schools of education and teacher preparation programs are unable to connect to the rapidly shifting needs of U.S. students (Levine, 2006). Yet these institutions play a vital role in teacher preparation. Recognizing the relative influence and importance of these institutions, the United Nations highlighted,

> Institutions of teacher education fulfill vital roles in the global education community; they have the potential to bring changes within educational systems that will shape the knowledge and skills of future generations. Often, education is described as the great hope for creating a more

sustainable future; teacher-education institutions serve as key change agents in transforming education and society, so such a future is possible. (UNESCO, 2005, p. 12)

With all these different tensions and expectations for teacher preparation programs, this book addresses the role of internationalization as a conceptual framework for U.S. teacher education in a time of globalization. Though we would argue that all teachers should be more cognizant of international education, we especially believe that it is helpful for new teachers to have a strong foundation in order to ensure that the students they work with will be better prepared for an increasingly interdependent world. The vagaries of globalization will continue to evolve—but our argument, developed through an exploration into teacher education curricula, charges that international education will provide a framework for teachers to prepare their students for these changes. Further, the work of internationalizing U.S. teacher preparation programs is already late to the discussion, creating a dichotomy between teachers and students.

CONCEPTUAL FRAMEWORK

The migration of people has brought more foreign-born students to schools, and while the story of the United States has always been one of immigration, the movement of people has changed. In years past, waves of immigrants would come to neighborhoods dominated by people of the same ethnic, national, or cultural background and then move to suburban neighborhoods as their socioeconomic status improved. What has changed in the twenty-first century is that there is a greater melding of different groups and movement to a variety of environments beyond the three or four common urban destinations popular to immigrants in the past. Singer, Hardwick, and Bretell (2009) studied the trends of immigration to new "gateway" cities and found that "in 2005 nearly 96 percent of all immigrants lived in a city or suburb within a metropolitan area" (p. 7). Until the 1990s, 46 percent of immigrants lived primarily in New York, Los Angeles, Miami, and Chicago. By 2005 only 37 percent of immigrants were moving to these cities (Singer et al., 2009, p. 7). This dip shows that migration to traditional destinations for the commonality of experience and culture is changing. People are choosing to spread out and build new lives in locations that were not often seen as hubs of immigration, including cities such as Atlanta, Austin, Charlotte, Minneapolis-St. Paul, Phoenix, Portland, Sacramento, and Washington, D.C. This has offered new challenges to communities that in past years had not seen the growth of international populations in their schools.

Communities that are seeking to integrate new members from other countries face a series of shifting challenges in comparison to the migration of prior generations of immigrants. For instance, the patterns of residence of foreign born are altering, and a growing number of immigrants and refugees are living in suburban areas. Suburban communities have mixed attitudes and perceptions toward immigrant and refugee newcomers than were present in prior generations when immigrants settled primarily in urban communities. The official response to new immigrant flows and attempts to "manage" immigration locally has been challenged in recent times, as we can see with the changing laws in Arizona or Virginia on undocumented immigrants. Finally, the "role of social, political, and ethnic networks in migrant decision making as shown in patterns of settlement, identity retention, and processes of adjustment" (Singer et al., 2009, p. 17) have been altered as well.

What might be different today is that people are not necessarily coming from one country or culture. Whereas in the history of the United States, there have been movements of people from Ireland, China, or the Scandinavian countries, today people are coming from far more diverse places. Yet lack of global awareness on the part of Americans leads us to group people into larger categories, without a clear understanding of the nuances of culture. For example, the grouping of all people under the category of Asian fails to account for the fact that we have immigrants from China, Korea, Vietnam, Cambodia, and Laos. People from India, Pakistan, Sri Lanka, and other South Asian countries are also usually grouped together, but their histories, cultures, religions, and identities are impossible to systematize. Common misperceptions such as that all Asian students are alike and all are good at mathematics proliferate in education. Saying this, the burden on teachers becomes much harder. Layering upon the already troubled nature of some schools, the complexity of immigration, the tensions that arise with students of multiple countries, perspectives, attitudes, and experiences, hampers teachers' ability to teach effectively. This leaves teachers struggling to cope with this intercultural and international student body. We do not expect teachers to know every capital of every country or every cultural or national holiday. But relying on the argument that comprehensive understanding of all children is impractical and international understanding too complex prevents teacher preparation from moving toward understanding how to react and interact in this global environment. The goal of this book is to address the practical application of pedagogy, practice, and policies of education that will make teachers better equipped for this far more heterogeneous and international student body.

Who Are the Teachers?

The Department of Education estimated that by 2013, one million new teachers will enter U.S. schools (Hull, 2003). As we reach that ten-year mark, we are still seeing challenges that encompass high levels of turnover, rapid rates of retirement, and a seeming disconnect between the skills teachers need and those provided to them by colleges of education (Hull, 2003). Teacher preparation programs will need to focus on the changing ways to increase the dispositions of good teachers in the twenty-first century, including relationship building and movement away from "scripted curriculum, test prep manuals and one day trainings" (Duncan-Andrade, 2009, p. 452). This becomes more complex when the school student populations look, sound, and have dramatically different experiences from the teacher population. This is something to be especially cognizant of when success in teaching depends, in part, on building strong relationships between students and teachers.

With people moving with their children across and around the globe for various reasons and "from many different national and cultural backgrounds . . . individuals, commercial organizations, educational organizations, and national systems grow increasingly reliant on interaction with those in other parts of the globe, and understanding of what it means to be 'international' becomes ever-more relevant to increasing numbers of individuals worldwide" (Hayden, Rancic, & Thompson, 2000, p. 120). Yet the U.S. teacher population has been largely homogenous, where 88 to 90 percent of teachers, 75 percent of whom are female, descended from European origins, primarily based in a middle-class economic frame, and fewer than 10 percent have fluency in another language besides English. Most teachers live away from the communities in which they teach, making the cultural understandings less clear between teachers and students (Cushner, McClelland, & Safford, 2009). Additionally, the average age of teachers in the United States is forty-three years old, and the National Education Association has noted that the teaching corps in public schools does not reflect the diversity of the student population (National Education Association, 2010).

Who Are the Students?

The teaching force might be more homogenous, but the student population is vastly diverse, coming from homes where language, culture, customs, and other social and economic markers define the spectrum of human difference. In a school population where more than forty-nine million students are being served by the public school system, 22 percent of students in U.S. schools have at least one foreign-born parent, and 6 percent of students are themselves foreign born (U.S. Department of Education, 2008). Schools "should reflect—and reflect upon—the cultural and socio-economic realities of the communities of which they form an essential part" (Suarez-Orozco & Sattin, 2007, p. 2). Yet American schools are based on a nineteenth-century model developed with a monocultural focus. With the dramatically different school populations today, there has been a rapid rise in the number of students coming from other parts of the world. In the four-year span from 2006 to 2010, the number of children in American schools who have immigrated here has risen from one in five in 2006 to one in three in 2010, coming from countries as different as India, the Philippines, China, and El Salvador (U.S. Department of Education, 2008).

English language proficiency continues to be a major concern for policy makers and school districts when they think about new student needs, and while more than four hundred languages are represented in schools in the United States, research shows that one in nine students between Pre-K and twelfth grade requires assistance with English proficiency (Educational Testing Services, 2009). Languages in the schools represent those languages that are spoken both outside the United States (e.g., Asian, European, and African languages) and inside the United States (Native American languages). Nearly 80 percent of limited English proficiency (LEP) students speak Spanish; another 5 percent speak an Asian language. The number of K–12 students in the United States who are identified as being LEP has grown by nearly 650,000 in the past three years and is now approximately 4,985,000 (U.S. Department of Education, 2008). Another way to see the impact of these changes is to look at the immigration patterns of children, which show that between 1970 and 2000, immigrant children in U.S. schools more than tripled, moving from 6 percent to approximately 20 percent. Jaffe-Walter (2008) found that the majority of these youths are English language learners, and 94 percent of these children will reside in urban neighborhoods with the least well-qualified teachers and the lowest per-pupil funding rates.

INTERNATIONALIZING EDUCATION

International education has been defined from a variety of perspectives, and not all are in agreement with one another. Haywood (2007) contends that it is a complicated, messy configuration of "political astuteness, communication skills across languages, elements of multicultural understanding, global awareness and responsibilities involved with national and global citizenship" (p. 79). Others have focused on the pedagogical and skills-based future that students are growing up in, where it is considered the "intentional preparation of American students to be contributing citizens, productive workers, and competent leaders in the interconnected world of the 21st century" (Asia Society, 2010). Murphy (2000) has said that it is time to give up on a simple definition and simply recognize that we all hold differing views of international education.

The theoretical definitions may shift from scholar to scholar, but there are alternative approaches focused on qualities of an internationally minded person. Hill talks of using international education to bring students, teachers, and scholars from different nations together to exhibit a sense of awareness on global issues. Doing so creates an "international-minded person," and becoming internationally minded is the core value of international education (2007).

To be internationally minded would be to present a "curriculum [that] emphasizes studies in world history and literature, world cultures, stressing the interdependence of nationals and peoples, and de-emphasizing the study of such topics from the perspective of only one country or of a select region. Secondly, its ethical aim is actively to espouse and uphold certain universal values and to make them an integral part of the life of the schools, its community and particularly the children in its care" (Hill, as cited in Gellar, 2006, p. 31). In order to do this, frameworks such as Snowball's (2007) that highlight the qualities of an internationally minded teacher would need to be addressed by teacher education. For instance, Snowball (2007) characterizes an internationally minded educator as one who manifests:

1. An understanding of the international context of education, appreciating both the unique profile of each school and the diversity amongst education systems, as well as roles played by major educational organizations, regionally and globally;
2. A value for students' multilingual abilities and demonstrates understanding of the processes involved in language acquisition and development in the first and subsequent languages;
3. The employment of strategies that facilitate the academic achievement of students from diverse cultural groups;
4. Familiarity with international student characteristics, including stage theories of development, age-level characteristics, and student variability in learning; and
5. Sensitivity to the difficulties transition can cause and, in addition to handling personal stresses effectively, is skilled in supporting parents and students.

These qualities cannot be developed in one course and with the guidance of one teacher educator. For teachers to develop these skills, the onus of responsibility lies with schools of education and teacher educators.

WHY INTERNATIONALIZE TEACHER EDUCATION?

Our work with preservice and in-service teachers for over twenty-five years leads us to believe that it is important to try to identify the elements of an international educator and be more proactive about engaging teacher education programs to develop these qualities. The elements of international educators include what Merryfield (2001) calls the "globally competent teacher educator" who manifests "cross-cultural experiences, knowledge of diverse cultures, and an understanding of globalization, perceptual, interpersonal, and communication skills that enhance their abilities to work with and learn from people different from themselves and certain shared beliefs and values that support diversity, equity and global interconnectedness" (Merryfield, 2001, p. 2). The twenty-first century requires that students are able to understand what is needed to work in a globalized environment (Trilling & Fadel, 2009) and that outcomes for students stress global awareness. This global awareness highlights the themes of international mindedness where students are expected to work in collaboration and with respect to other cultures, nationalities, lifestyles, and religions (Partnership for 21st Century Skills, 2009). The call is clear, but learning for the twenty-first century and engaging in a global perspective cannot happen if our teacher education programs are stuck in the past.

Levy (2007) in his analysis of preservice and in-service teacher preparation programs in the United States commented, "Despite the influence of globalization, teachers who are prepared for multicultural settings normally focus on diverse domestic student populations, which may include some students who have recently immigrated . . . it is not clear how the knowledge and skills used with diverse national students would apply" (p. 217). Internationalizing teacher education allows for a more complete and holistic picture of the influences affecting student learning, including political, cultural, economic, and other factors. Teacher educators and teachers require more systematic curricula and better deconstruction of the issues affecting international mindedness and globalization before it can be infused and supported in teacher education programs.

Some schools of education have tried to use their platform to prepare teachers to understand these complexities through the offering of multiculturalism and cultural competency courses. Social justice has also become a lightening rod under which teacher education programs have tried to address these issues with teachers, but critiques have shown that such efforts are largely rhetorical in nature and often succumb to the demands of political pressure where the primary emphasis on teacher educators is to prepare teachers to substantially improve K–12 academic achievement as proven through standardized testing (McDonald & Zeichner, 2009). Yet such courses are often far from helpful, especially in light of the dramatic shifts in populations and the piecemeal efforts that are strongly dependent on a teacher's natural tendencies to appreciate or be open-minded to such endeavors. While a natural disposition or openness to working with the new student populations is desirable, it should not preclude formal preparation to teach effectively. As noted, Singer et al.'s (2009) research on migration indicates a far more complex set of variables affecting international families as well as influencing student learning and engagement in the classroom community. These variables need to be visible parts of teacher education.

The National Research Council highlighted three implications for teaching when it comes to helping students learn, and these implications apply to the context of internationalizing teacher education as well. First, research findings document that teachers must work with the preexisting understandings students bring with them if they are to be successful. Second, there must be a level of depth that provides for better coverage of the material. Finally, a metacognitive topic such as internationalization must be integrated across the curriculum rather than in one specific subject (National Research Council, 2000). As the bellwether for teaching children, this model is unfortunately not being replicated in how teacher preparation programs work with their students in preparing them for a global and interconnected world.

Teacher education programs dance around the ideas of internationalization that are encapsulated into themes like social justice, culturally responsive teaching, global citizens, and democratic classrooms. Critiques have noted the use of language that supports these ideas, but there is limited practice and implementation in classrooms. There may well be dissonance between all these issues as they pertain to preparing new teachers, as it lacks a coherent framework addressing the international orientation of the current student and family populations coming to U.S. schools. Further, the work appears to be focused on internationalizing our students for competition in a global society instead of internationalizing our teachers who are responsible for making this leap from a tradition-bound U.S. teacher education system.

DEVELOPING AN INTERNATIONAL EDUCATOR

The teacher educator plays an integral role in the development of a teacher corps that is concerned with and aware of internationalization as a framework for student learning. For teachers who "view themselves as brokers between children and their rapidly changing environment" (Mansilla & Gardner,

2007, p. 62), developing a knowledge base is imperative so that teacher educators have a framework through which the concepts of internationalization can be transmitted to teachers. Although there are multiple frameworks for considering the development of internationally minded teachers, for the purpose of this book we frame the discussion around certain transdisciplinary elements such as the development of social justice perspectives, inclusion, respect, empathy, global issues, responsibility and agency, and the ability to take multiple perspectives. We also look at the systemic issues affecting education—assessments, curricula, language learning, and social and economic conditions that affect learning. We have often depended on one course or a single experience in the field to foster these elements. Instead, we argue that such learning is an iterative and developmental process that requires systematic planning and implementation to be effective.

To focus our efforts on the development of an international educator, we first need to uncover preexisting beliefs and experiences related to international perspectives. Preexisting knowledge and beliefs create a foundation from which all other knowledge develops (National Research Council, 2000). The accuracy of the original knowledge and beliefs filters the acceptance of new or sometimes more accurate information. Helping teacher candidates "clear the lens," as part of teacher education preparation, is crucial to the acceptance and development of new perspectives. If this were a methods course, we would expect a preassessment of skills and knowledge of content, we would direct our teaching to further student skills and knowledge of the subject matter, and we would assess their final performance. Teaching for international understandings should be no different.

As we have come to understand, many U.S. teacher education programs continue to focus their efforts on traditional domestic views of multicultural education primarily around issues of race and class (Levy, 2007). The evidence about our growing U.S. student population shows that we are limiting teacher candidate preparation if we use a traditional model. To strengthen and deepen teacher candidate knowledge, a greater emphasis on international perspectives on culture, traditions, religion, policies, and other dimensions of international student experiences should be a visible part of teacher education. Furthermore, international elements should be integrated across all course work, from foundations through pedagogy and practice. Rather than focusing on fragmented skills, methods, and content, teacher educators should work to develop the metacognitive capacities of teacher candidates, fostering broader integration of relevant international practices and perspectives (National Research Council, 2000). Many teacher education programs fail to articulate and share a coherent philosophy for teacher development, much less one that is focused on an international point of view.

STRUCTURE OF THIS BOOK

This book is a theoretical and practical exploration of how internationalizing teacher education would look while deconstructing traditional arguments that have prevented teacher education programs from engaging in this transformation. The fact remains that we have a critical need to move our teaching corps into this new domain, based on the student populations, the global competition, and the closer ties people have across historical borders. This book focuses energy in two parts: the first section focuses on preparing for teaching the changing population and the knowledge, skills, and attitudes that are needed, and the second section explores the debates that arise in situations that are complex.

Section 1 seeks to examine the intersections between international and multicultural education by addressing the issues of critical languages, intra-intercultural competence for teaching and learning, technology for teachers and students, and finally, learning supports for vulnerable yet resilient children. Section 2 introduces further questions still to be answered in U.S. schools and teacher education as to how we might engage teachers in building relationships with international families and communities, understanding how to balance international standards and assessments with U.S., state, and local standards, furthering the secondary models in the United States; addressing the future of the STEM subjects (science, technology, engineering, and mathematics); and finally bridging the pedagogical diversity of various cultures and countries.

The chapters are based in the literature and utilize empirical research as appropriate. There is a huge gap in the literature on this subject, while there is also a recognizable need to provide a conceptual framework that includes elements in international education, which could contribute to successful implementation.

GOALS

As we set out to write this book, we find that we want to prompt conversations among teacher educators to think about the ways in which teacher education can systematically meet the needs of a rapidly changing school system, and to move beyond the rhetoric of recognizing that the global is the local and vice versa. It often appears that teacher educators themselves are unsure of how to translate the shifting tides of education and yet are expected to work with teacher candidates to then prepare them for their new classroom populations.

This book, with its exploration of multiple topics that affect teachers and the connections between current practices in teacher education and what we foresee as the future of teacher education, aims to open up that conversation.

Furthermore, we anticipate the fresh examination of curricula including field and clinical experiences in light of the goals of internationalization and international mindedness. By promoting the development of faculty capacity to teach to and speak to internationalization, we hope that curriculum changes and broader understandings of how to prepare teachers will emerge through consensus and further collaboration.

Internationalizing teacher education has often been a conversation on the fringes of teacher education or historically associated with specific subject matter such as social studies. But today, even leaders in the field are calling for greater engagement with international education. Levine (2010) recently noted that U.S. teacher education must change to adapt to changes in economy, demographics, as well as globalization. With this book, we hope to bring the conversation inside rather than outside the common dialogue about teacher education. There is a clear recognition that internationalization is a domestic need in the United States today, and we have to be prepared to teach to that. Models of teacher education in Australia, Hong Kong, and Singapore among others are addressing this new reality. If the United States is to lead rather than just keep up, the conversation has to move from rhetoric to action, and we are doing a disservice to our students to limit our conversations on the topic. Internationalizing teacher education is the next step in the process and evolution of teaching and learning.

REFERENCES

Asia Society. (2010, February 17). *Opinions on Global Learning Reveal an Interesting Gap*. Retrieved from http://asiasociety.org/education-learning/partnership-global-learning/making-case/opinions-global-learning-reveal-interesting-gap-3.

Cushner, K. H., McClelland, A., & Safford, P. (2009). *Human diversity in education: An integrative approach* (5th ed.). New York: McGraw-Hill.

Duncan-Andrade, J. (2009). Youth and social justice in education. In W. Ayers, T. Quinn, & D. Stovall (Eds.), *Handbook of social justice in education* (pp. 449–54). New York: Routledge.

Educational Testing Services. (2009). *Guidelines for the assessment of English language learners*. Princeton, NJ: Author.

Gellar, S. (2006). International education: A commitment to universal values. In M. Hayden, J. Thompson, & G. Walker (Eds.), *International Education in Practice* (pp. 30–35). New York: Routledge.

Hayden, M. C., Rancic, B. A., & Thompson, J. J. (2000). Being international: Student and teacher perceptions from international schools. *Oxford Review of Education, 26*(1), 107–23.

Haywood, T. (2007). A simple typology of international-mindedness and its implications for education. In M. Hayden, J. Levy, & J. Thompson (Eds.), *The Sage Handbook of Research in International Education* (pp. 79–89). Thousand Oaks, CA: Sage.

Hill, I. (2007). International education as developed by the International Baccalaureate Organization. In M. Hayden, J. Levy, & J. Thompson (Eds.), *The Sage Handbook of Research in International Education* (pp. 25–37). Thousand Oaks, CA: Sage.

Hull, J. W. (2003). *Filling in the gaps: Solving teacher shortages*. Atlanta, GA: Council of State Governments.

Jaffe-Walter, R. (2008). Negotiating mandates and memory: Inside a small schools network for immigrant youth. *Teachers College Record, 110*(9), 2040–66.

Kissock, C., & Richardson, P. (2009, December). *It is time to internationalize teacher education*. Paper presented at the International Council on Education for Teaching Fifty-Fourth World Assembly, Muscat, Oman.

Levine, A. (2006). *Educating school teachers*. Washington, DC: Educational Schools Project.

———. (2010). Teacher education must respond to changes in America. *Phi Delta Kappan*, October 2010.

Levy, J. (2007). Pre-service teacher preparation for international setting. In M. Hayden, J. Levy, & J. Thompson (Eds.), *The Sage Handbook of Research in International Education* (pp. 213–22). Thousand Oaks, CA: Sage.

Mansilla, V. B., & Gardner, H. (2007). From teaching globalization to nurturing global consciousness. In M. Suarez-Orozco (Ed.), *Learning in the global era: International perspectives on globalization and education* (pp. 47–66). Berkeley: University of California Press.

McDonald, M., & Zeichner, K. (2009). Social justice teacher education. In W. Ayers, T. Quinn, & D. Stovall (Eds.), *Handbook of social justice in education* (pp. 595–610). New York: Routledge.

Merryfield, M. M. (2001, March). *Implications of globalization for teacher education in the United States: Towards a framework for globally competent teacher educators*. Prepared for the Fifty-Third Annual Meeting of the American Association of Colleges for Teacher Education, Dallas, TX.

Murphy, E. (2000). Questions for the new millennium. *International Schools Journal, 19*(2), 5–10.

National Education Association. (2010). *Today's teacher issues: Latest statistics on teachers*. Retrieved on September 15, 2010, from http://educationalissues.suite101.com/article.cfm/nea__todays_teacher_issues#ixzz0r7uTPp00.

National Research Council. (2000). *How people learn: Brain, mind, experience, and school*. Washington, DC: National Academy Press.

Partnership for 21st Century Skills. (2009). *P21 Framework definitions*. Tucson, AZ: Partnership for 21st Century Skills.

Reagan, T. (2005). *Non-western educational traditions: Alternative approaches to educational thought and practice* (3rd ed.). Mahwah, NJ: Erlbaum.

Singer, A., Hardwick, S., & Bretell, C. (2009). *Twenty-first century gateways: Immigrant incorporation in suburban America.* Washington, DC: Brookings Institution.

Snowball, L. (2007). Becoming more internationally minded: International teacher certification and professional development. In M. Hayden, J. Levy, & J. Thompson (Eds.), *The Sage Handbook of Research in International Education* (pp. 247–55). Thousand Oaks, CA: Sage.

Suarez-Orozco, M. M., & Sattin, C. (2007). Introduction: Learning in a global era. In M. Suarez-Orozco (Ed.), *Learning in the global era: International perspectives on globalization and education* (pp. 1–46). Berkeley: University of California Press.

Trilling, B., & Fadel, C. (2009). *21st century skills: Learning for life in our times.* San Francisco, CA: Jossey-Bass.

Tye, K. A. (1999). Global education at the beginning of the twenty-first century. In K. A. Sirotnik & R. Soder (Eds.), *The beat of a different drummer: Essays on educational renewal in honor of John I. Goodlad* (pp. 59–73). New York: Peter Lang.

UNESCO. (2005). *Guidelines and Recommendations for Reorienting Teacher Education to Address Sustainability.* Paris: UNESCO.

U.S. Department of Education. (2008). *The biennial report to Congress on the implementation of the Title III state formula grant program: School years 2004–06.* Office of English Language Acquisition, Language Enhancement, and Academic Achievement for Limited English Proficient Students, DOE, Washington, DC.

Section 1

PREPARATIONS FOR TEACHING INTERNATIONAL POPULATIONS

What Are the Knowledge, Skills, and Attitudes?

In our experience, U.S. teachers are often keenly aware of the international students in their classrooms. They recognize the potential obstacles presented by differences of language, culture, religion, and interests, but they also seem to be seeking better ways to understand the differences of systems, structures, and curricula they have had limited exposure to in their preparation for the classroom. We have also met teachers who are unsure of how assessments are handled, the nuances of differing ways of teaching, and the variety of structures that govern educational systems in different parts of the world. While U.S. teachers are called upon to teach for the twenty-first century, it is clear that their teacher preparation programs often do little to expose them to experiences with international students; strategies for language acquisition; or knowledge of how culture, religion, and context influence learning in the classroom.

Within this vacuum, this book seeks to explore the attributes U.S. teachers should acquire to better answer the questions they have about teaching international students, while also laying a foundation to better understand the complexities and confluences of working with all students. This section addresses the first point—namely, the attributes, or the knowledge, skills, and attitudes that might be useful for teacher educators to understand while working with teachers.

In this context, one might ask, knowledge of what? To that, we answer: this book focuses on deepening the dialogue on the role of internationalism in teacher education and refocusing efforts to bridge the historical notions of diversity with greater clarity on the impact of "being international" in the United States today. Knowledge might mean the extent to which teacher educators understand and use intercultural competence measures to connect a more homogeneous teaching population with an increasingly heterogeneous student population.

To the question of skills, we look to the role of language in classrooms. Oftentimes, we have heard teachers say, "but if they only knew English, we would be able to serve them more easily," and, while this book seeks to address language, it also moves beyond learning the language to uncover issues stemming from the power of language dominance. Further, we address the issue of U.S. teachers' language proficiency beyond English and the importance that multilingualism has for teaching and learning. There is also a need to decipher the sophisticated nature of standards and assessments that drive the systems that students emerge from, just as it drives the system here in the United States. For classroom teachers to fold that knowledge into their repertoire of skills requires teacher educators to decipher the role of international standards and assessments as well.

Finally, we look to a country similar to ours in terms of history, population, governance, and language, with a growing international population of its own, but with a national and proactive strategy for preparing teachers to work with its global student body. Many countries might offer us a perspective to work on internationalizing its teacher force, but our colleague in Australia offers a keen sense of some initial steps the United States might adopt or adapt for its teacher education programs. Building positive teacher attitudes around working with global populations does not occur overnight, yet there are actions and directions teacher education in the Unites States can go to ensure that we begin to deepen teacher understandings of international student populations and that may well serve all student populations in the United States.

There is a sense of urgency when we speak with teachers about international students in their classrooms. Too often teachers are focused on their own responsibilities of classroom management, content area specialization, and testing to have the luxury for adequate space to better understand the issues addressing the global students in their classroom. The responsibility for that space needs to be made before they graduate from the teacher education programs. This first section offers ways to build the knowledge, skills, and attitudes for preservice teachers to work with international students.

· 1 ·

A Comparison of K–12 Multicultural and International Education in the United States

Natasha G. Kolar

Teacher educators are likely to agree that good teachers understand how students can benefit from the knowledge, understanding, and skills outlined in their courses' syllabi (Darling-Hammond, Banks, Zumwalt, Gomez, Sherin, Griesdorn, & Finn, 2005). They are also likely to concede that excellent teachers are aware of the "hidden curriculum" implicit in how teachers frame course material, use pedagogy to shape classroom culture, and inevitably model certain values and beliefs. This chapter provides a basic rationale for multicultural education and international education in the K–12 context, guided by the assumption that all U.S. teachers should be equipped to understand the value of these approaches to their students' personal, social, and professional development. The two approaches are contrasted in their origins, guiding principles, and intended results; and they are ultimately framed as separate parts of the same continuum of learning. The chapter concludes with an emphasis on the value of professional learning communities as a setting for developing globally minded multicultural educators, citing teachers' general preference for context-specific peer learning.

A SNAPSHOT OF MULTICULTURAL EDUCATION IN UNITED STATES

While the need for multicultural education in the United States is situated in current realities, our national and local communities are the result of hundreds of years of cultural clashes. U.S. history is riddled with instances of racial injustice and ethnic oppression, beginning with the genocide of Native

American populations through foreign colonization and the enslavement of Africans to labor on settlers' newly acquired land (Finzsch, 2008; Eltis, 2008). Japanese-American internment camps during World War II, the suspicion that Mexican Americans are largely "illegal aliens," and the rendition of Arab Americans during the War on Terror have further added to interracial tensions in the United States (Ringel, 2004). This is but a glimpse into the European American tendency to be suspicious and repressive of groups who might pose a threat to their hegemony.

This deeply rooted history of privileging the white majority, at the expense of ethnic minorities, is foundational in the case for multicultural education in the United States. According to Verma and Papastamatis (2007), the United States mainstream has dealt with cultural minorities in four ways during the course of its history: marginalization (evidenced in the segregation of African Americans), assimilation (depicted in the melting pot metaphor), integration (while validating immigrants' cultural uniqueness), and finally multiculturalism. Multiculturalism involves aspects of integration, but there is an added goal of eliminating the institutional racism that impairs "the occupational and cultural progress of long-settled immigrant groups and their children" (Verma & Papastamatis, 2007, p. 83). The history of the U.S. public school system has been shaped by both the institutional injustice and the progressive movement toward social reconstruction described above.

Sleeter and Grant (1987) define multicultural education as a "reform movement to change the content and processes within schools" to reflect an appreciation of diversity, social justice and human rights, equal opportunities for all people, and equitable power distribution "among members of all ethnic groups" (pp. 421, 429). This definition highlights multicultural educators' intent for sociological problems to be recognized and remedied, a motivator that will be contrasted later in this chapter with international education's potential tendency toward survivalistic opportunism.

Multiculturalists have made great strides in remedying social ills in the U.S. system of education, and the civil rights movement led to the abolition of certain forms of institutional prejudice; however, race still weighs heavily on student and teacher demographics. For example, the monumental 1954 *Brown vs. Board of Education* ruling that declared racial segregation of students unconstitutional has yet to completely transform U.S. classrooms. An analysis of statistics from the 1998–1999 school year by the Civil Rights Project of Harvard University shows that U.S. schools have failed to significantly integrate racial groups (Orfield, Wald, & Sanni, 2001). The study determined that 70 percent of black students attend schools with over 50 percent minority enrollment, while the majority of white students attend schools with less than 20 percent minority enrollment. Although such segregation is no longer mandated, the U.S. government's failure to reverse the situation has allowed a continuation of "ethnic polarization and educational inequalities" (Orfield, Wald, & Sanni, 2001, p. 2). Furthermore, U.S. Census Bureau (2011) data from the 2007–2008 academic year indicate that black and Hispanic teachers represent only 15 percent of teachers in the United States, compared to the 44 percent of nonwhite students enrolled in public school, contributing additionally to the racial imbalance in our system of education (National Center for Education Statistics, 2010). Students may not be consciously taking note of these demographics, but educators must be mindful of how student perceptions are shaped by their exposure (or lack of exposure) to students of other cultures as well as the racial composition of school leadership.

Demographic trends in the United States add to the urgency and relevance of preparing all teachers to advocate for social reform in their schools and districts. Based on immigration and fertility rates, the U.S. Census Bureau projects that the majority of children will be ethnic minorities by the year 2023 (Bernstein & Edwards, 2008). In order to prepare for this rapid increase in ethnic and cultural diversity among schoolchildren, the National Association for Multicultural Education (NAME) (2009) is calling for initiatives to ensure the success of all students. Strategic multicultural education policies, teacher preparation, curricula, and pedagogy will be critical to facilitating this demographic transition. The next section will compare the value of several approaches to multicultural education, concluding that teacher preparation is most powerful when it results in critical multicultural educators.

APPROACHES TO MULTICULTURAL EDUCATION

Sleeter and Grant's (1987) typology identifies five approaches to multicultural education that have emerged as a result of the civil rights movement in the United States. Since its introduction, this framework has been used preeminently among scholars and practitioners (Banks, 1997; Leistyna, 2002). This section will explore three approaches: "human relations," "teaching the culturally different," and "critical multicultural education" (Leistyna, 2002, p. 9). Understanding and weighing the value of the various approaches is useful for educators as they consider making responsive changes to their individual spheres of influence (Inglis, 2008).

Human Relations Approach

This approach is guided by a rather rosy view of cultural and racial diversity, as it aims to nurture intercultural tolerance and a sense of unity in diversity

(Leistyna, 2002). Self-reflection, simulations, and intergroup collaboration are strategies used to increase students' multicultural sensitivity and personal self-worth (Junn, Morton, & Yee, 1995). Educators guided by this perspective focus on creating a harmonious social community.

Teaching the Culturally Different

Teaching the culturally different is an approach that comes from the alternative perspective that diversity is an educational challenge that needs to be strategically managed (Leistyna, 2002; Hennon, 2000). The primary goal is to assimilate culturally different students into the conventional classroom once they have acquired the remediation and human capital necessary for their success in a meritocracy. To prepare for the classroom and the workforce, these students receive assistance from educators in areas such as English language ability, core academic knowledge, and socialization skills. Supporting students' home culture is not usually a high priority to educators, and parents are encouraged to promote their child's assimilation.

First-generation immigrants may come to mind as natural beneficiaries of this approach. However, an emblematic example of "teaching the culturally different" is seen in the invention of preschool in 1958, originally an intervention to narrow the academic achievement gap between white and African American students (Hanford, 2009). The concept of preschool, as well as the subsequent Head Start program, was based on the perception that low-income and minority youth had poor IQ scores, grades, and graduation rates "because of the culture of poverty in which they were socialized" (Banks, 1997, p. 51). This theory, the "cultural deprivation hypothesis," led educators to believe that these students might require an extra two years in the classroom to become kindergarten ready. Longitudinal studies have shown that the original preschool pilot, the Perry Preschool, raised participants' high school graduation rates by 20 percent and lowered the likelihood of future arrest by 50 percent (Hanford, 2009). Although these results have engendered broad support for universal access to preschool in the United States, the "cultural deprivation hypothesis" that led to its inception has been hotly contested.

Critics now argue that African American, Hispanic, and other minority children have, in fact, "rich and elaborate cultures that are evident in their languages and communication styles, behavioral styles, and values" (Banks, 1997, p. 52). Their academic shortcomings may actually result from the failure of educators to reflect alternative cultures in school infrastructure, curricula, and pedagogy. Teacher preparation is critical in this equation, when considering that academic achievement can increase "when teachers use knowledge about the social, cultural, and language backgrounds of their students when planning and implementing instruction" (Gilette & Schultz, 2008, p. 233). This, and other strategies that value and accommodate for student differences, are more likely to be used by proponents of the following approach to multicultural education.

Critical Multicultural Education

Critical multicultural education is an endeavor to replace assimilation policies that mold "at-risk" children to fit into mainstream white school culture with strategies to accommodate the "cognitive, learning and motivational styles" of the diverse populations represented (Banks, 1997, p. 52). This approach calls for a redesign of the entire schooling process in order to eliminate institutional prejudices and nurture "a conscious, socially responsible, and politically active student body and citizenry" (Leistyna, 2002, p. 14). Teacher education programs can embrace these goals in several ways.

Institutional prejudice might first be addressed by improved efforts by teacher preparation institutions to recruit, support, and place minority teachers across the nation. A 2004 policy paper by the National Collaboration on Diversity in the Teaching Force noted that "students of color tend to have higher academic, personal and social performance when taught by teachers from their own ethnic groups," as teachers who generally demonstrate "higher performance expectations for students of color from their own ethnic group" (p. 504). The collaborative also suggested that the "significant barriers" to the credentialing and success of a diverse qualified teaching force must be acknowledged and mitigated by legislators.

Second, teachers should be encouraged to see themselves as agents of change and responsively "consider the ways students construct knowledge in relation to their surrounding contexts" (Westheimer, 2008, p. 757). One context that exemplifies the power of critical multicultural education to empower marginalized student groups is the bilingual education model. Mexican Americans in Texas, who have a self-described history of being treated "as an inferior species by all institutions of society," describe a feeling of being valued in the bilingual model as language and culture experts and enabled to "repudiate the past and evoke a very different future" (Cummins, 2000, p. 8). Teachers in such schools encourage these students to question hegemonic "values, assumptions, and interest reflected in bodies of knowledge and representations" through "critical pedagogy," of which the revolutionary Brazilian educator Paolo Freire was an early champion (Leistyna, 2002, p. 16). The nascent potential for critical pedagogy to enrich international education will be considered later in this chapter.

A SNAPSHOT OF INTERNATIONAL EDUCATION IN THE UNITED STATES

Like multicultural education, international education in the United States is partly motivated by an increasingly diverse foreign-born citizenry (Stewart, 2007; Ohio International Education Advisory Committee, 2008). Stewart (2007) observes, "Knowledge of other cultures will help students understand and respect classmates from different countries and promote effective leadership abroad" (para. 6). It is this long-established focus on "leadership abroad" where international education diverges from multicultural education. Like the internationalization of higher education, K–12 international education involves a great variety of activities, including "bringing international concerns to [the] teaching . . . and service activities of an institution. . . . It also means constant effort to reduce curricular parochialism . . . [and facilitate] intellectual, cultural and educational exchanges between two or more nations in the world" (Spaulding, Mauch, & Lin, 2001). The internationalization of both preservice and in-service teacher education requires the development of relevant curricula, pedagogy, and teacher educators who can nurture these capacities in the nation's teacher corps.

U.S. participation in international education exchange and collaboration began in the 1870s (Fuchs, 2007). The early years were characterized by emerging networks dedicated to the promotion of "peace, and mutual understanding" (p. 200). In 1919, the League of Nations was founded, providing cohesion and leadership in this global venture. The league facilitated mutually beneficial international education partnerships, challenged themes of intolerance in national social studies curricula, and attempted to develop a standardized international history textbook. However, U.S. engagement in these idealistic activities was not hailed by all, however. An isolationist Senate was reproachful of President Woodrow Wilson's convictions about the United States' responsibility to advance the cause of world peace (Goehner, 1999).

Although President Wilson and the League of Nations failed to ward off a second world war, the league's advancement of international education had a lasting impact on the United States. The stimulation of peace education, the ideal of global citizenship, and curricula for tolerance paved the way for mainstream policy initiatives and alternative school models we find in the twenty-first century. We will consider these approaches in the next section, followed by a review of an alternatively nationalistic approach to international education.

APPROACHES TO INTERNATIONAL EDUCATION

While global and international education both fall under the heading of international education for the purpose of this chapter, there are some distinctions to be made about the two approaches. The language of the former lends itself to framing topics, such as human rights, global warming, poverty reduction, and arts and culture as concerns currently facing residents of planet Earth regardless of the their national residence. The latter explicitly positions the nation-state at the center of its language, facilitating activities such as the consideration of topics from the perspectives of multiple national governments, the comparison of historical events as experienced by people living in different countries, and any programs that prepare students to strengthen the economy and security of the United States. Both perspectives can be useful, and teachers should be cognizant of when to choose a global or an international frame for their curriculum.

Education for Global Consciousness

Education for global consciousness enables students to identify themselves as members of not only their local or national community, but also an interdependent global community. This involves learning to respect, engage with, and feel a sense of solidarity with other members of this community. With the myriad threats facing the world today, it is not difficult to reframe many American challenges as global challenges. Stewart (2007) claims, "Every major issue people face—from environmental degradation and global warming, to pandemic diseases, to energy and water shortages, to terrorism and weapons proliferation—has an international dimension" (para. 5). Global consciousness education should extend beyond matters that directly affect students, though, and nurture empathy for groups of people of which they might otherwise never be aware.

Dr. Maria Montessori, founder of the Montessori model, highlighted the power of global consciousness in her philosophy of education. She prescribed an early childhood education in which "the child will develop a kind of philosophy which teaches him the unity of the universe. This is the very thing to organize his intelligence and to give him a better insight into his own place and task in the world, at the same time presenting a chance for the development of his creative energy" (cited in Grazzini, 2001, p. 7). Decades later, this vision is being brought to life in the Global Citizens' Action Project, an annual professional conference for Montessori middle school students (Kahn, 2008). The event exists to cultivate in students a passion to pursue social justice. A recent initiative from the Montessori School of Evergreen, Colorado, raises public awareness about land-mine issues in postconflict zones including Vietnam and Mozambique. This project demonstrates how students can take this learning from the classroom and conference room into their community (Stubbs, 2009).

Education that Furthers National Security and Economic Growth

Although developing global consciousness in students is an honorable approach to international education, it is often overshadowed by the demand for education that contributes to both national security and the stimulation of local and national growth in the global economy (Kagan & Stewart, 2004; Stewart, 2007; National Geographic—Roper Public Affairs, 2006; Ohio International Education Advisory Committee, 2008). As early as 1989, Virginia's governor, Gerald L. Baliles, perceived the deficits in American students' preparation for the workforce, warning, "We know neither the languages, the cultures, nor the geographic characteristics of our competitors" (cited by Gutek, 1993, p. 235). The Asia Society (2008b), a global organization promoting cooperation and exchange between Asia and the United States, urges that international education should equip students with the following capacities:

1. Knowledge of other world regions, cultures, economies and global issues;
2. Skills to communicate in languages other than English, to work in cross-cultural teams, and to assess information from different sources around the world; and
3. Values of respect for other cultures. (para. 3)

The demand for these skills and competencies is echoed by the Partnership for 21st Century Skills (2009) in their advocacy for U.S. education to move beyond a reading, writing, and arithmetic framework in preparing students to live and work in a global knowledge-based economy.

The stirring language used to express the current demand for K–12 international education in the United States is often reminiscent of the 1983 report *A Nation at Risk* (National Commission on Excellence in Education). Authors of the report warned Americans, "Our Nation is at risk. Our once unchallenged preeminence in commerce, industry, science and technological innovation is being overtaken by competitors throughout the world" (para. 1). Twenty years later, a postindustrial United States is faced with a new challenge. Advocates of international education charge policymakers to consider emerging competitors abroad, warning, "The U.S. lags behind other countries in imparting to its students the skills needed to be citizens and workers in the 21st century global age" (Kagan & Stewart, 2004, p. 230). The Asia Society (2008b) asserts, "This national challenge demands immediate action" (para. 1).

Because of the technology now available, many U.S. jobs can be efficiently outsourced to employees in other countries. Students, therefore, will face competition in the workplace from their peers all over the world. If they are successful in finding employment in this global economy, they will likely be "marketing products to customers around the globe and . . . collaborating with colleagues in multiple countries, either face to face or through technology" (Ohio International Education Advisory Committee, 2008). A number of state initiatives aim to prepare students for these responsibilities. They will be explored later on in their relationship to related multicultural education initiatives.

In addition to promising economic growth, advocates of international education point to concerns about national security. The activities of radical Islamic groups since September 11, 2001, and the U.S. War on Terror have spotlighted the importance of international and cross-cultural diplomacy. The U.S. military's human rights abuses against prisoners of war in Guantanamo Bay are an example of the danger of ethnocentrism and xenophobia. In its Strategic Plan for International Education, the Ohio International Education Advisory Committee (2008) claims, "Managing international conflicts requires a solid knowledge and awareness of people, their history, beliefs and values" (p. 9). Cross-cultural sensitivity is clearly crucial not only for politicians and deployed military, but also for conscientious voters and community members.

In order to educate the next generation to meet these challenges, teachers need to be alert to the continuing evolution of global interdependence, develop geographic and intercultural literacy, model a value for and proficiency in foreign language(s), and become critical consumers of world news (Gutek, 1993). Unfortunately, educational policy that perpetuates the "mass production learning of the industrial age is ill-suited for the information age," and it distracts teachers and teacher educators from the cultivation of these international educational outcomes (McGraw-Hill, *Businessweek*, & the National Center for Research in Vocational Education, 1998, p. 4). Schools and teachers serving low-income and minority students are likely to be most adversely affected by these archaic policies. The potential for international educators to face this dilemma with the tools and the spirit of critical multiculturalism will be explored in the next section.

UNITY OF PURPOSE: A PORTRAIT OF MULTICULTURAL AND INTERNATIONAL EDUCATION

In light of this foundation, I propose a framework for understanding the potential for greater coherence between international and critical multicultural education. At the first intersection, we consider the multiculturalist concern that increased internationalization of K–12 schools in the United States may further contribute to the achievement gap between students who attend high-performing schools and those (often ethnic minorities) tracked into remedial programs in underserved schools. The second intersection is a framework for understanding identity development proposed by James A. Banks, which places the progression from multiculturalism to globalism on the same continuum of learning. The third intersection is the demand for critical pedagogy, traditionally a tool of multicultural educators, to play a greater role in shaping the field of international education. The fourth and final intersection is the shared objective of multicultural and international educators to dramatically increase the diversity of perspectives represented in K–12 curricula. While the intentions and perspectives of multiculturalists and internationalists are not always congruent, these specific recommendations point to a potential synergy that has yet to be fully explored or realized in the field of education.

Equity in International Education

The No Child Left Behind (NCLB) Act was implemented in 2002 by the administration of President George W. Bush with the intention of narrowing the achievement gap between races and social classes (Hanford, Jones, Shapiro, & George, 2007; Wallis, 2006). Since then, schools and teachers have been required to prove that *all* students have learned state-mandated curricula through standardized test scores. If schools fail to meet adequate yearly progress (AYP) goals, they are in danger of being named a "failing school" by the federal and state government.

Opinions among educators and policy makers about the heretofore success of NCLB are varied. Advocates claim that this policy protects minority and "at-risk" students from being written off by teachers; opponents complain that test preparation has replaced meaningful education that would prepare students for twenty-first-century life and employment—especially low-performing students who are often tracked into repetitive remedial programs until able to pass a standardized assessment (Hanford et al., 2007). Multicultural educators note that, because predominantly minority schools tend to be marked by low test scores, this further contributes to disparity in the material students are presented with during their K–12 education: "Equality of access to international education is a concern . . . [because] schools that are struggling to meet state standards, and those in rural areas, often view international education as an 'add-on' or 'luxury' when compared to more pressing problems" (Orfield, Wald, & Sanni, 2001; Frey & Whitehead, 2009, pp. 279–80). So, while the expansion of international education opportunities in U.S. schools may improve the prospects of some students, as well as contribute to national security and economic growth, an unintended result may be the widening opportunity gap between the privileged and the marginalized.

However, this dire portrait of future disparity need not be realized if educators are trained to advocate both for equitable educational opportunities for all students and progressive course work that will equip them to participate in a global workforce. When international education is implemented in impoverished minority schools, the power to elevate students' sense of possibility is dramatic. In one New Jersey school, students perceive themselves as "modern day explorers, just as Columbus had been in his time. Their ship was their computer and their ocean was the World Wide Web" (Asia Society, 2008a, para. 18). These students claim that they do not expect their origins to be hindrances to their future success, an outlook that is likely to contribute to their resilience. This concomitance of educational equity and innovation in global studies has exciting potential for social transformation.

Stages of Ethnic and Global Identification

At this point it is critical to describe James A. Banks' (2004) "stages of cultural identity typology," which places multiculturalism and globalism on the same continuum. Based on this perspective, educators should facilitate students' transition from "cultural ethnocentrism" (stage 2) to "multiculturalism and reflective nationalism" (stage 5), by cultivating in students the "knowledge, skills, and attitudes needed to function effectively within their own cultural communities, within other cultures within their nation-state, [and] in the civic culture of their nation" (p. 297). Subsequently, teachers should empower students to approach the stage 6 ideal of "globalism and global competency." Individuals in this stage have a central commitment to universal social justice, and a sense of solidarity with "all human beings in the world community" (p. 297). As teachers study child development and approaches to instructional differentiation, this model of identity formation should be included in course content.

Studies have shown that students generally begin to develop their cultural identity and prejudices at a very young age. Because students develop these sensibilities at different rates, teachers should be prepared to differentiate learning activities and the complexity of topics explored to individual students. It is generally true, though, that most three- and four-year-old children have already "begun to construct their gender and racial identity" (Araujo & Strasser, 2003, p. 179). Feelings about their self-worth may be characterized by either confidence or shame. Early childhood educators, whether conscious of it or not, play a role in shaping that self-concept. Their behavior also has the potential to model either prejudice or a celebration of diversity. With something as simple as materials in the classroom, from ethnically diverse dolls to picture books promoting intercultural respect, and from crayons that reflect a rainbow of skin tones to inclusive social rules, teachers can impact their students' preconscious beliefs (Araujo & Strasser, 2003).

A study by Ponterotto, Utsey, and Pederson (2006) concluded that the following three characteristics are indicators of an "enhanced quality of life for Americans living in an increasingly diverse society": cross-cultural sensitivity, a commitment to social justice, and the pursuit of culturally diverse experiences (cited by Brummett, Wade, Ponterotto, Thombs, & Lewis, 2007, p. 73). Educators can nurture in students multiple "forms of belonging . . . identities and solidarities" through a range of meaningful entry points (Guarneri, 2002, p. 46). Lucas (2009) suggests that elementary educators approach "ethical and moral . . . issues of [living in] community" with a local-to-global lens (p. 80): students can begin by exploring classroom and familial responsibilities, proceed to understanding their local and national civic duties, study and develop empathy for children in the developing world, and ultimately find a platform to champion international human rights.

Of course, in order for teachers to achieve these student outcomes, it becomes necessary that they first be pursued in preservice teacher education (and continue to be explored in in-service professional development activities). Kegan's constructive-developmental lens for teacher identity development requires that teachers "(1) become aware of their identities and the political, historical, and social forces that shape them; (2) assume agency, find their voice, and take the authority to shape their own professional paths and identities" (Rodgers & Scott, 2008, p. 742). Only as teachers consciously challenge their own assumptions about themselves and others can they honestly expect their students to do the same. As former Putney Graduate School teacher education director Morris R. Mitchell acknowledged, "A teacher teaches who he is" (Rodgers & Scott, 2008, p. 744).

Expanding the Horizons of Critical Pedagogy

Implementing developmentally appropriate critical pedagogy is the next step for teachers who have developed a mature multicultural and global consciousness, have considered ways to strategically design their classroom to foster these qualities in students, and have begun to understand the phases of cultural identity development. Teachers today should be trained to expand the principles of critical multiculturalism, which challenge unjust social structures in the local and national community, to the international and global level. Social justice education has the potential to give students a framework for understanding all power structures through the lens of universal human rights. Social justice education is particularly relevant to elementary school students. Studies have shown that "by the age of ten, attitudes about equality and human dignity are already firmly established" (Lucas, 2009, p. 79). It is irresponsible for K–12 educators to defer the topic of human rights to college and university professors, as is often done in the United States (Zimmerman, Aberle, & Krafchick, 2005; UNESCO, 1994). Secondary and tertiary educators can still plant seeds of empathy and solidarity in their students, but they are better suited to nourish nascent seeds to fruition.

The number of resources for teachers and schools to pursue these objectives is growing. For example, human rights content can be tailored to young students through the lens of the UNICEF Convention on the Rights of the Child (Lucas, 2009). Meanwhile, Mansilla and Gardner's (2007) reflection on Harvard's Project Zero, a collaboration to document best practices in nurturing global consciousness, features a high school social studies unit exploring the effects of globalization on China and India. Working from a global-to-local scale, students analyze the UN's Millennium Development Goals, U.S. corporations' policies of outsourcing, the fair trade movement, and personal consumer relationships to these issues. This sample unit demonstrates the relevance of critical pedagogy to international education.

At a time when neoliberalism guides educational policies, opportunistic states such as Ohio and Indiana focus their rationale for international education on its potential to promote local participation in the global marketplace (Rizvi & Engel, 2009; Frey & Whitehead, 2009). Many preschools and elementary schools boast foreign language programs that prepare students for the international business internships they might pursue in high school and college (Ohio International Education Advisory Committee, 2008). While this strategic initiative is impressive indeed, unless these emerging leaders are taught to be global citizens who challenge hegemonic policies and unjust practices, the United States is in danger of repeating its historic tendency toward colonization (McLaren & Farahmandpur, 2001). According to McLaren (1997), a self-proclaimed revolutionary multiculturalist, "The globalization of capitalism is not in any way accountable to democratic interest" (para. 6). He refers to the North America Free Trade Agreement, which has enabled International Garment Processors, a company serving big names such as Gap, Guess, and Levi Strauss, to move factory operations from Texas to Mexico and cut its workers' hourly wages form $6.00 to $1.25 per hour. McLaren complains, "Global capitalism is excluding large numbers from formal employment while the poor [are] trapped within post-Fordist arenas of global restructuring and systems of flexible specialization" (p. 3). While this perspective may be to the political left of many students' conclusions, students should be taught to wrestle with diverse perspectives in the context of international education and to consider the implications of globalization on marginalized people/groups.

Curriculum Reform: Toward a Diversity of Perspectives

One of the most distinctly complementary objectives of multicultural and international educators is an increased multiplicity of perspectives represented in K–12 curricula in the United States—curricula that has unfortunately tended to be both Eurocentric and nationalistic. Both groups begin the continuum of reform with the introduction of relatively benign celebrations of heroes, holidays, and the cuisine of either foreign countries or minority populations in the United States. Cesar Chavez Day, Black History Month, and international festivals and fashion shows are examples of this approach. Critics argue that these activities fail to facilitate cross-cultural skills and competencies, though; even more importantly, this approach tends to exoticize minority and foreign populations (Kagan & Stewart, 2004; Araujo & Strasser, 2003). On the other hand, Banks (1997) suggests that the annual repetition of these topical studies may play an important part in developing students' multicultural awareness, with implications for international education. He posits that international "heroes, myths, symbols, and school rituals" could help students "develop attachment to and identification with the global community" (p. 137).

Banks' (1988) ethnic additive approach is one step above the "heroes and holidays" approach previously described. In this vein, educators disrupt Eurocentric curricula that privileges white males, introducing the literature, achievements, and ideas of other groups. This is arguably a precursor to internationalization, as textbook developers may first focus on a diversification of American perspectives before looking outside national boundaries. Regardless of textbook limitations, teachers have a responsibility to adapt curricula in their classroom. In preservice foundations courses, as teachers are developing their personal philosophy of education, they should be motivated to design inclusive coursework that "allows students to see themselves represented in the curriculum" (Darling-Hammond et al., 2005, p. 191).

The "transformation approach" and the "decision making and social action approach" are next on Banks' (1988) continuum. Teacher responsibilities involve synthesizing "the diverse cultural elements . . . that make up American Society" while empowering students to think critically about these realities and work toward social change (p. 2). In this stage, coordination has the potential to effect deeper and broader change than multicultural content reform in isolation. Howard Zinn's *A People's History of the United States of America* (1980) is a textbook exemplar that involves a plurality of voices and experiences, a vision of the United States as part of a larger global system, and provocative critical pedagogy. Similarly, Guarneri (2002) offers a model of an American history course syllabus, which makes connections between domestic "multiculturalism" and global diversity. It also contextualizes the events of U.S. history, such as the civil rights movement, as "variations on global developments" (45). Zinn's and Guarneri's work is most appropriate for college students but should also be considered for use in the high school setting. More research needs to be conducted to understand the role of elementary educators in empowering students to grasp these complex issues.

Adapting state and national standardized assessments to include content from diverse perspectives would add an incentive for schools and teachers to adopt inclusive curricula. Additionally, if states would adopt unified multicultural and international education standards that reflect the wisdom of both perspectives, curriculum developers would be better motivated to create integrated materials for use in K–12 classrooms. Two frameworks to use for considering this work are the National Association for Multicultural Education's (NAME) "Criteria for Evaluating State Curriculum Standards" and the Partnership for 21st Century Skills' (2009) "21st Century Interdisciplinary Themes." NAME envisions its first four concerns with a strictly national lens: inclusiveness, diverse perspectives, alternative epistemologies, and self-knowledge. The social justice theme alone refers directly to global realities, with this suggestion to educators: "Prepare students to 'think globally and act locally' by fostering a critical understanding of the ways local knowledge and actions are situated within and have an impact on global contexts" (p. 2). On the other hand, an international dimension (but no form of critical multiculturalism) is integrated into each of the five 21st Century Interdisciplinary Themes, which include civic, economic, environmental, global, and health literacy. Both frameworks would better serve policy makers if critical multiculturalism and international education were integrated rather than isolated.

Some state and district policies do a better job of modeling an integrated approach. The School District of Philadelphia (2009) approximates a multicultural international education standard in this Multiracial-Multicultural-Gender Education Policy: "Teach students to respect their own cultural heritages and to appreciate other peoples from their neighborhood, city, state, nation and the world" (II.C.3.). This standard is in line with the wisdom of Banks' stages of cultural identity typology. Furthermore, the Alaska Standards for Culturally Responsible Schools (Alaska Native Knowledge Network, 1998) includes examples of integrated multicultural and global citizenship education. One standard states, "Culturally-knowledgeable students demonstrate an awareness and appreciation of the relationships and processes of interaction of all elements in the world around them" (p. 8). Another standard suggests, "A culturally-responsive curriculum fosters a complementary relationship across knowledge derived from diverse knowledge systems . . . [contributing] to an ever expanding view of the world" in students (p. 15). Ultimately, the value of these three examples is their global situating of local multiculturalism, which facilitates a richer curricular portrayal of both the local and the international community and a more nuanced nurturing of students' cultural identity.

Technology and Travel

New technologies, such as video conferencing and social networking, have major implications on the field of education in the United States. Teacher educators should work to stay at the cutting edge of these developments, enabling themselves to integrate useful applications into "content pedagogical courses that teachers take, so that they are using the tools within the disciplines themselves, not just learning about them in the abstract" (Darling-Hammond et al., 2005, p. 200). Professional networks are another way for teachers to stay apprised of the potential for new technology to improve their pedagogy.

For example, a sister school initiative can be a cost-effective method of developing multicultural and international awareness in students and staff. Partnerships may involve exchanging materials, practicing foreign language skills, developing cross-cultural curricula and projects, and engaging in community service (Asia Society, 2008b). They have the potential to reflect both multicultural and international education goals, as they can be arranged both at the domestic and international level (Parrett & Hartsock, 1990; Johnson, 2005; Bernard, 2006; Asia Society, 2008b). Banks' (2004) stages of cultural identity typology suggests the logical progression of identification first with local partners and later with the global community. Students and staff living in relatively homogenous communities can gradually expand their worldviews through increasingly interactive partnerships with ethnically diverse populations in the United States and abroad (Bernard, 2006; Orfield, Wald, & Sanni, 2001).

Study abroad, which is typically associated with higher education, can have a transforming effect on at-risk middle and high school students. The Ron Clark Academy, located in a low-income neighborhood in Atlanta, takes students to six continents during their enrollment (Truesdell, 2008). Clark claims that these trips enable students to "see the world differently—and . . . make them want more" (para. 2). One student testifies to feeling smarter and more confident after being exposed to a foreign culture. Another student moved from hating social studies to naming it as his favorite subject. In order to increase funding for middle and high school study abroad, more research should be done to document their impact on students' future success. For such programs to thrive and multiply, a well-traveled and culturally savvy teaching corps is necessary.

Some master's of education programs, such as the Literacy Education and Diverse Settings (LEADS) program at Ohio State University, involve a cultural immersion component. LEADS students, who are predominantly white with little experience serving a socioeconomically and racially diverse student body, participate in a one-year community-based internship with the nearby Mt. Olivet Church (Haberman & Post, 1998). This diverse 1,400-member church manages a private school and a number of educational outreach programs. While benefiting from the service of LEADS interns, the church also challenges the interns' "sense of cultural authority" (p. 353). Those managing this symbiotic partnership admit that it is "impossible for our students to unlearn years of racist socialization and develop anti-racist and sophisticated bicultural identities in one year," but the initial steps toward this end are modeled well for other teacher education institutions to consider (p. 353).

Extending the vision for cultural immersion to international education for teachers, there are a variety of opportunities for midcareer professionals to travel abroad and have experiences designed to enrich and educate. The Fulbright Teacher Exchange Program and the Toyota International Teacher Program are two such opportunities. The Fulbright Teacher Exchange Program, sponsored by the U.S. Department of State, Bureau of Educational and Cultural Affairs, is open to full-time elementary and high school teachers. It gives participants the chance to trade teaching positions with a participant from another country for up to one academic year. The program overview proposes,

> International collaborations such as these foster enduring relationships and continuously provide students with opportunities to increase their subject knowledge and understand its relevance in the greater context of the world. Participating teachers develop and share their expertise with

colleagues abroad, and schools gain from the experience of having an international resource in their communities. (Academy for Educational Development, 2009)

One participant in the Toyota program responded to her experience in the Galapagos Islands with a congruent perspective: "International opportunities such as these completely expand our worldviews and shift our priorities. . . . I have become more passionate about making my students global citizens with knowledge of and sensitivity to international issues" (Institute of International Education, 2011). Toyota's is the first corporate-sponsored program of its kind in the United States, effectively sending teachers abroad to learn about "environmental stewardship and global connectedness." Other global businesses would be wise to consider the skills and competencies fundamental to the success of their workforce and take an active role in shaping the teachers who will educate their future employees. In the meantime, teachers should keep abreast of the increasing number of grants available to them for international education and consider the value of cross-cultural relationships and experiences to their professional growth—not to mention their students' development.

CONCLUDING DISCUSSION OF PROFESSIONAL LEARNING COMMUNITIES

In conclusion, the advancement of both multicultural and international education at the K–12 level in the United States has serious implications for teacher education. Our nation's history of social injustice, currently evolving student demographics, and persisting inequities in education necessitate that multicultural content and pedagogy frame both classroom culture and course content. Meanwhile, the globalized marketplace and social fabric of the twenty-first century requires that international education, including cross-cultural communication and collaboration, critical media literacy, global awareness, and foreign language fluency, be nurtured throughout the entire education process, beginning with preschool (Partnership for 21st Century Skills, 2009). Furthermore, in order for interracial harmony and equitable opportunities for all Americans to be realized, students must be disciplined in a critical multiculturalism that extends into the fields of international relations and business.

Reflecting on the potential for a synergistic approach to multicultural international education, it remains to be stated directly that a teacher's responsibility to nurture multicultural global consciousness in his colleagues is as critical as his responsibility to shape such sensibilities in students. While the role of foundations classes and educational philosophy courses are essential to framing the teacher's perspective before she enters a classroom, these three to five years of lectures and discussions are a fraction of the twenty to forty years of dialogic lifelong learning teachers will experience together in the distinctive context of their school and city. In fact, research shows that a preference for learning by example is practically in the DNA of American teachers. Haberman and Post (1998) write,

> Teachers' preferred way of learning is to observe colleagues whom they regard as credible because they are successful with similar students in the same school system. Their focus is on craft knowledge. They are the ultimate pragmatists. Their test for knowledge is that they have seen it "work." (p. 364)

Understanding this reality leads to a consideration of next steps for teacher educators and school administrators.

An important role of teacher preparation institutions is to develop in future teachers the capacity to be engaged in a professional learning community. Mentoring relationships and reflective classroom observation are designed to be lifelong professional development habits, rather than just preservice activities that all too often end with the completion of student teaching. School administrators have the potential to create context-specific peer-learning processes that encourage veteran teachers, who have demonstrated excellence in multicultural international education techniques, to share their strategies with new or struggling teachers. Encouraging a schoolwide culture of collaboration and innovation can lead to surprisingly powerful results. According to extensive large-scale research, "successful professional learning communities [are linked to] reduced drop-out rates among students, lower absenteeism rates . . . and reduced gaps in achievement gains between students of varying socio-economic backgrounds" (Westheimer, 2008, p. 761). It should come as no surprise that students respond positively to a school culture in which innovative, collaborative relationships trickle down from the boardroom to the teachers' lounge to the classroom. If teachers learn together to thoughtfully understand and engage with an evolving global system and national citizenry, there is no limit to the power their students will have to positively shape their local and international community and hold U.S. enterprises to an ethical and moral standard we have failed to meet in the past.

REFERENCES

Academy for Educational Development. (2009). *Fulbright classroom teacher exchange*. Retrieved from http://www.fulbrightteacherexchange.org/cte.cfm.

Alaska Native Knowledge Network. (1998, February 3). *Alaska standards for culturally-responsive schools.* Retrieved from http://ankn.uaf.edu/publications/standards.html.

Araujo, L., & Strasser, J. (2003). Confronting prejudice in the early childhood classroom. *Kappa Delta Pi Record, 39*(4), 178–82.

Asia Society. (2008a, November 17). *Harnessing information technology with international education.* Retrieved from http://www.asiasociety.org/education-learning/policy-initiatives/state-initiatives/technology-and-global-learning.

Asia Society. (2008b, December 20). *Recommendations to the president and secretary of education.* Retrieved from http://www.asiasociety.org/education-learning/policy-initiatives/national-initiatives/recommendations-president-and-secretary-e.

Banks, J. A. (1988). Approaches to multicultural curriculum reform. *Multicultural Leader,* 1(2), 1–3.

———. (1997). *Educating citizens in a multicultural society.* New York: Teachers College Press.

———. (2004). Teaching for social justice, diversity, and citizenship in a global world. *The Educational Forum, 68*(4), 289–98.

Bernard, S. (2006, November/December). Global state of the states: Appreciating the world around you. *Edutopia: What Works in Public Education.* Retrieved from http://www.edutopia.org/world-at-your-fingertips-education-technology-opens-doors.

Bernstein, R., & Edwards, T. (2008, August 14). An older and more diverse nation by midcentury (press release). Washington, DC: U.S. Census Bureau. Retrieved from http://www.census.gov/newsroom/releases/archives/population/cb08-123.html.

Brummett, B. R., Wade, J. C., Ponterotto, J. G., Thombs, B., & Lewis, C. (2007). Psychosocial well-being and a multicultural personality disposition. *Journal of Counseling & Development, 85*(1), 73–81.

Cummins, J. (2000). *Language, power, and pedagogy.* Clevedon, England: Cambrian Printers.

Darling-Hammond, L., Banks, J. A., Zumwalt, K., Gomez, L., Sherin, M. G., Griesdorn, J., & Finn, L. (2005). Educational goals and purposes: Developing a curricular vision for teaching. In L. Darling-Hammond & J. Bransford (Eds.), *Preparing teachers for a changing world: What teachers should learn and be able to do* (pp. 169–200). San Francisco: Jossey-Bass.

Eltis, D. (2008). The U.S. transatlantic slave trade, 1644–1867: An assessment. *Civil War History, 54*(4), 347–78.

Finzsch, N. (2008). "Extirpate or remove that vermine": Genocide, biological warfare, and settler imperialism in the eighteenth and early nineteenth century. *Journal of Genocide Research, 10*(2), 215–32.

Frey, C. J., & Whitehead, D. M. (2009). International education policies and the boundaries of global citizenship in the U.S. *Journal of Curriculum Studies, 41*(2), 269–90.

Fuchs, E. (2007). The creation of new international networks in education: The league of nations and educational organizations in the 1920s. *Paedagogica Historica: International Journal of the History of Education, 43*(2), 199–209.

Gilette, M. D., & Schultz, B. D. (2008). Do you see what I see? Teacher capacity as vision for education in a democracy. In M. Cochran-Smith, S. Fieman-Nemser, D. J. McIntyre, & K. E. Demers (Eds.), *Handbook of research on teacher education: Enduring questions in changing contexts* (5th ed., pp. 231–37). New York: Association of Teacher Educators.

Goehner, T. B. (1999). *Woodrow Wilson: Prophet of peace; teaching with historic places*. Washington, DC: National Park Service (Department of the Interior).

Grazzini, C. (2001). *Maria Montessori's cosmic vision, cosmic plan, and cosmic education*. Proceedings from the Twenty-Fourth International Montessori Congress. Paris, France: Association Montessori Internationale.

Guarneri, C. J. (2002). Internationalizing the United States survey course: American history for a global age. *History Teacher, 36*(1), 37–64.

Gutek, G. L. (1993). *American education in a global society: Internationalizing teacher education*. White Plains, NY: Longman.

Haberman, M., & Post, L. (2008). Teachers for multicultural schools: The power of selection. In M. Cochran-Smith, S. Fieman-Nemser, D. J. McIntyre, & K. E. Demers (Eds.), *Handbook of research on teacher education: Enduring questions in changing contexts* (5th ed., pp. 97–104). New York: Association of Teacher Educators.

Hanford, E. (Producer). (2009, October). Early lessons. In C. Winter (Ed.), *American RadioWorks*. Podcast retrieved from http://americanradioworks.publicradio.org/features/preschool.

Hanford, E., Jones, A., Shapiro, B., & George, D. (Producers). (2007, September). Put to the test. In M. B. Kirchner (Ed.), *American RadioWorks*. Podcast retrieved from http://americanradioworks.publicradio.org/features/testing.

Hennon, L. (2000). The construction of discursive space as patterns of inclusion/exclusion: Governmentality and urbanism in the United States. In T. S. Popkewitz (Ed.), *Educational knowledge: Changing relationships between the state, civil society, and the educational community* (pp. 243–61). Albany: State University of New York Press.

Inglis, C. (2008). *Planning for cultural diversity*. Paris: United Nations Educational, Scientific and Cultural Organization. Retrieved from http://unesdoc.unesco.org/images/0015/001597/159778e.pdf.

Institute of International Education. (2011). *Toyota International Teacher Program*. Retrieved from http://www.iie.org/en/Programs/Toyota-International-Teacher-Program.

———. (2011). *Toyota International Teacher Program Participant: Sue Cullumber*. Retrieved from http://www.iie.org/en/Who-We-Are/Stories/toyota-story-suecullumber.

Johnson, L. E. (2005). Using technology to enhance intranational studies. *International Journal of Social Education, 19*(2), 32–38.

Junn, E. N., Morton, K. R., & Yee, I. (1995). The "gibberish" exercise: Facilitating empathetic multicultural awareness. *Journal of Instructional Psychology, 22*(4), 324–29.

Kagan, L., & Stewart, V. (2004, November). International education in the schools: The state of the field. *Phi Delta Kappan*, 229–45.

Kahn, D. (2008). *Montessori wells of love and Amman Imman: Water is life*. Retrieved from http://montessori-amman-imman-project.blogspot.com/2008/01/global-citizens-action-project-schools.html.

Leistyna, P. (2002). *Defining and designing multiculturalism: One school system's efforts*. Albany: State University of New York Press.

Lucas, A. G. (2009). Teaching about human rights in the elementary classroom using the book "A life like mine: How children live around the world." *Social Studies, 100*(2), 79–84.

Mansilla, V. B., & Gardner, H. (2007). From teaching globalization to nurturing global consciousness. In M. M. Suarez-Orozco (Ed.), *Learning in the global era* (pp. 47–66). Berkeley: University of California Press.

McGraw-Hill, *Businessweek*, & the National Center for Research in Vocational Education. (1998). *New American high schools: Preparing students for college and careers*. Seventh annual *Businessweek* awards for instructional innovation. New York: McGraw-Hill.

McLaren, P. (1997). *Revolutionary multiculturalism: Pedagogies of dissent for the new millennium*. Boulder, CO: Westview.

McLaren, P., & Farahmandpur, R. (2001). Class, cultism, & multiculturalism: A notebook on forging a revolutionary politics. *Multicultural Education, 8*(3), 2–14.

National Association for Multicultural Education. (2001, November 11). Criteria for evaluating state curriculum standards. Retrieved from http://nameorg.org/position-statements.

———. (2011). Retrieved from http://nameorg.org.

National Center for Education Statistics. (2010, July). Status and trends in the education of racial and ethnic minorities. Washington, DC: U.S. Department of Education Institute of Education Sciences. Retrieved from http://nces.ed.gov/pubs2010/2010015/#1.

National Collaboration on Diversity in the Teaching Force. (2008). Assessment of diversity in America's teaching force: A call to action. In M. Cochran-Smith, S. Fieman-Nemser, D. J. McIntyre, & K. E. Demers (Eds.), *Handbook of research on teacher education: Enduring questions in changing contexts* (5th ed., pp. 501–7). New York: Association of Teacher Educators.

National Commission on Excellence in Education. (1983, April). Introduction to *A nation at risk*. Retrieved from http://www.ed.gov/pubs/NatAtRisk/risk.html.

National Geographic—Roper Public Affairs 2006 geographic literacy study (2006). New York: Roper Public Affairs. Retrieved from http://www.nationalgeographic.com/roper2006/pdf/FINALReport2006GeogLitsurvey.pdf

Ohio International Education Advisory Committee. (2008, Fall). *Strategic plan for international education in Ohio*. Retrieved from http://education.ohio.gov/GD/Templates/Pages/ODE/ODEDetail.aspx?page=3&TopicRelationID=1785&ContentID=59080&Content=72418.

Orfield, G., Wald, J., & Sanni, C. (2001, July 17). School segregation on the rise despite growing diversity among school-aged children (press release). Boston, MA: Harvard Graduate School of Education. Retrieved from http://www.gse.harvard.edu/news/features/orfield07172001.html.

Parrett, W. H., & Hartsock, J. (1990). Implementing global studies curriculum through international school-to-school partnerships. Presented at the Rural Education Symposium of the American Council on Rural Special Education and the National Rural and Small Schools Consortium, Tucson, AZ. Retrieved from http://www.eric.ed.gov/ERICWebPortal/search/detailmini.jsp?_nfpb=true&_&ERICExtSearch_SearchValue_0=ED339564&ERICExtSearch_SearchType_0=no&accno=ED339564.

Partnership for 21st Century Skills. (2009). *P21 framework definitions document*. Retrieved from http://www.p21.org/index.php?option=com_content&task=view&id=254&Itemid=120.

Ringel, L. S. (2004). Freedom challenged: Due process of law during war. *White House Studies, 4*(2), 231–52.

Rizvi, F., & Engel, L. C. (2009). Neoliberal globalization, educational policy, and the struggle for social justice. In W. Ayers, T. Quinn, & D. Stovall (Eds.), *Handbook of social justice in education* (pp. 529–39). New York: Routledge.

Rodgers, C. R., & Scott, K. H. (2008). The development of the personal self and professional identity in learning to teach. In M. Cochran-Smith, S. Fieman-Nemser, D. J. McIntyre, and K. E. Demers (Eds.), *Handbook of research on teacher education: Enduring questions in changing contexts* (5th ed., pp. 732–55). New York: Association of Teacher Educators.

School District of Philadelphia. (2008, December 23). Multiracial-multicultural-gender education. Retrieved from http://www.phila.k12.pa.us/offices/administration/policies/102.html.

Sleeter, C., & Grant, C. (1987). An analysis of multicultural education in the United States. *Harvard Educational Review, 57*(4), 421–39.

Spaulding, S., Mauch, J., and Lin, L. (2001). The internationalization of higher education. In P. O'Meara, H. D. Mehlinger, and R. M. Newman (Eds.), *Changing perspectives on international education* (pp. 190–212). Bloomington: Indiana University Press.

Stewart, V. (2007). Becoming citizens of the world. *Educational Leadership, 64*(7), 8–14.

Stubbs, E. L. (2009, August). *Peace seed connection: From tourism to activism*. Retrieved from http://www.amshq.org.

Truesdell, J. (2008, June). He Takes Students around the World. *People, 69*(24), 101.

UNESCO. (1994, October). Proceedings from the International Conference on Education '94: Declaration and integrated framework of action on education for peace, human rights, and democracy. Geneva, Switzerland: UNESCO. Retrieved from http://www.unesco.org/education/nfsunesco/pdf/REV_74_E.PDF.

U.S. Census Bureau. (2011). Public elementary and secondary school teachers: Selected characteristics. In *The 2011 statistical abstract*. Retrieved from http://www.census.gov/compendia/statab/cats/education.html.

Verma, G. K., and Papastamatis, A. (2007). Multicultural education: A European perspective. In G. K. Verma, C. R. Bagley, & M. M. Jha (Eds.), *International perspectives on educational diversity and inclusion: Studies from America, Europe, and India* (pp. 79–85). Routledge: New York.

Wallis, C. (2006, 10 December). How to bring our schools out of the 20th century. *Time*.

Westheimer, J. (2008). Learning among colleagues: Teacher community and the shared enterprise of education. In M. Cochran-Smith, S. Fieman-Nemser, D. J. McIntyre, and K. E. Demers (Eds.), *Handbook of research on teacher education: Enduring questions in changing contexts* (5th ed., pp. 756–83). New York: Association of Teacher Educators.

Zimmerman, T. S., Aberle, J. M., & Krafchick, J. L. (2005). FAIR: A diversity and social justice curriculum for school counselors to integrate school-wide. *Guidance & Counseling, 21*(1), 47–56.

Zinn, H. (1980). *A people's history of the United States: 1492 to present*. New York: HarperCollins.

· 2 ·

Intercultural Competence for Teaching and Learning

Kenneth Cushner

𝒟eveloping intercultural competence is an increasingly important skill for professionals in an ever-widening range of contexts and disciplines. This is especially so in the field of education where teachers must effectively teach students and interact with families from a wide range of backgrounds. What is even more important, however, is that young people acquire these sensitivities and skills, as it is they who will be required to interact and collaborate with a greater diversity of people worldwide in order to solve the many problems they will face that are global in nature. It is straddling both sides of this double-edged sword, so to speak—enhancing the understanding and skills of teachers while at the same time helping them to transfer this to the children in their charge—that is among the greatest challenges for teacher educators.

The chapter begins by differentiating among some commonly used terms before providing a more in-depth discussion of the concept of intercultural competence. It then expands upon an intercultural conundrum I have previously written about (Cushner, 2008) that suggests that although most teachers and teacher education students may lack the prerequisite attitudes and skills required for them to be effective in their intercultural interactions, young people may possess a solid foundation from which to build upon. The chapter concludes with a discussion of strategies that enhance the intercultural preparedness of prospective teachers. Throughout, the chapter draws heavily from cross-cultural and intercultural research and education, two fields that have become an increasingly critical component of this work.

WHAT IS INTERCULTURAL COMPETENCE IN THE MIX OF TERMINOLOGY?

The educational literature is replete with reference to studies related to cross-cultural, multicultural, and intercultural dimensions of teaching and learning, with such terms often used interchangeably. The term *cross-cultural* focuses primarily on the similarities and differences between cultures, comparing one against another (Landis & Wasilewski, 1999). Cross-cultural approaches lie at the historical base and are at the foundation of the intercultural field, having had the greatest influences in such fields as anthropology and psychology and, later, communication. The term *multicultural*, at least how it has been used in the United States, focuses the notion of group differences to those that occur within a particular nation. Multicultural understanding highlights the juxtaposition of knowledge about particular groups, addressing the exclusion of some from social institutions, educational opportunities, and curricula. It does not, however, necessarily address any interconnection between the groups. The term *intercultural*, in contrast, is more dynamic in nature, focusing on the penetration and interaction of an individual from one culture into another. The teaching-learning process, characterized by this dynamic interchange between teacher and student, coupled with the growing interdependence and movement of people worldwide, suggests that a focus on intercultural aspects of teaching and learning is essential to consider in the preparation of educators in an increasingly interdependent global society. The natural extension of these concepts in the field of education—intercultural competence—refers to the critical knowledge and skills that enable teachers to be successful within a wide range of culturally diverse contexts.

Over the years, researchers have attempted to identify the specific behaviors exhibited by individuals who demonstrate intercultural competence and who are effective at living and working across cultures. Early studies suggested that interculturally effective people were (1) able to manage the psychological stress that accompanies intercultural interactions, (2) able to communicate effectively across cultures—both verbally as well as nonverbally, and (3) able to develop and maintain new and essential interpersonal relationships (Brislin & Yoshida, 1994).

The publication of *The Sage Handbook of Intercultural Competence* (Deardorff, 2009) attests to the increased attention on the part of intercultural researchers and practitioners to better understand the concepts of intercultural sensitivity and intercultural competence, with the first chapter alone presenting at least twenty-two models (Spitzberg & Changnon, 2009). Most conceptualizations of intercultural competence consider the interplay between the cognitive, affective, and behavioral domains. Deardorff's (2006) pyramid model of intercultural competence, a good example of this, places affect or attitude (which she defines as respect, openness, and curiosity) as a prerequisite to knowledge acquisition (such cognitive dimensions as cultural self-awareness and culture-general as well as culture-specific knowledge), and the attainment of such skills as listening, observing, and interpreting. These all must be acquired before individuals are capable of a more enhanced behavioral repertoire of flexibility, empathy, adaptability, and more culturally competent communication and interaction. Ultimately, people who are interculturally minded move from the avoidance or tolerance of difference to a respect and appreciation of difference, and from an unconscious ethnocentrism to a more conscious awareness of their own and others' cultures (Bennett, 1993). And instead of being conscious of what not to do to avoid racism, sexism, and other prejudices, they understand what they can do to create respectful, productive intercultural relationships. Interculturally effective people, thus, are proactive in nature and seek out diverse perspectives and contributions when making decisions and taking actions.

All teachers and teacher education students should understand that culture socializes individuals in a variety of powerful ways that include the manner in which one learns how to learn and teach, how it has influenced their own perception and way of interacting in the world, as well as how others have encountered difference. In addition, we must understand that a foundation of acceptance, openness, and comfort with difference must be in place before people will ever welcome change and develop the skills needed to collaborate with people different from themselves.

MEASURING INTERCULTURAL COMPETENCE

The Intercultural Development Inventory (IDI; Hammer & Bennett, 2003) has been the most widely used assessment tool designed to assess the level of intercultural sensitivity of various groups and organizations, including teachers. The IDI is a valid and reliable instrument based on Bennett's developmental model of intercultural sensitivity (DMIS) that identifies where an individual falls along a continuum from highly ethnocentric to highly ethnorelative (Hammer & Bennett, 2003). Three stages lie on the ethnocentric side of the continuum—denial, defense, and minimization—and three stages reflect increasingly ethnorelative perspectives and skills—acceptance, adaptability, and integration. A brief description of each of these stages follows.

Denial refers to the inability or unwillingness to see cultural differences and is evident when individuals isolate or separate themselves into homogenous groups. Individuals at this stage tend to ignore the reality of diversity and are often characterized by well-meant, but ignorant, stereotyping and superficial statements of tolerance. At this stage, an individual's understanding of difference is minimal. Cultural difference, if it is considered, is typically attributed to a deficiency in intelligence or personality. Such a viewpoint can result in a tendency to dehumanize others, seeing others as simple, undifferentiated aspects or objects of their environment that make them easy targets for discrimination, exploitation, or conquer.

Defense, the next stage of the DMIS, while characterized by the recognition of cultural difference, is often coupled with a negative evaluation of others. Strong dualistic us/them thinking is common in this stage, and when forced into contact with others, individuals often become defensive.

Minimization, the last stage on the ethnocentric side of the continuum, is entered with the discovery of commonality. People at this stage begin to recognize and accept superficial cultural differences (e.g., eating customs, clothing), while holding on to the belief that all human beings are essentially the same. The emphasis at this stage, on the similarity of people and the commonality of basic values, exists around physical universalism ("We are all the same—we all eat, sleep, breathe, bleed red, and die"; "We are all people of color after all"), or around spiritual universalism ("Deep down we are all children of the same God, whether we know it or not"). People in this stage typically do not recognize the very real differences that do exist between people.

Bennett asserts that a paradigmatic shift in thinking occurs when an individual moves from the ethnocentric stages of the continuum, where difference is viewed as something to be avoided, to the ethnorelative side, where difference is something that is sought out. Individuals in the ethnorelative stage recognize that people live in culturally different contexts and search for ways to adapt to difference. This notion of cultural context is not fully understood in the ethnocentric stages.

Acceptance of difference is the first stage on the ethnorelative side of the continuum. Individuals at this stage have the ability to recognize and appreciate cultural difference in terms of both people's values and their behavior, understanding that there are viable alternative solutions to the way people organize their existence and experience. At this stage, the individual begins to demonstrate an ability to interpret phenomena within a cultural context and to analyze complex interactions in culture-contrast terms. Categories of difference are consciously expanded and elaborated, with people understanding that others are "not good or bad—just different." While people find that they may not necessarily agree with all they see practiced within another culture, they can at least understand what they encounter. Teachers at this stage, for instance, might understand that family or other collective influences may be greater for a Latino or Asian child than for an Anglo counterpart, and begin to question if this difference is influencing a particular set of behaviors observed in the classroom.

Adaptation is the stage when people begin to see cultural categories as more flexible and thus become more competent in their ability to communicate and interact across cultures. Individuals use empathy effectively, can readily shift frames of reference, and are better able to understand others as well as be understood across cultural boundaries. Movement into this stage is typically driven by the recognition of the need for action, such as better teaching, or improved communication with families. Two forms of adaptation exist: cultural adaptation, referring to the ability to consciously shift perspective into an alternative cultural worldview and to use multiple cultural frames of reference in evaluating phenomena, and behavioral adaptation, where people are able to act in culturally appropriate ways. It is at this stage that we say that people are becoming bicultural or multicultural. For instance, at this stage, a teacher, or even a fellow student, may understand that the needs of refugee students are quite distinct from those of international exchange students—even though they may both be from abroad—and will, in turn, respond differently to them.

Integration, the final stage of the DMIS, reflects those individuals who have multiple frames of reference and can identify and move freely within more than one cultural group. Integration refers to the internalization of bicultural or multicultural frames of reference, with individuals at this level being able to mediate between multiple groups. People at this level are able to facilitate constructive contact between cultures and tend to become cultural mediators or cultural bridge builders. This level is more difficult to achieve and is both rare and hard to measure.

AN INTERCULTURAL CONUNDRUM: THE INTERCULTURAL COMPETENCE OF TEACHERS AND THEIR STUDENTS

There is every indication to suggest that the majority of today's teachers and teacher education students fall on the ethnocentric side of this scale and may not, without further education, have the requisite disposition to be effective intercultural educators or possess the skills necessary to guide young people to develop intercultural competence. Mahon's (2006) study of 155 teachers from the American Midwest placed all of them on the ethnocentric side of the scale at minimization or below. Her follow-up study of 88 teachers in the American West found 84 percent to be at minimization or below (Mahon, 2009). Another study of 233 teachers in a southern, urban U.S. district found 91 percent to be at minimization or below (Bayles, 2009).

A related study based on the DMIS but not using the IDI (Pappamihiel, 2004) found that even after taking one class in multicultural education and another one specific to the needs of English-language learners, early childhood teacher education students still exhibited a low level of intercultural sensitivity. When students were asked to compare how they would express caring behaviors to children in an ESL class compared to similar-aged children in a general education class, very few of the twenty-eight respondents reported that they would behave any differently in their interactions or demonstrated any indication that they understood, accepted, and valued cultural differences between these groups of students. Like others in minimization, they reported that they would treat all children alike by offering "hugs and smiles" as the predominant way to express caring to all.

Such findings are not limited to the United States. A study of 107 teachers in schools in Hong Kong found 55 percent in denial or defense and 43 percent in minimization, with only 2 percent on the ethnorelative side of the continuum (Grossman & Yuen, 2006). Yuen's (2009) more recent survey of 386 teachers in nine schools in Hong Kong revealed the majority to be in denial or defense, emphasizing cultural similarities with minimal recognition given to cultural differences.

Two studies looking at the intercultural sensitivity of young people reported some surprisingly results. Pederson (1998) used a modified version of the IDI with 145 twelve-year-old seventh graders and found 35 percent in high minimization and 35 percent in acceptance. And, of 336 high school students in an international school in Southeast Asia, Straffon (2003) found 71 percent to be in acceptance and 26 percent in cognitive adaptation, with only 3 percent on the ethnocentric side. Both of these studies showed that the greater the amount of exposure to difference (city versus suburban and rural schools in the Pedersen study and the amount of time in international schools in the Straffon study), the higher the level of intercultural sensitivity.

So, herein lies an intercultural conundrum: the majority of teachers—those we make responsible for advancing the knowledge, skills, and attitudes of young people—appear to be stuck on the ethnocentric side of the continuum, while their students show evidence of being more sophisticated in terms of intercultural development. This presents some interesting challenges for intercultural researchers, and especially teacher educators, to consider in the coming years.

Knowing that we find most teachers in minimization on the ethnocentric side of the continuum is of considerable concern. Minimization seems to be a comfortable place to be, with people making such positive-sounding statements as "I don't see difference—I treat all children alike," or "I don't discriminate. When you really get down to it, we're all the same." This, in reality, is a color-blind notion that ignores the very real experiences encountered by individual children and families and that may impact their learning in significant ways. What makes this stage especially problematic is that it becomes difficult to advance to more sophisticated levels precisely because people believe they are saying all the right things. Yet it is exactly the ability to discriminate that Mahon (2006) suggests is essential if teachers are to fully understand the influence that such factors as culture, race, ethnicity, and socioeconomic status have on the experiences that students, their families, as well as teachers bring to the school context. Teachers must understand how their own rather narrow perspective and experience may influence their ability to accurately perceive and understand the children in their charge as well as the inherently narrow environment in which they work. It is also essential that they understand their resistance to difference—a characteristic of individuals in the ethnocentric stages of this model.

ADVANCING ALONG THE CONTINUUM TOWARD INTERCULTURAL COMPETENCE

Students studying in universities in the United States spend a significant amount of their time in what many consider to be the most internationally diverse organizations in existence today. Unfortunately, meaningful interaction between domestic and international students tends to be rare, especially for those studying to be teachers. Participation in study abroad is also low among education students. Consider the following data in regard to the preparation of teachers whom we increasingly expect to integrate an intercultural and international dimension in their teaching: although 81 percent of incoming university freshmen students say they plan or wish to study abroad during their undergraduate years, fewer than 5 percent ultimately do (American Council on Education, 2008); of the roughly 260,000 students who did study abroad in the 2008–2009 academic year, only 4 percent of those were education majors, and that number was down from the previous year (Open Doors, 2010); and while the number of international students choosing the United States for study continues to increase, with 690,923 in residence in the 2009–2010 academic year, only 2.6 percent of them are studying in colleges of education (Open Doors, 2010). Yet, the desire for international experiences, and the recognition of their importance in teacher education, has been recognized and supported by a study reporting that two-thirds of in-service teachers feel that study abroad should be part of the undergraduate experience, and the majority of students in education would like to see more study abroad opportunities available to them (Schneider, 2003).

Direct, meaningful experience has repeatedly been identified as an essential element in the development of intercultural competence and the attainment of a global perspective (Cushner, McClelland, & Safford, 2012; Brislin & Yoshida, 1994). A study of undergraduate and postgraduate teacher trainees in Britain (Holden & Hicks, 2007), perhaps not surprisingly, found that firsthand experience living or working abroad had a direct positive influence on an individual's knowledge and interest in global matters, a finding that has been reported elsewhere (Fry et al., 2009; Thomas, 2001; Merryfield et al., 1997). We know that most U.S. teachers and teacher education students represent the majority culture, that they are not having the kinds of firsthand intercultural encounters that are so needed to enhance their intercultural development, and that the majority, by far, are at minimization or below. If we are serious in our conviction that teachers acquire international knowledge and intercultural competence, then we are obliged to enhance the kinds of experiences we provide or require of them.

We know that intercultural development is an evolutionary and not a revolutionary process that can be achieved in one course or one single experience. Knowing this should greatly influence the manner in which both children and teacher education students are educated toward a more ethnorelative orientation. Utilizing a developmental scale such as the DMIS and its associated assessment instrument, the IDI, we are better able to determine where on a continuum an individual falls and then to prescribe curricular interventions that are specific to the educational needs of a particular group. Development thus comes about after recognizing where one is on the developmental continuum and then engaging in systematic, oftentimes repetitious and well-planned exposure to intercultural interactions that are designed to nudge one to increasingly complex levels. Moving too quickly along the continuum might be akin to a scuba diver plunging immediately to a depth of one hundred feet without taking the requisite time to equalize pressure and accommodate to the new environment—the shock can just be too traumatic for one to accept. Alternatively, gradual movement or immersion enables the diver to adjust to the changing circumstances and thus to function more effectively in the new environment. So, too, should it be with intercultural development. Understanding and integrating what we know about intercultural development into the education of young people and teachers will result in a more culturally effective and culturally competent citizenry.

How best to bring about such transformative culture learning has been the focus of cross-cultural trainers and intercultural educators for decades (Brislin & Pedersen, 1976; Brislin & Yoshida, 1994). Mezirow's theory of transformative learning (1991) suggests that the way learners interpret and reinterpret their experience is central to meaning making, with reflection being a critical element of the learning process. Such learning involves challenging the assumptions, or schemata, one holds in an effort to determine whether those beliefs, often acquired early in life, continue to hold true as adults. In order to construct new schemata, learners need situations or discrepant events that do not fit the paradigms they currently hold. Learning thus results from the reciprocal process of experience and reflection, with new encounters leading to transformation, and subsequently further learning. This is what well-planned international or domestic intercultural encounters provide—they immerse participants in potentially disorienting cultural situations that do not align with existing cultural schemes, thus encouraging transformative learning that occurs as a result of experience, reflection, and transformation.

Integrating meaningful international and intercultural experiences in the preservice teacher education curriculum, although difficult due to the already overcrowded curriculum, the plethora of state requirements, and assessment mandates, is becoming a greater focus in many colleges of education. Consistent with what the research says about study abroad in general, there is a growing body of evidence to support the notion that participation in carefully planned, intercultural immersion programs, either through well-developed short-term study abroad or a more intensive and long-term international student teaching placement, impacts preservice teachers profoundly in personal and professional ways. Such experiences provide opportunities for students to experience life in another context, to learn about another's view of the world from an insider's perspective, and to examine alternative approaches and philosophies of education. Among the outcomes that have been documented as a result of such experiences include increased intercultural communication competence, as well as enhanced cultural empathy, flexibility, personal confidence, professional competence, and a greater understanding of both global and domestic diversity (Cushner & Mahon, 2009; Mahon & Cushner, 2007; Stachowski & Sparks, 2007; Kambutu & Nganga, 2008).

However, in offering such experiences to students we must be mindful that we differentiate between the more common and frequent surface-level or tourist-oriented encounters and the more in-depth immersion experiences that allow for the reflection and introspection that are more likely to result in impact and growth. Field-based experiences are often utilized in teacher education programs to expose students to diverse school settings. The relatively surface-level encounters that characterize most of these experiences, although intended to make students more comfortable with diversity, have been criticized by some as being limited in scope and lacking depth of involvement and reflection (Villegas & Lucas, 2002), and by others as being brief and not well applied to the real world (Zeichner, 1993). These surface-level "tourist" encounters, like many short-term study abroad programs, can have a tendency to be haphazard and more entertainment- or thrill-based, thus lacking in the depth required for the development of intercultural competence. Such encounters minimize meaningful interaction with hosts and often perpetuate the tendency people have to view others from their own ethnocentric perspective (Cushner, 2004; Kambutu & Nganga, 2008). Mindful and well-planned intercultural immersion experiences, on the other hand, require intention, focus, reflection, and consistent effort throughout, from initial planning to implementation. Carefully planned experiences that immerse participants in a new cultural context over a sustained period of time, such as that provided by international student teaching, can provide for meaningful disorientation, reflection, and transformation.

But what about those who, due to financial concerns, family and work obligations, or other constraints find it impossible to student teach overseas or participate in study abroad? What other ways can be utilized to achieve the same or similar outcomes? Two powerful culture learning strategies that can be easily integrated into the teacher education experience will be considered—collaboration with international students on U.S. campuses and the use of technology.

International–Domestic Student Partnerships

Although most universities in the United States have significant international student populations, and campus international offices often encourage interaction between international and domestic students, the unfortunate truth is that such intercultural interactions rarely occur with the depth and successful outcomes that are assumed. In the United States, although domestic students tend to report positive yet stereotypical views about international students, they nevertheless perceive a range of threats and anxieties (Spencer-Rodgers, 2001; Spencer-Rodgers & McGovern, 2002). Halualani (2008) and Halualani et al. (2004) found that while students even on multicultural university campuses that promote diversity report participating in intercultural interactions, these tend to be rare, are perceived as less important, are separate from their personal friendship networks, or are in short-term one-time exchanges with international students. Many assume that merely because they are surrounded by diversity it automatically translates into substantial encounters and subsequent learning.

Such findings seem to be universal and not limited to the United States. In Australia, studies have found that domestic students were not as interested in intercultural contact as were their international student counterparts (Nesdale & Todd, 1993). In New Zealand, Ward and her colleagues (2005) report that although domestic students tended to have positive perceptions of international students, their subsequent interactions and intercultural friendships were rare. Similar studies in England, Ireland, Spain, and South Africa report that communication and language challenges, as well as the possibility of making cultural faux pas, led to domestic students avoiding international students (Peacock & Harrison, 2009; Dunne, 2009; Le Roux, 2001; Sánchez, 2004; Hyde & Ruth, 2002).

The literature across the board suggests that even when institutions stress the importance of intercultural interaction, both among domestically diverse students as well as between domestic and international students, these interactions are limited, oftentimes fleeting, and are a source of anxiety for students, teachers, and administrators alike. Providing the venue for international and domestic students to come together over a sustained period of time has benefits for both, as I have found by requiring my students to become conversation partners with interested international students throughout the course of a semester. Students are expected to meet with their partner for one hour a week, each with a task at hand. International students are given the opportunity to practice oral communication and get to know a domestic student on a more personal level than is likely to occur during their everyday encounters. Domestic teacher education students are asked to learn about their partner's culture and inquire about their adjustment to life in the United States. My students kept journals where, in part, they reflected on the process of culture learning and the implications of the experience, paying particular attention to how this applied to their role as a future teacher. Following are sample reflective statements:

> Our conversations together have been more informative than any world history class I have ever taken.

> I will not refer to anyone as my "global partners" since they are now my friends. My friends have taught me a lot about adjustment to life in the United States and how this applies to the lives of children and teachers in school today. . . . I know that I will now better understand the needs of children who may be struggling with their adjustment. . . . I think it is important for all teachers to seek opportunities to be around, work with, and learn from diverse groups of people. Teachers who interact with different cultures will have more effective communication skills with their students from different cultures as well as their families.

> I remember my conversation partner telling me how much trouble he had with his classes here in the U.S. because he was very uncertain about what the teachers wanted from him. He is constantly being asked to redo his work although many times he is not even quite sure what they are asking of him. I think as a teacher in my own classroom this is something I need

to understand. After seeing him struggle I see how frustrating this can become over something that can be so easily solved if the teacher just spent a little more time trying to communicate their expectations.

From this experience with my global partner, I have become more aware of how important it is for me to be mindful of second language learners and their adjustment to a new type of classroom setting. I realized that the language barrier made it very difficult to communicate clearly, and that it can take a very long time to get an idea across to each other. I got frustrated sometimes because we had to work so hard at understanding each other. I realized why people from the same cultures tend to band together—they find a sense of comfort and likeness with one another. I'd probably do the same thing.

It is amazing how much I have learned this semester about Turkey and the transition foreigners have to make when they come to the United States. Not only have I realized how stereotypical my thinking has been until I met my partner—the first Muslim I've ever met—but I also started to understand how difficult it is to make a transition into a new culture. Surprising though—we have much in common that I did not think about prior to our encounter. . . . I never considered that not all Muslims are the same. I used to lump all of them into one category. . . . As a future teacher, I will now be able to relate this experience and what I have learned about Muslims to my students. . . . I was anxious at the beginning of the experience, but I am glad the way it turned out. I feel silly for thinking that all Muslims were the same because I know that all White people or all Christians are not the same.

When I asked Jieun if it was easy for her to meet people, she said, "No. I mean it is easy to meet Chinese or Korean people. But, Americans, no. Not many are in my classes because I am in English learning courses. Not many Americans there!" We talked about her experiences in school and whether she enjoyed college in the U.S. better, or in Korea. She remarked, "College is different. Here is a lot more friends and hanging out and stuff. Not at home." I then looked around the student center at the small groups of people laughing and talking with their friends. It would be incredibly intimidating to walk up to a group of young adults that already appear to be friends and even more so if I couldn't speak their language or relate to their experiences. I then realized how a child must feel that has no connections to other young children when they enter this country. As their teacher, it will be my duty to not only be sensitive to their situation but be knowledgeable about their culture.

When I first received this assignment, I was terrified to actually go through with it because I figured it would be so uncomfortable. I was worried that I would not be able to understand him, that I would not know what to talk about and if the whole experience would be awkward. What I did not realize at that time was that this must be how he feels every day coming to a new country where he never knows if he is going to understand what anyone is talking about, or if he will know what to say next. At my first meeting, I at least told myself that it will be over in an hour or so, and then I can go back to my friends and to people that I am comfortable with. I now realize how selfish this thought was because he did not have that opportunity once he came to the United States. . . . I have learned to understand the transitions that it takes to come from a foreign country to the United States. I feel that to learn something like this, one cannot just read about it in a text or article, but actually meeting the person allowed me to really see what that transition is like for him as well as it may be for future students I may have in my classroom.

The comments above reflect a mere sampling of the statements my students have made documenting the personal as well as professional impact that a relatively simple and easy assignment such as this can provide—and it is a win-win for all students. A recent article by Keengew (2010) reports comparable findings based on a similar assignment.

The Role of Technology in Advancing Intercultural Competence

We are currently in the early phases of enhanced intercultural exposure as a result of a number of phenomena, including the increased movement of people across borders, greater attention to cultural diversity in school curricula worldwide, as well as increased access to global media. The ubiquitous nature of new technologies may be playing a critically important role in laying the foundation for fostering global awareness and enhancing intercultural understanding among young people in schools and communities around the world and might help explain the intercultural conundrum referenced earlier that young people appear to be more interculturally sensitive than their teachers. It is no secret that the percentage of children in the United States who use the Internet at home has increased sharply in recent years, rising from 22 percent in 1997, the first year for which such estimates are available, to 42 percent in 2003, to more than 90 percent in 2009 (Rideout et al., 2010). While much of this use is for information-gathering purposes, social networking sites such as Facebook (which now boasts more than five hundred million regular users), and more and more mobile phones, text messaging, interactive gaming, and Twitter in use, makes it increasingly easy for young people (and others) to maintain regular and frequent contact with one another. But this is a global phenomenon as well, with Internet penetration rates increasing everywhere—especially in Africa where it has increased 2,357 percent, the Middle East where it has increased 1,825 percent, and Latin America where it has increased 1,033 percent since 2000 (Miniwatts Marketing, 2010).

International linkages in education have existed at least since the 1920s when a number of global learning networks began in Europe and the United States. Such efforts made use of available technologies and modes of communication that enabled classrooms to exchange cultural artifacts such as letters, photos, and flowers from their local area with children in other parts of the world. Today's technology makes it increasingly easy to bring children into more frequent and regular interaction with one another—oftentimes in very meaningful ways. A number of engaging Internet-based school linkage initiatives exist that are currently involving millions of young people. iEARN, the International Education and Resource Network (www.iearn.org), is one of the world's largest global networks currently facilitating projects with more than 40,000 teachers and 2 million children in 20,000 schools in 115 countries. Zong (2009) has used iEARN to have U.S. teacher education students join online discussion forums with students and teachers in a number of countries and reports that these online discussions facilitated a deeper level of global awareness as well as increased interest in teaching about cross-cultural understanding, children's rights and welfare, hunger and poverty, peace and conflict resolution, and global interconnectedness.

A few other examples of Internet-based resources include the Global Nomads Group, which facilitates interactive educational programs with students in forty countries, reaching more than one million young people; ePals, a global community that has linked more than eight million students and teachers in 120,000 classrooms in more than two hundred countries and territories through a number of electronic exchange programs; and Peace Corps World Wise Schools that has helped more than three million U.S. students collaborate with Peace Corps volunteers all over the world.

The resources identified above are but a few of the opportunities available that educators can utilize to bring children into close, sustained contact with one another (Peters, 2009). Such efforts are beginning to find their way into teacher education programs that are concerned with preparing teachers to understand others and to teach more effectively in an increasingly interdependent world.

CONCLUSION

Developing intercultural competence, both in our teaching force as well as in young children, is a complex undertaking that requires a significant amount of planning and strategic implementation if it is to be successful and accomplished in a meaningful way. It is especially important that we understand that most preservice and in-service teachers themselves have limited international and intercultural experience—something that is essential to further development. We are balancing on two sides of a double-edged sword and as such must begin our efforts early in the teacher education process. Our preservice teachers must themselves become comfortable, knowledgable, and skilled first, and then consider how best to turn this into content that is integrated into the curriculum and integrated into the education of the students in their charge.

REFERENCES

American Council on Education. (2008). College bound students' interests in study abroad and other international activities. Retrieved November 18, 2010, from http://www.acenet.edu/AM/Template.cfm?Section=Home&Template=/CM/ContentDisplay.cfm&ContentFileID=3997.

Bayles, P. (2009). *Assessing the intercultural sensitivity of elementary teachers in bilingual schools in a Texas school district*. Doctoral dissertation, University of Minnesota, Minneapolis.

Bennett, M. (1993). Towards ethnorelativism: A developmental model of intercultural sensitivity. In M. Paige (Ed.), *Cross-cultural orientation* (pp. 27–69). Lanham, MD: University Press of America.

Brislin, R., & Pedersen, P. (1976). *Cross-cultural orientation programs*. New York: Gardner Press.

Brislin, R., & Yoshida, T. (1994). *Intercultural communication training: An introduction*. Thousand Oaks, CA: Sage.

Cushner, K. (2004). *Beyond tourism: A practical guide to meaningful educational travel*. Lanham, MD: Rowman & Littlefield Education.

Cushner, K. (2008). International socialization of young people: Obstacles and opportunities. *International Journal of Intercultural Relations, 32*(2), 164–73.

Cushner, K., & Mahon, J. (2009). Developing the intercultural competence of educators and their students: Creating the blueprints. In D. Deardorff (Ed.), *Handbook of Intercultural Development* (pp. 304–20). Thousand Oaks, CA: Sage.

Cushner, K., McClelland, A., & Safford, P. (2012). *Human diversity in education: An intercultural approach* (7th ed.). Boston, MA: McGraw-Hill.

Deardorff, D. (2006). Identification and assessment of intercultural competence as a student outcome of internationalization. *Journal of Studies in International Education, 10*(3), 241–66.

———. (2009). *The handbook of intercultural competence*. Thousand Oaks, CA: Sage.

Dunne, C. (2009). Host students' perspectives of intercultural contact in an Irish university. *Journal of Studies in International Education, 13*, 222–39.

Fry, G., Paige, M., & Stallman, E. (2009, August 15–19). *Beyond immediate impact: Study abroad for global engagement.* Sixth Biennial Conference of the International Academy for Intercultural Research, Honolulu, Hawaii.

Grossman, D., & Yuen, C. (2006). Beyond the rhetoric: A study of the intercultural sensitivity of Hong Kong secondary school teachers. *Pacific Asian Education, 18*(1), 70–87.

Halualani, R. (2008). How do multicultural university students define and make sense of intercultural contact? A qualitative study. *International Journal of Intercultural Relations, 32,* 1–16.

Halualani, R., Chitgopekar, A., Morrison, J., & Dodge, P. (2004). Who's interacting? And what are they talking about?—intercultural contact and interaction among multicultural university students. *International Journal of Intercultural Relations, 28,* 353–72.

Hammer, M., & Bennett, M. J. (2003). Measuring intercultural sensitivity: The Intercultural Development Inventory. *International Journal of Intercultural Relations, 27,* 403–19.

Holden, C., & Hicks, D. (2007). Making global connections: The knowledge, understanding, and motivation of trainee teachers. *Teaching and Teacher Education, 23,* 13–23.

Hyde, C., & Ruth, B. (2002). Multicultural content and class participation: Do students self-censor? *Journal of Social Work Education, 38,* 241–56.

Kambutu, J., & Nganga, L. (2008). In these uncertain times: Educators build cultural awareness through planned international experiences. *Teaching and Teacher Education, 24,* 939–51.

Keengwe, J. (2010). Fostering cross cultural competence in preservice teachers through multicultural education experiences. *Early Childhood Education Journal, 38,* 197–204.

Landis, D., & Wasilewski, J. H. (1999). Reflections on 22 years of the "International Journal of Intercultural Relations" and 23 years in other areas of intercultural practice. *International Journal of Intercultural Relations, 23*(4), 535–74.

Le Roux, J. (2001). Social dynamics of the multicultural classroom. *Intercultural Education, 12,* 273–88.

Mahon, J. (2006). Under the invisibility cloak: Teacher understanding of cultural difference. *Intercultural Education, 17,* 391–405.

———. (2009). Conflict style and cultural understanding among teachers in the western United States: Exploring relationships. *International Journal of Intercultural Relations, 33*(1), 46–56.

Mahon, J., & Cushner, K. (2007). The impact of overseas student teaching on personal and professional development. In K. Cushner and S. Brennan (Eds.), *Intercultural student teaching: A bridge to global competence* (pp. 57–87). Lanham, MD: Rowman & Littlefield Education.

Merryfield, M., Jarchow, E., & Pickert, S. (Eds.). (1997). *Preparing teachers to teach global perspectives: Handbook for teacher educators.* Thousand Oaks, CA: Corwin Press.

Mezirow, J. (1991). *Transformative dimensions of adult learning*. San Francisco, CA: Jossey-Bass.

Miniwatts Marketing Group. (2010). *World Internet marketing research*. Accessed February 8, 2011, at http://www.internetworldstats.com.

Nesdale, D., & Todd, P. (1993). Internationalising Australian universities: The intercultural contact issue. *Journal of Tertiary Education Administration, 15*, 189–202.

Open Doors. (2010). *Institute for International Education Open Doors 2010 fast facts*. Accessed January 5, 2011, at http://www.iie.org/en/Research-and-Publications/Open-Doors.

Pappamihiel, N. E. (2004). Hugs and smiles: Demonstrating caring in a multicultural early childhood classroom. *Early Child Development & Care, 174*, 539–48.

Peacock, N., & Harrison, N. (2009). "It's so much easier to go with what's easy": "Mindfulness" and the discourse between home and international students in the UK. *Journal of Studies in International Education, 13*, 487–508.

Pederson, P. V. (1998). *Intercultural sensitivity and the early adolescent*. Doctoral dissertation, University of Minnesota. *Dissertation Abstracts International*, 9826849.

Peters, L. (2009). *Global education: Using technology to bring the world to your students*. Washington, DC: International Society for Technology in Education.

Rideout, V. J., Foehr, U. G., & Roberts, D. F. (2010). *Generation M2: Media in the lives of 8- to 18-year-olds*. Kaiser Family Foundation. Accessed at http://kff.org/entmedia/upload/8010.pdf.

Sánchez, J. (2004). Intergroup perception of international students. *Academic Exchange Quarterly, 8*, 309–13.

Schneider, A. I. (2003). Internationalizing teacher education: What can be done? A research report on the undergraduate training of secondary school teachers. *International Studies Perspectives, 5*, 316–20.

Spencer-Rodgers, J. (2001). Consensual and individual stereotypic beliefs about international students among American host nationals. *International Journal of Intercultural Relations, 25*, 639–57.

Spencer-Rodgers, J., & McGovern, T. (2002). Attitudes towards the culturally different: The role of intercultural communication barriers, affective responses, consensual stereotypes, and perceived threat. *International Journal of Intercultural Relations, 26*, 609–31.

Spitzberg, B., & Changnon, G. (2009). Conceptualizing intercultural competence. In D. Deardorff (Ed.), *The handbook of intercultural competence* (pp. 2–52). Thousand Oaks, CA: Sage.

Stachowski, L., & Sparks, T. (2007). Thirty years and 2,000 student teachers later: An overseas student teaching project that is popular, successful, and replicable. *Teacher Education Quarterly 34*(1), 115–32.

Straffon, D. A. (2003). Assessing the intercultural sensitivity of high school students attending an international school. *International Journal of Intercultural Relations, 27*, 487–501.

Thomas, G. (2001). *Human traffic: Skills, employers, and international volunteering*. London: Demos.

Villegas, A., & Lucas, T. (2002). Preparing culturally responsive teachers: Rethinking the curriculum. *Journal of Teacher Education, 53*(1), 20–32.

Ward, C., Masgoret, A.-M., Ho, E., Holmes, P., Newton, J., & Crabbe, D. (2005). *Interactions with international students: Report prepared for Education New Zealand.* Wellington: Center for Applied Cross-Cultural Research, Victoria University of Wellington.

Yuen, C. (2009). Dimensions of diversity: Challenges to secondary school teachers with implications for intercultural teacher education. *Teaching and Teacher Education, 26*, 732–41.

Zeichner, K. M. (1993). *Educating teachers for cultural diversity.* NCRTL Special Report. East Lansing, MI: National Center for Research on Teacher Learning, Michigan State University.

Zong, G. (2009). Developing preservice teachers' global understanding through computer-mediated communication technology. *Teaching and Teacher Education, 25*, 617–25.

• 3 •

The Critical Role of Language in International Classrooms

Rebecca K. Fox

During the early years of the twenty-first century, as globalization continues to create rapid changes in demographics worldwide, these changes are also reflected in schools. The demographic changes in the United States have resulted in a culturally, ethnically, and linguistically diverse student population (Ball, 2009; Fry, 2006; Passel & Cohn, 2008). As such rapid changes in student demographics continue to alter the dynamic of international classrooms in the United States and around the world, there is an urgent need to address the critical role that language plays in education because language is at the core of classroom interactions. We need to understand more about the nature, scope, and role that language plays in our classrooms because language lies at the heart of our work as international educators across borders.

"The National Center for Educational Statistics (2006) reported that by 2020, more than 50 percent of the U.S. public school population will be classified as students of color—from Latino, African American, Pacific Islander, and American Indian backgrounds" (Ball, 2009, p. 46). Even though we have experienced enormous changes in our student population, our teachers remain largely white and middle class and come from backgrounds that are very different from those of their students. Therefore, there is an urgent need for teachers to have the preparation, knowledge, and pedagogical education necessary to be successful in today's cognitively and linguistically complex classrooms (Ball, 2009).

This chapter shares several important perspectives about language to help educators better understand its expanded and multidimensional role in today's international classrooms. By considering the changing nature and richness of our classrooms, and the languages spoken and taught in those classrooms, teachers and teacher educators will come to better understand the complex nature of the environments in which we are now teaching in the United States and worldwide. Educators need to be aware of the multidimensional tapestry of languages, perspectives, backgrounds, cultures, and religions and use it to help all students succeed academically. To do so, teachers need to be aware of students' backgrounds, strengths, and needs.

LANGUAGE

Language is considered to be one of the many distinctive characteristics of humans, it lies at the heart of our individuality, and it serves to partially define who we are. Language is a powerful communication tool that allows us to interact on many levels with others and to express our beliefs, our ideas, and our emotions. It also serves to frame our understandings, express our views and perceptions of the world, and provide a window into our thinking. Language and culture are integrally and inextricably intertwined, and language is the strongest medium of communication used to scaffold and support learning in the classroom setting. Intrinsically, language is connected to our sense of identity as individuals, as well as to members of a determined group or culture. While language allows us to express the ways in which we view and interpret the world, it can serve either as a cohesive force in society or as a divisive element, capable of promoting discord and separation among determined groups (Byram, 2008).

As our world becomes more and more connected across cultures, speakers of many languages are students in U.S. classrooms and around the world. English is more and more present as the language of both communication and instruction in world classrooms. In these classrooms, where language is at the core of the teaching and learning process, teachers have the distinguished privilege and responsibility of supporting their students' learning. They are also charged with the development of their students' language to sustain learning and promote its development as a lifelong skill. To that end, not only is it important that educators in internationalized classrooms understand language, second-language acquisition, bilingualism, and the developmental patterns that accompany them, but it is also essential that a deep understanding of language be an integral part of teacher education programs at all levels. If teachers are to incorporate a more global curriculum in their classrooms, then they need to be prepared to address the specific learning needs of the students in those classrooms (Levy, 2007). Just as preservice teacher education and professional development for experienced teachers should be part of a continuous and active learning process throughout educators' careers (Hayden, 2007), knowledge about language acquisition and application of international education and international mindedness should be included so that it might be applied to all educational settings in the United States and in extended international classrooms.

Authors throughout this volume have addressed the changing nature of international classrooms today and have talked about classrooms that are comprised of students from multiple countries who have different perspectives on the world, and whose educational experiences differ greatly from those in U.S. settings of previous decades. These students might speak any of the more than six thousand languages spoken in the world today (Lewis, 2009) and might have had differing opportunities and points of access to education in their home countries. For example, not all of these languages have a written form or are spoken by a large group; however, any number of their speakers might find themselves in U.S. classrooms. U.S. and immigrant students thus possess different perspectives and understandings of the world, and teachers need to be prepared to work effectively with this melding population of intercultural and international learners now in their schools.

DEFINING LANGUAGE TEACHING IN U.S. CLASSROOMS

Education has traditionally thought of language teachers as belonging to one of three categories of educators. The first are those who teach the principal language of the country in which they are living (e.g., English in America or other English-speaking countries, German in Germany, French in France or other francophone countries). The second category are those who teach the principal language of a country to immigrants whose native language is other than the one of schooling in that country. The third category is made up of those who teach foreign/world languages (e.g., Japanese, French, or Chinese in U.S. schools to native speakers of English; German or Spanish in French schools to native speakers of French).

The roles of language teachers have changed in multiple ways in recent decades. While we still have language arts or English for speakers of other languages (ESOL) or foreign language teachers and departments, the work we do as language teachers has become blurred across disciplines and school structures; instructional practices have changed and developed in different ways. For example, in some regions there may be significant changes in the structure of the school day, with block scheduling implemented in some schools, allowing for subjects to be taught in longer blocks that incorporate approaches such as project-based learning. This has altered some of the ways that language and other subjects are covered in the curriculum. In many schools and regions, instead of isolating language or language classes as a single subject, there is an increasing focus toward the integration of language across the curriculum (e.g., writing across the curriculum, reading across the disciplines, and word study in context). Other content disciplines have also experienced similar integration across subject matter, such as mathematics and science across the curriculum. While we have seen this cross-scheduling most often at the elementary level, secondary and high school classes and class schedules largely remain subject or discipline specific. Yet a few high schools have created some cross-disciplinary subjects that integrate disciplines, such as integrated biology, English, and technology (IBET) or chemistry, history, and humanities (CHUM), enabling students to develop and apply content language and cross-disciplinary knowledge and skills in project-based learning scenarios. This approach is a rich one that supports the development of language across curricula through content-based instruction, which is particularly beneficial to English language learners (Collier, 1995).

The second group of language educators comprises faculty teaching in programs for students whose home language is other than the language of instruction, or the country's majority language. In the United States, these programs have been most often known as English as a Second Language (ESL). They are now increasingly referred to as English for Speakers of Other Languages (ESOL) because English may not necessarily be the second language of many of these immigrants. It may in fact be the third, fourth, or even the fifth language spoken. These faculty may also teach in any one of many types of language programs, such as bilingual, ESL/ESOL, or sheltered English programs, that might be referred to differently across the country and offered in different formats. According to Ovando, Combs, and Collier (2005), the most prominent characteristic that defines the differences among these programs in bilingual/ESOL education adopted by school districts is how much the primary, or home, language (L1) of the students is used for instruction. Therefore, in some states around the nation, students may be learning in bilingual or dual immersion classrooms, where in others English may be taught in programs such as ESOL pull out or push in. In the latter, an ESOL teacher may co-plan and co-teach with mainstream teachers; English language learners (ELLs) are in classrooms with their native English-speaking peers where they learn language through content instruction. Students may be taught through bilingual education or dual language immersion programs, with bilingualism being the goal and language instruction being taught through content. The important message is that ELLs in today's classrooms do not fall into one distinct category, nor does English acquisition end at the time that a learner exits, or graduates from, ESOL classes. Second-language acquisition can take from seven to ten years or more (Thomas & Collier, 2003), and teachers need to be aware of the multiple levels and types of language that children in their classrooms might have.

The third group of language teachers, traditionally referred to as those who teach foreign languages, has also changed in the scope and nature of their positions in schools in recent years. What was always called foreign language (FL) education is now increasingly referred to as world language (WL) education. Due to rapidly changing global population trends, our concept of what is *foreign* and what is *the world* has changed dramatically in recent years. What may have been previously viewed as a language only spoken in another, or foreign, country may now be considered a world language because many speakers of that language speak and use it in the homes and immediate cultural communities in many areas of the world. In addition, students who speak a language in the home or have some oral competence in that language (often Spanish or Chinese) are increasingly being enrolled in foreign/world language department classes in their U.S. schools. These classes may be named Spanish for native speakers or heritage language classes. Even the concept of "foreign" is changing in scope, and many communities of language speakers are fostering the maintenance of a group's home country language through "heritage" language schools that meet outside the scope of the traditional school day. This has a long-standing practice in the Jewish community where Hebrew has been taught on the weekends. Increasingly Chinese, Korean, Greek, and other communities are gathering to preserve their heritage and support the development of language fluency in their children.

Elementary world language educators are also called to teach in many different kinds of programs where "language" per se is no longer the sole focus of our elementary programs. Rather, in immersion, partial immersion, foreign language in the elementary school (FLES), and other program models, language is the tool for developing content knowledge, communicative competence in the target language, vocabulary, critical thinking skills, concept building, and international mindedness. Teachers of world languages work with grade-specific curricula to enhance and expand children's vocabulary and extended understanding of specific topics. Their job is to teach language while helping students develop as citizens of the world by learning its products, practices, and perspectives (Shrum & Glisan, 2010) through experiential projects and learning. The development of deep cultural knowledge is among a world language educator's most important goals, alongside the development of spoken and written language in the target language.

So, as we think of "language" as it is taught in U.S. schools, there is less and less a clear delineation of its specific placement in the curriculum than in the past. Furthermore, language departments, as such, are actually teaching speakers of many languages and are not the distinct entities some people may have perceived them to be in the past. Not all native speakers of English are in English classrooms, learners in ESOL classrooms come from multiple backgrounds and language groups from around the world, and foreign/world language classes have learners who are new to that target language or may have learners who have been exposed to that language at home and possess varying levels of knowledge already when they enter that language classroom.

WHO ARE THE STUDENTS? CHANGING STUDENT POPULATIONS IN THE U.S. SETTING

The students in U.S. classrooms, as well as in international classrooms around the world, are speakers of multiple languages. Around the world, English is increasingly present as the language of both communication and instruction in world classrooms today. For example, in the United States, English language learners are many and varied. Some arrive in the United States with many years of schooling in their home countries and with strong literacy in their first language. While some may have had some exposure to English as a foreign language (EFL) in their home countries, others may not have studied it at all. While some immigrant families are in higher socioeconomic brackets and have many benefits, many have come with little more than the clothes they are wearing and often work two and three jobs to make ends meet.

Many school-aged learners come from war-torn countries and have lived in poverty with inconsistent opportunities for schooling. Some immigrant children experience the extra challenge of learning a second language while simultaneously trying to make up for lost education and catch up to peers of their same age that are native speakers of English (Collier, 1995; Crawford, 2004; Gándara, 2005; Ovando, Combs, & Collier, 2005). Thus, English language learners arrive in the United States with very different backgrounds, with differing levels of literacy development and schooling in their home countries (Crawford, 2004), and in addition they may have experienced interrupted schooling (Fox, Kitsantas, & Flowers, 2008), creating gaps in basic schooling and academic development. Achieving success is difficult for English language learners of any age; however achievement for students who have experienced interrupted schooling can be more difficult than for students who had high or grade-level academic proficiency in their first language (Collier, 1995; Garcia, 2000; Thomas & Collier, 2003).

If we look at some of the recent trends in population, we see that significant changes have occurred in the past decade and a half. In the time period between the mid-1990s and the 2003–2004 school year, the number of ELLs increased by nearly 60 percent. In the year 2000, one in nine of all U.S. residents were immigrants, and school-aged children of immigrants comprise one in five of all children in the United States (Capps, Fix, Murray, Ost,

Passel, & Herwantoro, 2005). Many immigrants come from non-English-speaking countries, and therefore learning English becomes an enormous challenge while simultaneously adjusting to English-speaking schools, culture, and society. It is an additional challenge to learn English for those young immigrants who are still in the process of learning their first language. Because a large number of these students often struggle in school, they have received many deficiency-oriented labels, such as "limited English proficient" or "language minority children" (Baker & Jones, 1998). However, from the perspective that even many native English-speaking children enter school lacking sufficient facility in English (O'Neal & Ringler, 2010), it is important to note here that nonnative English-speaking and bilingual children may have many strengths in domains which monolingual native English speakers may not have. Second-language acquisition research points to the added cognitive benefits of bilingual ability (Baker, 2002). Nonetheless, it can take up to seven or ten years for ELLs to catch up to their English-speaking peers (Thomas & Collier, 2003; Hakuta, Butler, & Witt, 2000).

To provide further context about students and the language they bring to the classroom, not all ELLs were born outside the United States. In fact, an increasing number of young students born in the United States speak another language prior to arriving in school. These children may be easily overlooked as needing special language consideration or services if they are listed upon entering school as American born.

As a side note for our international readership, the United States is not alone in its quest for understanding the twenty-first century learners in our classrooms and providing for their language development. A similar phenomenon is occurring in international classrooms in countries around the world. In France, speakers of other languages are struggling to learn French in school; the same is true in Germany, and teachers are trying hard to find ways to help students acquire the language needed in order to find success in school and pass national exams. So, what is described above is not a unique happening in the United States. As world demographics continue to change, educators need to work together, along with researchers in second-language acquisition, university teacher educators, and policy makers, to find solutions that lead to academic success for all learners.

STUDENTS AS SPEAKERS OF "WORLD ENGLISHES"

With the rapid spread of English as a language of communication across the globe, new questions, understandings, terminology, research, and debate have emerged regarding the varieties of English, or world Englishes (WEs), that exist in our world today (Jenkins, 2009; Kachru, 2005; Kachru & Smith, 2008; McArthur, 1998). In fact, whereas English was spoken as a native language in the mid-sixteenth century by a group of people inhabiting the British Isles (Jenkins, 2009), today "English has acquired both a range and a depth unparalleled in human history" (Kachru, 2005, p. 156) and is spoken in almost every country of the world. Jenkins (2008) reports that whereas there are about seventy-five countries and territories where English is spoken as a first language, or as an official (governmental) second language, the majority of its speakers today actually are those who do not speak it as a first language. The proficiency levels of this large group of English speakers can range from basic conversational to full bilingual competence, with many different accents and syntactical applications of the language. Groups of these English speakers have been described in many ways: speakers of English as a foreign language (EFL), English as a second language (ESL), English as a lingua franca (ELF), and perhaps, less commonly, English as an international language (EIL) (Jenkins, 2008). Published in 1997, Crystal's *English as a Global Language* indicated that L2 speakers of English outnumbered the total number of L1 speakers, and the numbers of English speakers have continued to rise (Crystal, 2003).

The development of English as a world language, and its growth, development, and world varieties, has enormous bearing on our U.S. classrooms because teaching and learning English today does not mean one "standard" English, nor English of a single regional variety. Language learning cannot be slated to occur "in that department over there"; nor can it be assumed that a fluent speaker of English has had the same approach to oral and written forms of the language as an American. This means that educators need to be "aware of the rich variation that exists in English around the world" and give students "the tools to educate themselves further about using their English for effective communication across varieties" (Kachru, 2005, p. 166). The work of Kachru and others has pushed us as educators to look beyond the errors that English learners might make in their oral and written language and to consider instead the characteristics of their English varieties and how their language might reflect the sociocultural reality of the world today.

The concept of WEs from the perspective of teaching and learning English around the world calls us to grapple with the notion of "standard English." Braj Kachru's concept of concentric circles of world Englishes, as explained by Y. Kachru (2005), helps to also consider the promotion of several inner circle models of English that are also clearly motivated by "the exploitation of the economic power of English" (p. 160). The concept of WEs is important as we think of the changing learners in international classrooms, particularly when we think of the historical and political background of the

English that might be spoken in a given area of the world, the linguistic features of WE varieties, sociocultural contexts of use of English, intelligibility among the varieties, interaction between English and local languages, and the language use of WE among multilinguals.

The teaching and learning of WEs is a subtopic within the range of these topics. Most of the research on the teaching and learning of WEs has focused on how these varieties are used in different spheres of human activities. Some research has been devoted to the construction of multicultural identity in the teaching of WEs. Kachru's work has provided important research on WEs and the connection with second-language acquisition (SLA) and the implication of such connection to the teaching and learning of WEs.

Although more research is clearly needed, and international classrooms could—and should—provide one viable "educational laboratory" in which to conduct language research, the connection of WEs and second-language acquisition research has provided new suggestions to language teaching and learning, and to teacher education regarding the importance of context, culture, and sociolinguistic and psycholinguistic variables that should be taken into account when studying speakers of English and English language learners and their language acquisition process. Kachru's view is that the inclusion of the perspective of those who speak WEs in our research and work with English language learners could lead to a paradigm shift in the teaching and learning of English. First, however, teachers need to understand speakers of WEs more specifically and then adopt an inquiry stance on their classroom language learning. Such steps will contribute to the understanding of the nature and scope of language needs in international classrooms. This research has the potential to be one of the most effective new areas for us to investigate so that we can transfer this knowledge to pre- and in-service teacher education programs and contribute to their ability to prepare teachers to work effectively with learners of English so they can meet the challenges of twenty-first-century globalization.

A BRIEF LOOK AT SECOND-LANGUAGE ACQUISITION RESEARCH

We have talked about English as a world language and discussed the concept of world Englishes and their many varieties and forms. We have also talked about teaching and learning world languages. When we consider languages, whether English as a world language or speakers of many languages in foreign/world language classrooms, we need to look at the learners and how language acquisition occurs and develops. Byram (2008) asserts that "foreign language education cannot be separated from language education in general" (p. 16) because all learning serves to develop the individual.

The field of research referred to as second-language acquisition first established itself as a field of inquiry sometime in the 1960s (Ellis, 1997). Second language acquisition research has provided valuable insights about language learning (Dulay & Burt, 1977; Ellis, 1997; Hall, 1997; Krashen, 1982). SLA research has continued to evolve, but it has not always resulted in agreement or consensus among researchers in the field. It does, however, provide us with a theoretical foundation that educators can use to inform classroom practices, and a steady line of research that language educators can use to discuss and debate how individuals acquire language. Thus, research in SLA has shown that a strong relationship exists between language acquisition and the processes involved in acquiring a second language. By understanding SLA research, educators are able to critically examine the principles and approaches they use in their classrooms and consider the results of those efforts. As part of their teacher education programs, WL and ESOL teachers learn about second-language acquisition theory and research. These concepts and the body of second-language acquisition theories and research are at the core of what these language educators do, from curriculum development and learning-centered instruction, to assessment practices and teaching methodologies. Speakers of world languages and world Englishes are regularly enrolled in mainstream English and world language classrooms together, and mainstream teachers do not always have this body of research in their teacher preparation. Now, with the changing demographics in our international classrooms, there is an even greater need for all teachers to understand SLA research so that teachers can deeply understand learners and engage in effective learning practices in their classrooms.

In the 1940s and 1950s, language learning was largely based on a behaviorist view that people learn through habit formation. They held that learning occurred through repetition, imitation, practice, and positive reinforcement (Skinner, 1957). Later, cognitive theorists such as Noam Chomsky gave rise to the idea that language acquisition isn't just a conditioned behavior. According to Chomsky, all children have a predisposition to learn language through what he called a language acquisition device, or LAD (Chomsky, 1957). Chomsky's idea of "universal grammar" helped to move the study of language acquisition beyond the behaviorist theories of the time. He believed that language acquisition was more of a natural process that relied on an innate capacity for language learning. Although Chomsky has often been criticized for ignoring the role of culture in language acquisition, his research has influenced SLA theorists, particularly from a psycholinguistic perspective. His definition of competence was later expanded to form the broader concept we refer to in world language education as communicative competence (Shrum & Glisan, 2010). Other areas of competence have evolved over time, with the most recent model by Celce-Murcia, Dörnyei, and Thurrel (1995), including the elements of discourse competence, sociocultural competence, linguistic competence, actional competence, and strategic competence. The important message for language teachers that has emerged from this work is that language learners need far more than basic grammar or linguistic knowledge in order to be able to communicate meaningfully and express thoughts and ideas.

Krashen's work in language acquisition built on some of the cognitive views that Chomsky posed. Krashen's (1982) monitor model is widely known and has been particularly influential in the field of foreign/world language education with regard to implications for classroom instruction. Krashen's input hypothesis is comprised of five principal points: (1) the acquisition-learning hypothesis, (2) the monitor hypothesis, (3) the natural order hypothesis, (4) the input hypothesis, and (5) the affective filter hypothesis (Ellis, 1997; Shrum & Glisan, 2010).

An important message for language educators is that multiple studies in SLA have also provided evidence of skills and knowledge that are transferred from language to language (e.g., Baker, 2002; Cummins, 1979, 2002). For international students entering the U.S. school system, the interdependent relationship between English language acquisition and their educational development, in general, is multifaceted and complex. The importance of students' using their native language (L1) for literacy processes is often noted in the literature (e.g., Ortega, 2009; Crawford, 2004; Baker, 2002; Cummins, 2002; Gandara & Mendez-Benavidez, 2007). Yet there is considerable controversy about the most effective pedagogical approaches for ensuring the language and literacy development of ELLs in school environments where English is the language of instruction. We need teachers who understand and can teach diverse, multilingual students, and yet teachers of general subjects do not often have the background themselves to creatively meet these needs.

Other important research and SLA theories continue to provide a foundation for the work we do with language learners. For example, Cummins (1979) suggested in his theory of "common underlying proficiency" (CUP) that language attributes are not separated in the brain but are interactive and transfer readily from one language to another. That is, when children are in classes where the language of instruction is French, they do not solely go to a French part of the brain. Information and processes learned in one language can readily transfer to the other language. Thus, teaching a child certain math processes like how to add or multiply numbers in French can easily transfer to addition or multiplication processes in another language. Thus, a mathematical concept can be easily and immediately used in English or another language if those languages are sufficiently well developed and the learner has the vocabulary to express himself (Baker, 2002).

Other theories have helped us understand processes in acquiring second-language abilities for academic success in school. The thresholds theory and the concepts of basic interpersonal communication skills (now more often referred to as social language ability) and cognitive academic language proficiency (now more commonly referred to as academic language) are attributed to Cummins as well (Baker, 2002). These have also often been referred to as BICS and CALP and have helped teachers consider the different levels of language proficiency and their connections to academic success.

Cummins's threshold theory and his work in the area of the interdependence of languages have been supported by several researchers, such as Ovando, Combs, and Collier (2005), who believe that competence in two languages support students' overall academic success. Other researchers have found that bilinguals have more creativity and better problem-solving skills than monolinguals (as explained in Baker, 2002; Ellis, 1997; Collier, 1995). SLA researchers believe that bilinguals have an advantage because they have more than one way of thinking about a given concept, making them more "divergent" thinkers and more effective problem solvers (Baker, 2002). In addition, being able to communicate in two languages means that learners have access to multiple sources of information and resources (Collier, 1995; Ovando, Combs, & Collier, 2005). From out of the thresholds theory and this early work in the field of SLA, we have come to understand more about some of the natural, subconscious linguistic processes that occur inside a learner's head.

Not all theorists agree with Cummins and believe that language development and cognitive development are not simple processes and cannot be isolated. Sociolinguists believe that cognitive and linguistic acquisition exist in a relationship that is influenced by various factors. They view language development and proficiency as relating to an individual's total environment. Collier found that "social and cultural processes have a powerful influence on language development in an education context" (1995, p. 21). She developed a model to explain the interrelationships among the sociocultural, linguistic, cognitive, and academic dimensions of language acquisition. Her research indicates that overall, language acquisition involves "three domains of development—cognitive, academic, and language processes" (p. 21). An essential aspect of this theory is that social and cultural processes are at the center of learning, and all of the processes are interdependent. Shrum and Glisan (2010) also present language learning as a collaborative, social process. Learning and development are presented as both social and cognitive processes.

This has important bearing on the development of curricula and pedagogical practices in the classroom setting.

THE ROLE OF CULTURE AND OTHER FACTORS IN LANGUAGE DEVELOPMENT IN INTERNATIONAL STUDENTS

Language and culture are inherently connected. One cannot pursue the study of one without the inclusion of the other. Hofstede (1986) and Munro (2007) both emphasize that learning is culturally constructed, and language is at the core of learning. As teachers, our focus is on student learning. We know that each student is unique and has his own approach to learning. Learning is impacted by student perceptions and beliefs (Munro, 2007). Teaching is often influenced by Western thought and culture, and according to Hofstede, culture can be a source of conflict, not harmony. If developing international approaches is to become part of the foundation of our teaching practice and development of students' language, there is a targeted need for understanding multiple cultural perspectives and how they influence language acquisition and learning. There is also a need to weave multiple cultural perspectives into the curriculum and study the results of those teaching practices.

Teachers and students interact with a variety of cultures each day within the context of their schools. If we value the perceptions and beliefs of the learner, then we must recognize that classroom culture will influence their learning and development. Skelton (2007) suggests that every individual relates and responds to his or her "own" culture differently and that culture in itself is not static or stable. Teachers in international classrooms need to consider carefully the role that culture plays in organizing content and planning for integrated learning.

APPLYING SLA RESEARCH TO CLASSROOM PRACTICE

Teachers find themselves challenged in international classrooms to provide effective instruction that builds on a student's first language and culture to support academic success. If teachers are also challenged to respect and incorporate culture within the organization of instruction and to conceptualize and put into practice the interaction of language and cognitive development for their students, how can we begin to help them make changes in their teaching practice? How can we help them respond to change?

Teachers must recognize their changing classroom populations and what the complexities involve. Pre- and in-service teachers also need to understand

SLA theories and how to apply them with their learners so that they can develop curricula and support the academic development of language learners in their classes. One of the most interesting points of studying SLA is that it affords us the opportunity to view language acquisition and second-language acquisition through a wider lens. It is important to be able to determine which teaching practices are the most effective for all learners, particularly our international students.

Both mainstream and language teachers who work with international students need to have opportunities for interdisciplinary collaboration and communication in order to develop effective pedagogical practices. In their preservice programs, teachers are not likely to have taken courses with an international perspective of learning and culture (Levy, 2007). Because of the rising number of international students entering U.S. schools and given that the majority of them are in schools where English is the only medium of instruction, it becomes critical to help teachers examine and implement the most effective approaches for helping speakers of world languages develop high levels of academic language and help them achieve success in school.

Teachers of international students should work together to build on SLA research and combine some of the most effective methodological approaches for ELLs and world language classrooms to develop language. There are several recommendations that have emerged from SLA research and the literature on implementing effective language teaching for world languages (Shrum & Glisan, 2010) and ELLs (August & Shanahan, 2006; Thomas & Collier, 2003). These might serve as a springboard for future development.

First, teachers should support language learning in their classrooms in ways that call for students to engage with the content through interactive and experiential learning in multiple ways used in world language classrooms. Interactive approaches have been identified as being highly effective with ELLs, as well (Genesse & Riches, 2006). These might include bringing students into their learning by clearly stating goals and objectives, interactive formative and summative assessments, project-based and authentic learning activities with rich language that is carefully incorporated, and directed writing with individual feedback.

Second, to help international students maintain their home language and develop English language skills, teachers should strongly encourage their students to continue to develop their home/first language by reading regularly in their first language. Teachers should ask families to support this practice at home and work with them to provide support and materials. Many teachers still believe that ELLs should not use their first language when they are learning to read and write in English. The first/home language is an important scaffold for developing a second language and achieving bilingualism.

Building on Cummins' work (1979, 2002), and confirmed by extended analysis by Goldenberg (2008), the research suggests that literacy and other skills and knowledge transfer across languages.

Third, teachers should build on students' home culture and use their strengths to modify instruction and build students' language. The importance of oral language development is critical for all learners and particularly international learners of English. Teachers should promote the idea of using the students' home language for clarification and explanation to increase levels of comprehension and promote metalinguistic awareness.

The question still remains: how can we prepare teachers to work with speakers of multiple languages and encourage in-service teachers to enhance their understanding of multiple perspectives? In other words, how can we help teachers learn to develop cross-cultural learning (Hofstede, 1986), so that international education aims are put to an action in all classrooms to foster language acquisition and inspire international mindedness and world perspectives in both themselves and their students?

Differences between teachers and their students should not be ignored with a business-as-usual response. It is hoped that when teachers acknowledge their changing classroom population and the role that culture and language play in influencing learning, the need to foster international education aims will be seen as a necessity, not as an extra activity they need to add into their already busy days. This realization would result in teachers taking action to build relationships that cross cultural lines between themselves, their students, and students' parents so that all are working together for learning to occur. It would also result in teachers allowing students to interact with one another in a positive and safe environment to help them come to their own conclusions about both the similarities and differences they may share. Finally, this realization would encourage teachers to present their curriculum through multiple perspectives as well.

Fourth, time should be invested in getting to know students as individuals and to foster interaction between students. This is an important characteristic of good teaching, particularly in international classrooms. Relationships are at the heart of teaching, and these relationships can serve as an important building block upon which teachers can learn the individual needs of their students. Connecting with students and allowing them to make connections with their peers will support interactive learning and engages the students in the social aspect of learning.

If classroom practices are implemented that encourage engaged language learning and incorporate the aims of international education, the result will not only foster students' overall language and academic development, but will serve to also develop such twenty-first-century skills as international mindedness and communicative competence in languages and in content areas. Teacher education faculty need to consciously think about how to best work with pre- and in-service teachers so that they fully understand the role that language plays in our international classrooms. They must be mindful of the global context in which we live and expand our knowledge about the languages and countries of the students in our classrooms.

This clearly points to the necessity to tailor teacher preparation programs with appropriate teaching content in the areas of second-language acquisition, culturally appropriate pedagogy, and effective practices for intercultural competence in our international classrooms. Such changes also have implications for educational policy makers, as well. The time has come to join in a targeted quest to integrate intercultural goals with language teaching in order to prepare our twenty-first-century international students for the future.

REFERENCES

August, D., & Shanahan, T. (2006). *Developing literacy in second-language learners: Report of the National Literacy Panel on language-minority children and youth*. Mahwah, NJ: Erlbaum.

Baker, C. (2002). *Foundations of bilingual education and bilingualism* (3rd ed.). Clevedon, UK: Multilingual Matters.

Baker, C., & Jones, S. P. (1998). *Encyclopedia of bilingualism and bilingual education*. Clevedon, UK: Multilingual Matters.

Ball, A. (2009). Toward a theory of generative change in culturally and linguistically complex classrooms. *American Educational Research Journal, 46*(1), 45–72.

Brookfield, S. (1995). *Becoming a critically reflective teacher*. San Francisco, CA: Jossey-Bass.

Byram, M. (2008). *From foreign language education to education for intercultural citizenship: Essays and reflections*. Clevedon, UK: Multilingual Matters.

Byram, M., & Feng, A. (2005). Teaching and researching intercultural competence. In E. Hinkel (Ed.), *Handbook of research in second language teaching and learning* (pp. 911–30). Mahwah, NJ: Erlbaum.

Capps, R., Fix, M., Murray, J., Ost, J., Passel, J., & Herwantoro, S. (2005). *The new demography of America's schools: Immigration and the No Child Left Behind Act*. Urban Institute, Washington, DC. Retrieved from http://www.urban.org/UploadedPDF/311230_new_demography.pdf.

Celce-Murcia, M., Dörnyei, Z., & Thurrell, S. (1995). Communicative competence: A pedagogically motivated model with content specifications. *Issues in Applied Linguistics, 6*, 5–35.

Chomsky, N. (1957). *Syntactic structures*. New York: Mouton de Gruyter.

Collier, V. (1995). *Promoting academic success for ESL students: Understanding second language acquisition for school*. Woodside, NY: Bastos Books.

Crawford, J. (2004). *Educating English language learners*. Los Angeles: Bilingual Education Services.
Crystal, D. (1997). *English as a global language*. Cambridge: Cambridge University Press.
———. (2003). *English as a global language* (2nd ed.). Cambridge: Cambridge University Press.
Cummins, J. (1979). Cognitive/academic language proficiency, linguistic interdependence, the optimum age question. *Working Papers in Bilingualism, 19*, 121–29.
———. (2002). Cognitive theories of bilingualism & the curriculum. In C. Baker (Ed.), *Foundations of bilingual education and bilingualism*. Buffalo, NY: Clevedon.
Dulay, H., & Burt, M. (1977). Remarks on creativity in language acquisition. In M. Burt, H. Dulay, & M. Finnochiaro (Eds.), *Viewpoints on English as a second language* (pp. 95–126). New York: Regents.
Ellis, R. (1997). *The study of second language acquisition* (5th ed.). New York: Oxford University Press.
Fox, R., Kitsantas, A., & Flowers, G. (2008, Fall). English language learners with interrupted schooling: Do self-efficacy beliefs in native language proficiency and acculturation matter? *AccELLerate!, 1*(1), 14–16. Washington, DC: National Clearinghouse for English Language Acquisition. Available online at http://www.ncela.gwu.edu/accellerate/edition/1.
Fry, R. (2006). *The changing landscape of American public education: New students, new schools*. Washington, DC: Pew Research Center.
Gándara, P. (2005). *Latino achievement: Identifying models that foster success*. National Center for the Gifted and Talented, University of Connecticut.
Garcia, G. E. (2000). Bilingual children's reading. In M. L. Kamil, P. B. Mosenthal, P. D. Pearson, & R. Barr (Eds.), *Handbook of reading research* (Vol. 3, pp. 813–34). Mahwah, NJ: Erlbaum.
Genessee, F., & Riches, C. (2006). Literacy: Instructional issues. In F. Genessee, K. Lindholm-Leary, W. Saunders, & D. Christian (Eds.), *Educating English language learners: A synthesis of research evidence*. Cambridge: Cambridge University Press.
Goldenberg, C. (2008, Summer). Teaching English language learners: What the research does—and does not—say. *American Educator*, 8–44.
Hakuta, K., Butler, Y. G., & Witt, D. (2000). *How long does it take English learners to attain proficiency?* (policy report, 2000–2001). Santa Barbara: University of California Linguistic Minority Research Institute.
Hall, J. K. (1997). A consideration of SLA as a theory of practice: A response to Firth and Wagner. *Modern Language Journal, 81*, 301–6.
Hayden, M. (2007). Professional development of educators: The international education context. In M. Hayden, J. Levy, & J. Thompson (Eds.), *The Sage handbook of research in international education* (pp. 223–32). London: Sage.
Hofstede, G. (1986). Cultural differences in teaching and learning. *International Journal of Intercultural Education, 10*, 301–20.
Jenkins, J. (2009). *World Englishes: A resource book for students*. New York: Routledge.

Kachru, Y. (2005). Teaching and learning of world Englishes. In E. Hinkel (Ed.), *Handbook of research in second language teaching and learning* (pp. 155–73). Mahwah, NJ: Erlbaum.

Kachru, Y., & Smith, L. (2008). *Cultures, contexts, and world Englishes*. New York: Routledge.

Krashen, S. (1982). *Principles and practice in second language acquisition*. Oxford, UK: Pergamon Press.

Levy, J. (2007). Pre-service teacher preparation for international settings. In M. Hayden, J. Levy, & J. Thompson (Eds.), *The Sage handbook of research in international education*. Thousand Oaks, CA: Sage.

Lewis, M. P. (Ed.). (2009). *Ethnologue: Languages of the world* (16th ed.). Dallas, TX.: SIL International. Online version: http://www.ethnologue.com/.

Matsuda, A. (2005). Preparing future users of English as an international language. In A. Burns (Ed.), *Teaching English from a global perspective* (pp. 63–72). Alexandria, VA: Teachers of English to Speakers of Other Languages.

McArthur, A. (1998). *The English languages*. Cambridge: Cambridge University Press.

Munro, J. (2007). Learning internationally in future context. In M. Hayden, J. Levy, & J. Thompson (Eds.), *The Sage handbook of research in international education*. Washington, DC: Sage.

Noel, A. M., & Sable, J. (2009). *Public elementary and secondary school student enrollment and staff counts from the common core of data: School year 2007–08* (NCES 2010-309). National Center for Education Statistics, Institute of Education Sciences, U.S. Department of Education, Washington, DC. Retrieved April 20, 2011, from http://nces.ed.gov/pubsearch/pubsinfo.asp?pubid=2010309.

O'Neal, D., & Ringler, M. (2010). Broadening our view of linguistic diversity. *Phi Delta Kappan, 91*, 48–52.

Ortega, L. (2009). *Understanding second language acquisition*. London: Hodder Education.

Ovando, C., Combs, M. C., & Collier, V. P. (2005). *Bilingual and ESL classrooms: Teaching in multicultural contexts* (4th ed.). New York: McGraw-Hill.

Passel, J. S., & Cohn, D. V. (2008). *U.S. population projections: 2005–2050*. Washington, DC: Pew Research Center.

Shrum, J., & Glisan, E. (2010). *Teacher's handbook: Contextualized language instruction* (4th ed.). Boston, MA: Heinle.

Skelton, M. (2007). International-mindedness and the brain: The difficulties of "becoming." In M. Hayden, L. Levy, & J. Thompson (Eds.), *The Sage handbook of research in international education* (pp. 379–89). Thousand Oaks, CA: Sage.

Skinner, B. F. (1957). *Verbal behavior*. New York: Appleton-Century-Crofts.

Thomas, W., & Collier, V. (2003). *A national study of school effectiveness for language minority students' long-term academic achievement*. Santa Cruz, CA: Center for Research on Education, Diversity, and Excellence.

• 4 •

One Size Fits All: Balancing Internationalization and Standardization of the U.S. Education System

Laura C. Engel and Kate Olden

> We are in the process of rebuilding our economy and restoring our competitiveness. That means focusing not just on the immediate job creation, but what we can do to build a solid economic foundation for generations to come. Today's students, our future workers, need to be prepared for jobs in high-growth industries, to innovate, and to think creatively to help solve the great challenges of the next generation. (U.S. House of Representatives Committee on Education and Labor, 2009, p. 2)

INTRODUCTION

Since the late twentieth century, political, economic, and cultural forces associated with globalization have marked new changes in education and school systems around the world. The global economy, now widely referred to as "knowledge based," is argued to require more education than ever before. As such, education systems worldwide are now being asked to produce a more educated and skilled workforce to meet the perceived needs of the global marketplace and enhance national economic competition in the wake of a global financial crisis. Against these shifts, education policies have been developed and enacted to enhance academic achievement and create a more skilled workforce considered essential for what is an increasingly interconnected and interdependent world.

In response to what the United States perceives to be challenges of the new global economy, recent education policy trends aim to improve academic achievement through increased standardization, shown in the move to adopt common national standards and increased accountability measures.

Encouraged by the federal government, national academic standards have been established in both mathematics and English language arts and apply to a wide range of other subject areas, including history, science, geography, civics, the arts, and foreign languages. Forty-five U.S. states, two territories, and the District of Columbia are now incorporating these common core standards into their curriculum frameworks. In this chapter, we explore the core standards adopted by this majority of U.S. states against a critical framework of globalization and the incorporation of education policy within the changing nature of the knowledge-based economy.

In the chapter, we wish to argue that the impetus for developing core standards is based within a dominant economic rationale for education, linked with a particular interpretation of globalization (Rizvi & Engel, 2009; Rizvi & Lingard, 2009). Moreover, the standards' rather narrow focus on achievement, skills, and a traditional nationalistic view of multiculturalism overlooks perspectives drawn from internationalization and cosmopolitanism. Although we do not wish to suggest that the standards are in and of themselves problematic, our analysis illustrates the need for teachers and teacher educators to extend beyond the core standards to help young people to develop international mindedness (Skelton, Wigford, Harper, & Reeves, 2002) and to critically reflect on what it means to be citizens in a globalizing world. We organize the chapter into three sections. The first section briefly outlines the relationship between globalization and education, exploring the ways in which standardization is part and parcel of recent trends in public-sector reform, including in education. The next section provides a chronology of the development of the common core standards in the United States. The last section analyzes the rationale underlying the core standards, exploring the extent to which they offer a global dimension to learning.

GLOBALIZATION AND EDUCATION

In recent years, nation-states, and the way that they organize education, have been influenced by a range of political, economic, and cultural forces stemming from globalization. In their seminal work on globalization, Held and McGrew (2003) argued that globalization "reflects real structural changes in the scale of modern social organization" (p. 6). They argued that new modes of production in the economic realm, new developments in governance, and a changing role of the state, as well as new configurations of cultural interrelationships, characterize the present round of globalization. Across these directives, global transformations are thought to be steered by technological advancements, the development of a single global economy, and changes in the nature of work (Dicken, 2003). These processes have altered the flows of capital, increased the numbers and importance of transnational actors, and put new emphasis on the need for a flexible, easily adaptable, multi-skilled workforce. Indeed, the new global economy is characterized by both flexibility and fluidity, "with multiple lines of power and decision-making mechanisms, analogous to a spider's web, as opposed to the static pyramidal organization of power that characterized the traditional capitalist system" (Morrow & Torres, 2000, p. 30).

In Harvey's (1989) earlier work on globalization, he illustrated shifts in production in the new global economy away from the Fordist era of mass industrialization, manufacturing, and Frederick Taylor's scientific management (Taylorization). In the new post-Fordist era, the emphasis is on skills suitable for the global knowledge-based economy. To this end, governments have placed new pressures on education systems to produce a skilled workforce suitable for an economy that values flexibility, instantaneousness, and speed. This is particularly the case in the wake of the global financial crisis, in which governments have stressed academic achievement to enhance their economic competitiveness on a global scale. In addition to these economic transformations, a range of new political and cultural changes have been unrolled. Among these shifts is the significant role that international organizations, both governmental and nongovernmental, now play in education policy formulation.

Ranging from major educational lenders, such as the World Bank, to the development of global educational performance indicators and benchmarks, such as the work of the Organisation for Economic Co-operation and Development (OECD), each of these organizations has become influential in developing powerful global networks that circulate particular ideas and ideologies about education worldwide. Through these global networks, education policies are now being exchanged and borrowed between national systems at a rapid rate (Samoff, 2003; Steiner-Khamsi, 2004; Phillips & Ochs, 2003). This is illustrated in the development of goals, benchmarks, and standards, which reinforce notions of global competition and place pressure on national education systems to converge around notions of best practice and performance guidelines.

The interrelationship between the national and the global in education is also evident within new developments of international comparisons of academic achievement. For example, in recent years, the growth of international large-scale assessments and the resulting production of league tables, in which countries are ranked based on their relative achievement in key subjects, have had significant impact on national education policy. Two international assessments, the Trends in International Mathematics and Science

Study (TIMSS), led by the International Association for the Evaluation of Educational Achievement (IEA), and the Programme for International Student Assessment (PISA), developed and led by the OECD, have become increasingly significant in the development of global performance indicators and benchmarks, as well as in guiding and steering national education policy. Every four years since 1995, TIMSS has assessed fourth- and eighth-grade students' mathematics and science achievement in over fifty education systems in order to compare across countries. PISA was developed by the OECD in order to compare fifteen-year-old students' scholastic performance across education systems. It is taken every three years, each year with a different focus. In PISA 2009, sixty-five countries and economies participated. These two assessments have influenced the exchange of particular ideas about education and are linked to policy trends toward outcomes-based education and increased standardization (Power, 1997).

Although education policy borrowing and lending is adapted and modified to fit the local contexts and circumstances (Steiner-Khamsi, 2004), education policy exchange has led to "the broad adoption of a common framework for describing, categorizing, analyzing, and assessing education," leaving education systems under increasing pressure and coercion to take new policy developments into account (Samoff, 2003, p. 62). In addition, policies of accountability, standardization, and performance management in education have been linked to the global spread of the influential doctrine of new public management. New public management encompasses three main tenets: a reduction in public spending, in part through privatization and decentralization; a stress on the efficiency and output of public services; and the construction of policy and implementation of public services geared much more toward global competition (Hood, 1991). The OECD's (1995) influential report, *Governance in Transition: Public Management Reforms in OECD Countries*, outlined the shift in practices of effective management and governance, in which accountability, transparency, and decentralization are argued to be central practices of good governance.

These trends represent what appears to be an overarching attempt to run the public sector, including education, more efficiently and more in line with economic models. As Kivinen and Nurmi (2003) argued, policy trends, such as marketization, performance, and accountability are increasingly being promoted, in which "the state is left with the double role of acting both as the sponsor and as the auditor who assesses output" (p. 84). Within this context of accountability and performance is an increasingly emphasized, perhaps dominating link, between education and the needs of the market leading to a growth in education policies focused on academic achievement, often conceived of in terms set out by international large-scale assessments and discourses developed by international organizations. Against these macrolevel shifts, in the United States, recent education policy trends have been aimed at improving academic achievement through increased standardization, illustrated by the adoption of common national standards and increased accountability measures. In the following sections, we explore the common core standards movement in the United States, in which we argue that the impetus for developing core standards is based within what is a dominant economic rationale for education.

THE COMMON CORE STANDARDS MOVEMENT

National standards in the United States represent a major accomplishment after years of faltering attempts to create a set of unified nationwide standards (Ravitch, 1995). Prior to the newly adopted core standards, a cohesive set of nationwide academic standards did not exist in the U.S. education system. Although the 2001 Education Reform Act, No Child Left Behind (NCLB), introduced new accountability measures in the United States, it required every state to set its own academic standards and use assessments aligned with those standards. This meant that standards varied widely between U.S. states. The development of the common core standards movement in the United States occurred alongside a global discourse focused overwhelmingly on the provision of quality education and a growing importance placed on academic achievement. In the discussion that follows, we lay out and briefly analyze the events and policies that have paved the way for the common core standards movement. The timeline in table 4.1 provides an overview of key events and policies leading up to the recent adoption of the common core state standards.

As shown in the timeline, the first official call to action for policy makers, educators, and citizens came in the form of a report commissioned by the secretary of education, entitled *A Nation at Risk*. This document, employing a rather alarmist discourse about the state of the U.S. education system in a context of increased global economic competition, laid out an argument that "the educational foundations of our society are presently being eroded by a rising tide of mediocrity" (National Commission on Excellence in Education, 1983, p. 1). The report noted many of the issues that remain at the heart of the core standards movement some thirty years later, including:

1. Inability of graduating high school seniors to succeed in college or the workplace;
2. Declining standardized achievement test scores in reading, writing, math, and science;

Table 4.1. Policies and Events Leading up to the Common Core Standards in the United States

Year	Policies/Events
1983	*A Nation at Risk* published
1989	National Education Summit adopted national goals for year 2000
	National Council of Teachers of Mathematics published the *Curriculum and Evaluation Standards for School Mathematics*
1994	Elementary and Secondary Education Act reauthorized Improving America's Schools Act
	Goals 2000: Educate America Act passed
1996	Second National Education Summit
2001	Elementary and Secondary Education Act reauthorized the Education Reform Act NCLB
2006	The *State of State Standards* published by the Fordham Institute
2008	Race to the Top instituted by the Obama administration
	Common core state standards begin to be formed
2010	Common core standards published, accepted by forty-six states and three territories

3. Insufficient acquisition of knowledge and skills with technology; and
4. The failure of U.S. students to excel on international tests.

The alarmist discourse used in the report was heightened in 1983 by the tension of the Cold War and the emergence of competitive world markets. In the early twenty-first century, these forces may have changed, but they have not subsided. For example, rhetoric in the United States continues to reflect a sense of ideological threat from fundamentalist and terrorist forces, particularly Islamist forces from the Middle East, and globalization continues to loom large as a planetwide economic, political, and cultural paradigm. In this way, *A Nation at Risk* served as the foundation for education policies and discourse focused on the provision of educational quality, which over the next decade turned toward a standards-based approach to education.

Professional organizations were the first to take up the challenge of establishing standards on a sectorwide basis, although they were only intended to influence the states' development and adoption of learning standards. The most visible of these efforts was that of the National Council of Teachers of

Mathematics, which began the process in 1986 and published its *Curriculum and Evaluation Standards for School Mathematics* in 1989. On a national level, however, it was broad goals, rather than specific standards, that were the focus of the first national education summit of all fifty states' governors, called for by President George H. W. Bush in 1989. At the same time that a Gallup poll noted that a majority of citizens wanted national education standards, a national curriculum, and national tests, critics and supporters alike began to muddle through the many questions arising from the debate:

> Should the country emphasize raising test scores and imposing tougher graduation requirements, or changing schools' structure and teaching methods to reach poor and minority children who are not learning now? Are the national goals being considered by the committee the right ones, or should the nation be paying more attention to the connection between poverty and school failure, as some contend? In any case, how will proclaiming national goals ensure that they are met? (Weinraub, September 29, 1989)

Resulting from this meeting was an agreement that a national education strategy and a set of nationwide education performance goals for literacy, math, social studies, and science were necessary. However, it was another five years before legislation began to connect such goals to federal educational financing.

In 1994, the national congress passed *Goals 2000: Educate America Act*, which stated,

> By the year 2000, all students will leave grades 4, 8, and 12 having demonstrated competency over challenging subject matter including English, mathematics, science, foreign languages, civics and government, economics, arts, history, and geography, and every school in America will ensure that all students learn to use their minds well, so they may be prepared for responsible citizenship, further learning, and productive employment in our Nation's modern economy. (Goals 2000, sec. 102.3)

The Educate America Act, along with the reauthorization of the Elementary and Secondary Education Act and the School to Work Opportunities Act, all passed in the same year, marked a paradigm shift in the kind of education encouraged by the federal government. That is to say, federal funds were now meant to stimulate and encourage state standards-driven reform that embraced the idea of all children being capable of high achievement (U.S. Department of Education, 1999).

The subsequent 1996 national education summit, which included fifty leading businessmen and CEOs, as well as governors from forty-four states, proposed the idea of national standards developed and voluntarily adopted by the states, without direct federal government involvement. It also moved the discussion from establishing broad goals to outlining specific standards that students need to meet at certain points in their education (Applebome, 1996). This movement toward specific standards received two notable infusions of support and encouragement from the federal government. The first came in the form of President Bush's Education Reform Act, or NCLB, in 2001, which provided many guidelines about the characteristics of standards that states must adopt in order to receive federal funds. The second came in 2009 with the Obama administration's Race to the Top initiative, funded by the American Recovery and Reinvestment Act of 2009. One of the four main funding objectives of this grant program is to underwrite reforms that lead to a state's "adopting standards and assessments that prepare students to succeed in college and the workplace and to compete in the global economy" (U.S. Department of Education, 2009, p. 2).

As a backdrop to these education policy shifts at the federal and state levels, discourse focused on the slipping status of the United States as an educational innovator. The 2006 edition of the Fordham Institute's *State of State Standards* found little advance in the reform of state standards since the inception of NCLB, leaving two-thirds of children attending schools in states whose standards were graded as C− or below (Finn, Jillian, & Petrilli, 2006). The report also suggested a correlation between the existence of strong state standards and gains made by those states' students on national achievement tests. This publication was quoted by several states as being particularly influential in their decision to join the common core standards initiative in 2008, headed by the National Governors Association Center for Best Practices and the Council of Chief State School Officers, whose work over the next two years resulted finally in the release of the common core state standards as they exist today.

GLOBAL DIMENSION IN THE CORE STANDARDS

In analyzing the core standards through a lens of globalization, namely, the extent to which the common core state standards embody a global dimension of learning, it appears that the common core standards are generated from an overwhelmingly economic rationale. Moreover, they seem to limit a global dimension of learning to a more traditional, nationalistic focus of multiculturalism. From a historical perspective, the common core standards were developed from a perspective that positioned the United States within a competitive global economic context. In fact, all of the policy documents, events, and legislation discussed above contain numerous references to the placement of the United States within a broader global economic framework. In many of the policy documents leading up to the common core standards, discourses reveal a sense of nostalgia for the past and a comparison of the United States and its perceived global competitors. However, it is worth noting that the very nature of the common core standards movement in the United States, as an effort of many independent parties (the states), sets it apart from education systems with strong central control over formal education, like Japan, which have been highly lauded during development of the standards.

In the Educate America Act of 1994, it was indicated that one goal of education must be that "all students will be knowledgeable about the diverse cultural heritage of this Nation and about the world community" (Goals 2000, sec. 102.vi). However, most of the documents relied on the economic arena for their inspiration and focus. Moreover, competition and a sense of threat to the well-being of the nation seems to drive much of the rhetoric in recent initiatives, such as Race to the Top, just as it drove the arguments in *A Nation at Risk* over thirty years ago. In a hearing held on December 8, 2009, the Committee on Education and Labor of the U.S. House of Representatives argued that the lack of standards undermines the American education system and the success of U.S. graduates in the global marketplace (U.S. House of Representatives Committee on Education and Labor, 2009).

In the aftermath of the global financial crisis, increased pressure is now placed on schools to enhance academic achievement and to align education and learning with the needs of the market, as illustrated in the jointly written Asia Society and Council of Chief State School Officers (2009) report entitled *International Perspectives on U.S. Education Policy and Practice: What Can We Learn from High-Performing Countries?*:

> Recognizing that education will be key to economic growth in a global knowledge and innovation-based economy and that low educational performance exacts measurable economic costs, countries around the world are focusing on increasing graduation rates, raising achievement, making educational systems more equitable, and rethinking the skills needed for the 21st century. (p. 2)

Moreover, in exploring the core standards materials, the focus on employment and skills appears in a number of places. For example, in the standards for English language arts, reading is to include not only literature but also "challenging informational texts in a range of subjects," and writing is to include not only longer research projects but also "short, focused projects (such as those commonly required in the workplace)" (Common Core State Standards Initiative [CCSSI], 2010a). There are subsections for speaking and listening, vital interpersonal skills, and a subsection for media and technology, which includes the ability to create media as well as to analyze it critically. In the "Key Points in Mathematics," (2010), there are repeated references to the importance of math skills for the workplace, for example "the ability to apply mathematics in novel situations, as college students and employees regularly do" (CCSSI, 2010b).

Central to the development of core standards, the overwhelming focus is on the performance of U.S. students on international large-scale assessments such as TIMSS and PISA, as mentioned earlier. As stated in different reports, nationwide standards have developed out of a reaction to the lagging scores of U.S. students compared to other countries on international assessments in math, science, and reading (National Governors Association, 2008). Furthermore, the standards themselves are internationally benchmarked in order to "establish a solid foundation for economic development in the 21st century" (National Governors Association, 2008, p. 5). In the same report, the International Benchmarking Advisory Group of the Common Core State Standards Initiative referred to the need to align educational standards with the perceived needs of the global economy:

> It is only through such benchmarking that countries can understand relative strengths and weaknesses of their education system and identify best practices and ways forward. *The world is indifferent to tradition and past reputations, unforgiving of frailty and ignorant of custom or practice.* Success will go to those individuals and countries that are swift to adapt, slow to complain, and open to change. (p. 7, authors' emphasis)

In an analysis of the extent to which a global dimension of learning is encompassed within the common core state standards, one of the five themes focuses on cultural diversity.

The theme of cultural diversity places importance on students developing an understanding of other perspectives and cultures. As stated in the English language arts standards (2010a),

> Students appreciate that the twenty-first-century classroom and workplace are settings in which people from often widely divergent cultures and who represent diverse experiences and perspectives must learn and work together. Students actively seek to understand other perspectives and cultures through reading and listening, and they are able to communicate effectively with people of varied backgrounds. They evaluate other points of view critically and constructively. Through reading great classic and contemporary works of literature representative of a variety of periods, cultures, and worldviews, students can vicariously inhabit worlds and have experiences much different than their own. (p. 7)

This aligns with Mitchell's (2003) argument that multiculturalism "has begun to move to a more strategic form of utilizing culture for economic purposes, and away from a sense of individual fulfillment and of the necessity of forming bonds of social and national cohesion" (p. 399). Moreover, the standards' call for the critical-thinking skills necessary for discerning citizens of a complicated world relies on the concept that there is always one right answer. In the English language arts standards (CCSSI, 2010a), for example, students are expected to be able to "assess the veracity of claims and the soundness of reasoning" (p. 7), while in the mathematics standards, one of the standards for mathematical practice is that students "construct viable arguments and critique the reasoning of others" (p. 6). These fall short of what Helen Haste called for in her twenty-first-century competencies, particularly "managing ambiguity," which she identified as "that tension between rushing to the clear, the concrete, and managing this ambiguous fuzzy area in the middle. And managing ambiguity is something we have to teach. Because we have to counter the story of a single linear solution" (Silverthorne, 2009).

The "Key Points in English Language Arts" (CCSSI, 2010a) makes only one mention of internationalism, within the reading subsection, which includes "classic myths and stories from around the world" in the list of types of literature to which students are to be exposed (http://www.corestandards.org/about-the-standards/key-points-in-english-language-arts). The specific English language arts standards for primary grades include the expectations that students can identify the underlying moral in myths and fables from diverse cultures, as well as compare and contrast similar stories as they are told in different cultures. Linked to a framework of the globalization and education policy, we might argue that in the above statement, the emphasis is on the relationship between cultural competence and employability, and in particular, developing language and culture skills in order to adapt to the changing nature of the global marketplace. The introduction to the English language arts standards (2010a) states explicitly that "a particular standard was included . . . only when the best available evidence indicated that its mastery was essential for college and career readiness in a twenty-first-century, globally competitive society" (p. 3). Although we do not wish to argue that this is in and of itself negative, it offers a rather narrow interpretation of global citizenship as linked first and foremost to the needs of the economy, overlooking key questions and challenges about citizenship in a complex and changing global world. Education has a significant role to play not only in providing students with the necessary skills for future employment, but it also plays a critical role in helping students to navigate the demands and challenges associated with the global world, which reach beyond such a narrow interpretation.

Moreover, as articulated in the standards, a global dimension of learning appears to rest on learning about the "other" ("other perspectives and cultures"). In this way, these standards do little more than reinforce a traditional, nationalistic conception of multiculturalism rooted in national solidarity (Beck & Grande, 2007). Framed in "us vs. them" rhetoric, there is risk of creating a superficial and nationalistic sense of culture and diversity, limited to an add-on study of food, flags, and festivals (Banks & Banks, 1997; Skelton et al., 2002). By framing the study of "the other," students may not be able to grasp the challenges of an interconnected and interdependent global society, which requires skills such as "being able to engage in culturally relevant and sensitive dialogue" (Fox & Diaz-Greenberg, 2006, p. 405).

A deeper global dimension might include not only moving beyond such simplistic notions of culture and identity but also offer students an opportunity to interrogate the complexities surrounding the relationship between identity, culture, and nation, which reach beyond us vs. them rhetoric. Building from Beck and Grande's (2007) work in Europe, a global dimension of learning might adopt a form of cosmopolitan solidarity, reaching beyond the national: "cosmopolitanism calls for new concepts of integration and identity that enable and affirm coexistence across borders, without requiring that distinctiveness and difference be sacrificed on the altar of supposed (national) equality" (p. 14). This form of cosmopolitan solidarity embraces both integration and difference and works to complicate questions of nationality and interdependence of people across borders. This perspective appears to be illustrated in Oxfam's (2006) curriculum for global citizenship, which states among its objectives not only content knowledge of other cultures and passive practices, like tolerance and valuing diversity, but also emotive and active goals for outrage at social injustice, participation in the community, and a willingness to act to make the world better. Further, a cosmopolitan perspective offers the opportunity to consider the global society (rather than merely the global economy), which students will form and which requires students to have the necessary cultural understanding and skills to communicate across boundaries both geographic and conceptual. After all, "as teachers, we need to be acutely aware of the need for preparing our students to work and live in a world context" (Fox & Diaz-Greenberg, 2006, p. 403).

DISCUSSION

Skelton et al. (2002) stated, "Today, helping our students develop a sense of international mindedness is more important than ever before. . . . International mindedness deserves the same rigorous exploration and treatment as math, science, language arts, and every other aspect of the curriculum that we consider important" (p. 5). As we argue in this chapter, the common core state standards recently adopted by a majority of U.S. states appear to constrain the kind of international mindedness Skelton and colleagues proposed. In exploring the policies leading up to the common core standards, the themes underlying the standards, and the standards themselves, it appears that they limit a global dimension of learning in two ways: first, to a skills-based approach (i.e., the skills required to compete in a global economy), and second, to a nationalistic perspective of culture and cultural difference, rooted in a more superficial form of multiculturalism rather than a critical understanding about global citizenship and cosmopolitanism.

Standards can be useful, and we do not wish to argue that standards are in and of themselves problematic. The common core state standards have made significant strides toward the understanding that the United States has a great deal to learn from other countries and that the ability to critique and discern is vital to the modern citizen (Marshall, 1964). However, from the perspective of Skelton and colleagues' international mindedness and Beck and Grande's (2007) notion of cosmopolitan solidarity, the new complex globalized world requires teachers and teacher educators to be critical of the underlying economic rationale of the core standards movement and to work to interpret and incorporate a critical global perspective into the standards. It is likely a faulty logic to assume that students will naturally form the skills to discern and reason fairly between divergent cultural models without such skills being explicitly developed. As teachers have a key role in not only creating skilled workers in the global economy, but also facilitating globally aware, critically minded citizens, it requires an extension and a deepening of the common core standards.

Fox and Diaz-Greenberg (2006) suggest the use of experiential training in teacher formation programs, allowing preservice teachers to know the explicit process through which they learned those same abilities they wish to encourage in their future students. They go on to suggest the use of critical pedagogical techniques and a perspective rooted in multicultural education to help teachers see beyond the standards and textbooks that could so easily fetter their classroom practice. Teacher formation programs are very much based on knowledge of learning standards and face a mounting conservative influence to focus on technique to the detriment of purpose and values, which has led to a narrowing of the part of the teacher training curriculum oriented toward the social foundations of education, such as equity, social justice, and citizenship (Neumann, 2009; Null, 2003). However, "being able to meet a standard successfully should include not only discussions about the degree to which that standard is met, but it should also entail dialogue and discussion about the pedagogical pathways that serve its implementation," which would require of U.S. teacher formation programs a much deeper critical element (Fox & Diaz-Greenberg, 2006, p. 418).

Lastly, although the focus of this chapter is on the United States and its recent adoption of the common core state standards, the application of economically driven, broadly applicable educational standards has not occurred solely in the United States but in many different national contexts. As one example, in 1995, South Africa instituted a National Qualifications Framework "as a means of addressing inequalities in learning across different racial groups in society" (Chisholm, 2007, p. 297) and "to integrate the worlds of education and training through an overarching qualifications framework" (p. 298). Similar to the common core standards initiative in the United States, South Africa's program was part of a market-based policy agenda and was "a collaboration between institutions and individuals with weak ties to one another" (p. 300), which came together to form what Chisholm called "discourse coalitions" (p. 295).

Ultimately, however, the South African system did not achieve its goals because "an outcomes based framework is essentially an assessment framework, not a framework for provision," and the structure was found to have little effect on actual classroom-level teaching and learning behaviors (Chisholm, p. 303). Chisholm's research showed that well-resourced schools were more capable of applying the curriculum and teaching changes as suggested through the framework, while poorly resourced schools were less able to do so. With the example from the South African case and against the burgeoning framework for common national standards in the United States, it is worth raising questions about whether academic standards, particularly standards so deeply based in an assumedly inescapable world capitalist market, are able to inform any real reform of the structural inequalities that challenge so many students, not only in the developing world, but also in the United States.

REFERENCES

Applebome, P. (1996, March 27). Education summit calls for tough standards to be set by states and local school districts. *New York Times.* Retrieved April 4, 2011, from http://www.nytimes.com/1996/03/27/us/education-summit-calls-for-tough-standards-be-set-states-andlocal-school.html.

Asia Society and Council of Chief State School Officers. (2009). *International perspectives on U.S. education policy and practice: What can we learn from high-performing countries?* Retrieved April 3, 2011, from http://asiasociety.org/files/learningwiththeworld.pdf.

Banks, J. A., & Banks, C. A. M. (Eds.). (1997). *Multicultural education: Issues and perspectives* (3rd ed.). Boston, MA: Allyn & Bacon.

Beck, U., & Grande, E. (2007). *Cosmopolitan Europe*. Cambridge, England: Polity Press.

Chisholm, L. (2007). Framework and outcomes-based education in southern and eastern Africa. *Comparative Education, 43*(2), 295–309.

Common Core State Standards Initiative. (2010a). *Key points in English language arts*. Retrieved March 25, 2011, from http://www.corestandards.org/about-the-standards/key-points-in-english-language-arts.

———. (2010b). *Key points in mathematics*. Retrieved March 25, 2011, from http://www.corestandards.org/about-the-standards/key-points-in-mathematics.

Dicken, P. (2003). *Global shift: Reshaping the global economic map in the 21st century* (4th ed.). New York: Guilford.

Finn, Jr., C. E., Julian, L., & Petrilli, M. J. (2006). *2006 the state of state standards*. Washington, DC: Thomas R. Fordham Foundation.

Fox, R. K., & Diaz-Greenberg, R. (2006). Culture, multiculturalism, and foreign/world language standards in U.S. teacher preparation programs: Toward a discourse of dissonance. *European Journal of Teacher Education, 29*(3), 401–22.

Goals 2000: Education America Act, HR 1804, 103rd Cong., 1st sess. (1994).

Harvey, D. (1989). *The condition of postmodernity*. Oxford, England: Blackwell.

Held, D., & McGrew, A. (Eds.). (2003). *The global transformation reader: An introduction to the globalization debate*. Cambridge, England: Polity Press.

Hood, C. (1991). A public management for all seasons. *Public Administration, 69*, 3–19.

Kivinen, O., & Nurmi, J. (2003). Unifying higher education for different kinds of Europeans. Higher education and work: A comparison of ten countries. *Comparative Education, 39*(1), 83–103.

Marshall, T. H. (1964). *Class, citizenship, and social development*. Garden City, NY: Doubleday.

Mitchell, K. (2003). Educating the national citizen in neoliberal times: From the multicultural self to the strategic cosmopolitan. *Transactions of the Institute of British Geographers, 28*(4), 387–403.

Morrow, R. A., & Torres, C. A. (2000). The state, globalization, and educational policy. In N. Burbules & C. A. Torres (Eds.), *Globalization and education: Critical perspectives* (pp. 27–56). London: Routledge.

National Commission on Excellence in Education. (1983). *A nation at risk*. Washington, DC: Department of Education.

National Governors Association, the Council of Chief State School Officers, & Achieve Inc., International Benchmarking Advisory Group. (2008). *Benchmarking for success: Ensuring U.S. students receive a world-class education*. Washington, DC: National Governors Association.

Neumann, R. (2009). Highly qualified teachers and the social foundations of education. *Phi Delta Kappan, 91*(3), 81–85.

No Child Left Behind Act of 2001, HR 1, 107th Cong., 1st Sess. (2001).

Null, J. W. (2003). Education and knowledge, not "standards and accountability": A critique of reform rhetoric through the ideas of Dewey, Bagley, and Schwab. *Educational Studies, 34*(4), 397–413.

OECD. (1995). *Governance in transition: Public management reforms in OECD countries.* Paris: OECD.

Oxfam. (2006). *Education for global citizenship: A guide for schools.* Retrieved May 16, 2011, from http://www.oxfam.org.uk/education/gc/files/education_for_global_citizenship_a_guide_for_schools.pdf.

Phillips, D., & Ochs, K. (2003). Processes of policy borrowing in education: Some explanatory and analytical devices. *Comparative Education, 49*(4), 451–61.

Power, M. (1997). *The audit society: Rituals of verification.* Oxford, England: Oxford University Press.

Ravitch, D. (1995). *National standards in American education: A citizen's guide.* Washington, DC: Brookings Institution.

Rizvi, F., & Engel, L. C. (2009). Neo-liberal globalization, educational policy, and the struggle for social justice. In W. Ayers, T. Quinn, & D. Stovall (Eds.), *The handbook of social justice in education* (pp. 529–41). Lanham, MD: Rowman & Littlefield.

Rizvi, F., & Lingard, B. (2009) *Globalizing education policy.* London: Routledge.

Samoff, J. (2003). Institutionalizing international influence. In R. F. Arnove & C. A. Torres (Eds.), *Comparative education: The dialectic of the global and the local* (pp. 409–45). Oxford, England: Rowman & Littlefield.

Silverthorne, S. (2009, August 13). Re: 5 personal core competencies for the 21st century. [Web log message]. Retrieved from http://www.bnet.com/blog/harvard/5-personal-core-competencies-for-the-21st-century/3332.

Skelton, M., Wigford, A., Harper, P., & Reeves, G. (2002). Beyond food, festivals, and flags. *Educational Leadership, 60*(2), 52–55.

Steiner-Khamsi, G. (Ed.). (2004). *The global politics of educational borrowing and lending.* New York: Teachers College Press.

U.S. Department of Education. (1999). *Federal education legislation enacted in 1994: An evaluation of implementation and impact; executive summary.* Retrieved March 15, 2011, from http://www2.ed.gov/offices/OUS/PES/1994legislation.html.

———. (2009). *Race to the top program: Executive summary.* Retrieved March 15, 2011, from http://www.ed.gov.

U.S. House of Representatives Committee on Education and Labor. (2009, December 8). Hearing: *Improving our competitiveness: Common core education standards.* Retrieved February 9, 2011, from http://frwebgate.access.gpo.gov/cgi-bin/getdoc.cgi?dbname=111_house_hearings&docid=f:53732.pdf.

Weinraub, B. (1989, September 29). Bush and governors set education goals. *New York Times.* Retrieved March 17, 2011, from http://www.nytimes.com/1989/09/29/us/bush-and-governors-set-education-goals.html.

• 5 •

Global Perspectives on the Internationalization of Teacher Education

Through an Australian Lens

Libby Tudball

INTRODUCTION: THE CHALLENGES FOR TEACHER EDUCATORS

Higher education across the globe is undergoing rapid change, but while universities rush to develop "international divisions," internationalized curriculum and policies, offshore programs, mobile academics, distance learning, and public statements that brand programs as international in focus, national interests still drive national education systems. Teacher education providers are also caught up in the rush to internationalize in diverse ways, responding to the needs of international students, but also ensuring that curricula focus on international dimensions and global concerns, yet there is a lack of rigorous research to date documenting how widespread the implementation of internationalized curricula and practice has been. In Australia and elsewhere, there is a need to problematize and further interrogate what internationalization means, how it is being translated into practice in teacher education courses, and by individual university-level teachers/lecturers in their work with students. All teacher educators should be able to articulate a view of what internationalization means to them, and how it is translated into action in their programs. Webb's (2005) view is that an institution will only become internationalized "through the creative utilization, imagination and agency of those who are staff in the university" (p. 117). Sanderson (2009) argues that we need to be able to answer the question, "What does an internationalized teacher know, do and believe in?" (p. 2). The answer will depend on the different roles academics play in the teacher education sphere. Internationalization can be connected, for example, to the education of international students, human rights education, education for equality, peace education, education for intercultural understanding, education for sustainable development, global education, cosmopolitan citizenship education, or cross-curriculum approaches to developing international mindedness.

In this chapter, perspectives on the internationalization of teacher education that guide the development of this concept are provided through an Australian lens and through discussion of the many ways that internationalization has become a necessary, inevitable, and lived experience in our programs. Discussion considers how teacher education can prepare beginning teachers to address new global challenges in their work with school students and what shifts in thinking and practices may be necessary. Internationalization is likely to be multifaceted, cross-disciplinary, and evolutionary in nature, in response to the times we are in, the places where we work, the students we teach, and the challenges that we face in our own contexts (Tudball, 2005). This chapter introduces some of the key contextual factors driving internationalization in Australia. Insights are provided through stories and examples from Australian students, curriculum goals, and policies, but also with reference to broader global perspectives on how the concept and practices of internationalization are evolving in teacher education and being connected to other issues on the international education agenda. Finally, recommendations are made for future trajectories.

For more than a decade, there has been a focus in global literature on the evolving concept of the "internationalization of education," which Bremer and van der Wende (1995) defined as "Curricula with an international orientation in content, aimed at preparing students for performing (professionally/socially) in an international and multicultural context, and designed for domestic students and/or foreign students" (p. 10). Van der Wende (1996) also sees internationalization as "any systematic effort aimed at making higher education responsive to the requirements and challenges related to the globalization of societies, economy and labor markets" (p. 18). Cambridge and Thompson (2004) maintained that *international education* (used in the broad sense of "internationalization") has more recently "been used to denote an ideology of education oriented towards 'internationalism' and 'international-mindedness'" (p. 161). In the Australian context, internationalization is no longer regarded as an optional extra. In universities across the nation, international/global dimensions are being included in vision and goal statements, and in policies and practices that often include elements of Knight's (1999) framework for approaches to internationalization, incorporating:

- *Activity*—including curriculum development, student and/or faculty exchanges, and international students;
- *Competency*—including the development of new skills, knowledge, values, and attitudes in students, faculty, and staff. The level of interest in defining global/international competencies continues to grow;
- *Ethos*—including the creation of a culture or climate on campus that promotes and supports international/intercultural initiatives; and
- *Process*—including the integration or infusion of international/intercultural dimensions into education through a combination of a range of activities, policies, and procedures. (p. 15)

More recently, Knight (2004) argued there should be a redefining of internationalization of education to include "internationalization at home"—activities that help students to develop international understandings and intercultural skills, onshore and locally—and "internationalization abroad"—all forms of education crossing borders, including mobility of students, teachers, scholars, programs, courses, and curriculum. There are increasing global flows of higher education students in and out of Australia, and methods of delivery also provide tangible evidence of internationalization at home and abroad, since both local and international students may study here in face-to-face mode, in online programs, and, increasingly, in Australian campuses and centers all over the world (Sanderson, 2009). In the Faculty of Education at Monash University, academics fly abroad to deliver courses at campuses in South Africa, Italy, Malaysia, and Singapore, and preservice teachers can experience their practicum through collaborations in countries, including the Cook Islands and South Korea. This is also a common trend in other Australian universities. However, the binaries defined by Knight (2004) of internationalization at home and abroad do neglect the larger agendas of global issues and ideas about capacity building and issues of transnational importance, which are also key challenges for teacher educators to address within the curriculum. Information and communication technologies have revolutionized the pace and form of international interactions, and both the forces of globalization and the realities of global interdependency have created new imperatives for internationalization that transcend Knight's binary.

While it is clear that many Australian academics in teacher education have moved beyond a parochial view of teacher education that merely prepares teachers for careers in their home nations, there is room for more widespread thinking and action to plan future directions in internationalization, and particularly to decide what should happen in program delivery and content. We recognize that our preservice teachers bring to our courses perspectives and experiences from all over the world, and they may leave the site of their initial teacher education during their courses for practicum experiences in diverse contexts, both in local and offshore culturally diverse schools, but how adequately are we utilizing their knowledge and empowering beginning teachers to teach in new and culturally appropriate ways? This question, along with the need to make considered decisions about what should be taught in an internationalized curriculum, provides further challenges for teacher educators.

THE AUSTRALIAN CONTEXT

Today, more than 23 percent of Australians were born overseas, and our population hails from over 230 nations. There are now new waves of immigrants from the African continent and from China and India. Australia is undoubtedly one of the world's most culturally diverse nations. We know that as our graduates commence their teaching, they may be scattered all over the globe (Marginson, 2011). In 2011, in a lecture theater packed with four hundred final-year education students, I asked who planned to travel overseas for their first teaching position; at least 70 percent of hands were raised. Two-way international migration and mobility now characterize our age. We are preparing preservice teachers for very different careers—to teach school students who in many parts of the world have greater access than ever before to new technologies, who need to be ready for global challenges not envisaged by previous generations, and who need different skills and capacities that are challenging teacher educators to redevelop and renew programs. In my teacher education faculty we have introduced bridging courses for international students to understand local school cultures, core units on education for sustainability, and programs including new media and integrated curriculum strategies, to lead new thinking and action in teaching and learning, including international dimensions. However, it is still true to say that many Australian academics have a long way to go before they can claim that their courses are leading internationalization, though most would agree that teacher education must prepare preservice teachers to be professional educators anywhere in the world, with an awareness of global concerns.

The highly culturally diverse nature of the Australian population—increasing global flows of students, the impact of high-speed Internet access, blogs, wikis, Moodles, mobile phones, iPads, and other new technologies—are all factors stimulating the need for international changes in pedagogy and programs. Preservice teachers (PSTs) can rapidly access information about curricula and programs in any part of the world where they plan to teach. PSTs who will return to Africa or China, for example, do require some knowledge of local curricula to complete practicum experience in Australia, but all PSTs should develop the capacity to apply broader knowledge gained in courses about pedagogy to other education contexts. They should be empowered to make transformative judgments about what will and will not apply in different international contexts where they commence their teaching.

South Australian academic Gavin Sanderson (2009) notes:

> Most of the research that has been carried out on internationalization in higher education over the past two decades has focused on activities at the organizational level, and the social and academic experiences of international students. Concurrently, the discourse emanating from universities speaks of their determination and capacity to equip all students with the knowledge, skills and attitudes required to make a success of life and work in what is frequently coined (rather restrictively) as the "global market economy." (p. 2)

While the increased numbers of international students, and the marketization and commodification of higher education, have provided key drivers for change, it has become increasingly clear that the global agenda for internationalization extends beyond these considerations. There is a genuine concern among many teacher education colleagues that programs must be authentic, purposeful, and focused on developing programs suited to 21st-century learning emphases and learners.

In Australian universities, there is now constant interaction and movement across cultures and nations, among staff and students. This includes transnational interactions at personal, academic, and institutional levels, but at the same time there are also large-scale global convergences and cross-border collaborations in education such as through the Programme for International Student Assessment (more commonly known as PISA) testing and global research projects, representing the intersection of internationalization and globalization. Altbach (2004) argues that internationalization is both a reflection of and an agent of globalization. In developing teacher education programs, academics are responding to a complex range of forces that have encouraged rethinking of program focus and delivery to ensure that internationalization becomes a reality in practice. At the same time, teacher educators need to recognize that school educators are also responding to the internationalization agenda within both local curricula and internationally accredited programs, including the International Baccalaureate and the Council of International Schools (CIS), through offshore programs and exchange, and with a greater emphasis on developing school students' global skills and competencies. In 2009, in a ministerial forward to a Victorian state government school-level policy document, which should also drive action in the preparation of teachers, the then state minister Bronwyn Pike said, "Knowledge of multicultural perspectives and of emerging global issues, and an open, respectful, compassionate attitude to difference are vital . . . (and) . . . students who possess the skills, knowledge and attitudes of a global and multicultural citizen will have a competitive edge and contribute to our national advantage" (Department of Education and Early Childhood Development, DEECD, 2009, p. 1). This policy was not defined as "internationalization," yet the expectations are consistent with how the concept is evolving in theory and practice (Tudball, 2005).

THE CONTEXT AND DRIVERS FOR INTERNATIONALIZATION: OUR CHANGING WORLD

At the Asia Education Foundation National Forum in Australia (June 2005), Sophie Palavestra, a senior high school student from Canberra, made a speech that drew on the work of respected Australian educator, the late Professor Hedley Beare, in expressing her ideas about the future of education. The following extracts provide an alert that teacher education programs must respond to as part of the push toward internationalization. Sophie said,

> I want you to understand . . . how I think about my future and my worldview. Wherever I live and work, I will certainly be mixing in a multinational, multi-faith, multi-cultural setting. During my lifetime, a planet-wide economic system will operate, controlled not so much by big nations as by big business networks and regional centers of trade like Singapore, Los Angeles, Tokyo, and Sydney. By the time I am 35 more people will live in Shanghai than in the whole of the south Pacific—including Australia and New Zealand. The really prosperous countries will trade in technical skills, problem-solving skills and in strategic brokerage. These workers will be the knowledge workers—working across national borders—working inter-culturally—speaking more than one language—probably including an Asian language. That's the kind of job I want. The Asia/Pacific area will be a strong focus of my world. China already has a population ten times that of Japan. The Asian continent (from India to Japan) already accounts for half the world's population. . . . There are three billion people in Asia. Half of them are under 25. They are my contemporaries. They will be my partners—my competitors. It will not matter what nationality I have, because my world is smaller, people move about, and most workplaces will be internationalized. My world is likely to be borderless. I will probably be employed in an internationally owned firm, and it is likely that in my home we will speak Japanese, Korean, Spanish, or Chinese.

Our environment will be changed. In the 1950s, when my parents were born, only two cities in the world, London and New York, had more than 8 million inhabitants. . . . In 2015, there will be about thirty-four such cities, half of them in Asia. Environmentally what happens within the border of one country is no longer solely that country's business. Environmental responsibilities will be enforced internationally. By the time I am 50, the world could be threatened by "green wars," unless my generation does something to balance up the unequal access to clean water, good topsoil, electric power and food distribution.

Tourism and travel collectively are becoming the world's biggest industry and globally will employ the largest number of people. It has been predicted that in 25–30 years there will be 5–10 million Chinese tourists, alone, visiting Australia each year. What skills and understandings will Australians working in the tourism and travel industry need? By far the world's largest Muslim country is Indonesia with a population of over 220 million—larger than that of Japan and Russia—we will have to learn about Islam at school. And because the "tigers of Asia" are largely Confucian economies, schools will need to teach about those characteristics of Confucian societies, which produce economic success and community cohesion. A lot of the older textbooks used around the world were Eurocentric in their thinking and are out-of-date. My schooling must teach me about living comfortably in a multi-cultural world.

Do you know what an international curriculum looks like, and how it can be taught? My school says I need to be a global citizen. So do you know what to teach me? . . . And do you know *how* to teach me? Are you confident that you can design a curriculum, which will equip me to live in my world? My name is Sophie. And I am sitting in one of your classrooms today. (Adapted from Beare, *Creating a Future School*, 2001)

Sophie's speech demonstrates the need for radically new emphases in schools and teacher education, and for new approaches to selection of content, and teaching and learning strategies, because of internationalization, global trends, and issues. Today's world is multifaceted and rapidly changing. It is no longer possible to successfully operate in a complex global economy from a monocultural and monolingual base. Our beginning teachers require different personal, social, and vocational competencies, and so do the students they teach. They need the skills and knowledge to know how to negotiate confidently the cultural, religious, and linguistic differences within communities. We are preparing teachers for a mobile and uncertain world, where new skills are required, new forms of learning are necessary, and one of the few constants is change. More importantly, programs and pedagogy must be developed to provide authentic and purposeful responses to the forces of internationalization and the need to prepare students for a rapidly globalizing world.

AUSTRALIAN POLICY IMPERATIVES FOR INTERNATIONALIZATION

While global emphases are important in teacher education programs, through an Australian lens, imperatives exist for a much greater focus on Asia. In the national policy statement *Engaging Young Australians with Asia* (Curriculum Corporation, 2005), it is argued that "the countries of the Asian region are of critical importance, since they are our closest neighbors and major trading partners" (p. 2). Noted Australian General Peter Cosgrove (2000) declared that "good neighbors learn to speak each other's languages . . . respect each other's religious and cultural beliefs . . . allow for differences and be inclusive . . . spend time with each other . . . [and] understand that contentious issues should be resolved through negotiation" (p. 4). People from diverse countries in Asia "represent the cultural heritage of a growing number of Australians. Their rich traditional and contemporary cultures provide opportunities for our social, creative and intellectual development" (Curriculum Corporation, 2005, p. 2). These messages are as relevant to teacher educators elsewhere in the world as in Australia. However, the point is also made that "now more than ever we live in one world. We face issues that can only be addressed internationally: sustainable futures, the changing world economy and security of people and environments" (Curriculum Corporation, 2005, p. 4). In the Melbourne Declaration on Educational Goals for Young Australians (MCEETYA, 2008), it is stated that "global integration and international mobility have increased rapidly in the past decade. As a consequence, new and exciting opportunities for Australians are emerging. This heightens the need to nurture an appreciation of, and respect for social, cultural and religious diversity, and a sense of global citizenship" (p. 4).

A further goal is for school students to be "active and informed citizens" (p. 1), with "the knowledge, skills and understanding to participate in local, national, regional and global community contexts" (p. 1). This requires a clear focus on civics and citizenship in teacher education that has not been sufficiently evident across the nation to date. In the "Shape of the Australian Curriculum Version 2" (ACARA, 2010) paper, it is recognized that the Australian national curriculum currently being developed will be an evolving document that responds to the times we are in. Teacher educators will also need to respond to the times we are in with an eye on local and international issues. It is clarified in the section on "general capabilities" that

> The disciplines provide a foundation of learning in schools because they reflect the ways in which knowledge has, and will continue to be developed and codified. However, 21st century learning does not fit neatly into

a curriculum solely organised by learning areas or subjects that reflect the disciplines. Increasingly, in a world where knowledge itself is constantly growing and evolving, students need to develop a set of skills, behaviours and dispositions, or general capabilities that apply across subject-based content and equip them to be lifelong learners able to operate with confidence in a complex, information-rich, globalised world. (ACARA, 2010, p. 18)

This suggests a clear policy implementation challenge for educators at all levels to look at teaching and learning in new ways.

EDUCATION FOR SUSTAINABILITY: AN UNAVOIDABLE PERSPECTIVE IN INTERNATIONALIZATION?

A further key driver for internationalization in higher education and in the Australian context is the need for universities to build students' capacities to understand issues of global concern. This is connected to a rising view that universities should play a role in education for the public good (Nixon, 2011). There have, for example, been constant instances worldwide of educators taking action to increase education for sustainability (EFS) in schools and universities, demonstrating the serious concern educators have about the importance of this field. Henderson and Tilbury's (2004) review of school programs for sustainability documents international instances of diverse actions. They note for example that "the Scottish Eco-schools program encourages teachers to link subject areas such as health education, enterprise, international, personal and social education, citizenship and sustainable development" (p. 27). But how frequently and effectively do we encourage PSTs to make these links and know how to plan EFS? A number of education theorists have described "action competence" as a critical method in teaching school students about sustainable development (Jensen & Schnack, 1997; Lundegard & Wickman, 2007). Action implies a set of intentional behaviors, and competence implies being ready, willing, and able to inspire change (Jensen & Schnack, 1997). Rauch (2002) agreed that "action competence aims to promote pupils' readiness and abilities to concern themselves with environmental issues in a democratic manner, by developing their own criteria for decision-making and behavior, and to prevent pupils from adopting patterns of thinking without reflection" (p. 45). The clear need to model and develop strategies such as these in teacher education internationally is evident, so that PSTs see that their role in action competence can facilitate and motivate students to take positive action in promoting sustainable development.

In Australia, the agreed national goals for schooling also urge attention to education for sustainability as a key element of school and teacher education programs, a focus that is also clearly on the international education agenda. The goal states that "complex environmental, social and economic pressures such as climate change that extend beyond national borders pose unprecedented challenges, requiring countries to work together in new ways" (MCEETYA, 2008, p. 5). In the preface to *Teaching for Uncertain Futures: The Open Book Scenarios Project* in Australia, Headley Beare's leadership in thinking is once again present where he argues that "business as usual is not a survival option. More particularly, schools cannot afford to be complacent, as they are responsible for educating the next generation of the world's citizens" (Beare, 2008, p. 9). In a wake-up call for educators, Beare reminded us that in the future, "students will be globally oriented in a way we never conceived of in the 20th century, and what they must learn at school has changed dramatically.... Their lifestyle patterns will need to be radically overhauled too" (p. 9). Put simply, the resources that middle-class Europeans, Australians, and North Americans currently use in their lives and work are not sustainable, so schools must act urgently to provide students with thoughtful alternative models for the future, and so must teacher education programs, internationally. Increasing instances of extreme weather events, droughts, floods, earthquakes, and crop failures in Australia and elsewhere are heightening concerns. The evidence is overwhelming that it is the responsibility of teacher educators to find space for issues of global concern within our programs, as Sophie's speech noted. In February 2007, the United Nations published a 1,200-page assessment of the globe's health (United Nations Foundation & Sigma XI, 2007), containing contributions from 2,500 scientists, citing 6,000 reports and reviews by 750 experts. It concludes that climate change trends are almost certainly the result of human activity and that global temperatures and sea levels are rising, so the planet faces the loss of places of human habitation, snow will vanish from all but the highest peaks, and there will be an increasing incidence of extreme and violent weather (Chandler, 2007, p. 1). Minchin (2007) reaches the enigmatic view that "the human and economic costs of climate change are likely to be highest in poor countries, which have typically contributed least because of their much lower greenhouse gas emissions" (p. 1), and the challenges for teacher education in those parts of the world will be immense. Beare (2008) does however provide a note of optimism, stating that there is "growing evidence that many members of Generation Y—those in secondary school and those in their twenties—are taking initiatives and making interventions, altruistically, selflessly and courageously, in ways never characteristic of the baby boomer generation before them.... They are showing a propensity to get up and do something creative and constructive about the state of the world" (p. 3). School and teacher education programs will need to increase efforts to address these issues in positive ways.

RESPONDING TO THE IMPACT OF THE KNOWLEDGE ERA: AN IMPERATIVE FOR INTERNATIONALIZATION

In the landmark publication *The World Is Flat* (2005), Thomas Friedman signaled that we are in a new era, because internationalism is reality:

> Transnational engagement, flows, interactions which have implications for schools, universities and communities. . . . The net result of this convergence is the creation of a global, Web-enabled playing field that allows for multiple forms of collaboration—the sharing of knowledge and work—in real time, without regard to geography, distance, or, in the near future, even language. No, not everyone has access to this platform, this playing field, but it is open today to more people in more places on more days in more ways than anything like it ever before in the history of the world. (pp. 176–77)

In Australia, there are many instances where teachers are working in teams to create more open and collaborative learning environments rather than a controlling, authoritarian atmosphere where the lone-wolf teacher delivers knowledge and information in closed classrooms. Teachers are increasingly "facilitators of learning," not tellers, and beginning teachers need to be ready to work in new learning spaces, where their students are knowledge creators, and the teacher need not be the fount of all knowledge. The labor market in the new global economy rewards knowledge workers who can self-learn, problem solve, and adapt to rapid change, so our teacher education programs must ensure that PSTs have the strategies to lead this kind of learning in schools across the world. C21st learners are no longer content to sit and read from a single text that may be years out of date; they expect to have access to up-to-the-minute engaging resources, YouTube clips, instant news, photographs, multiple sources, and the opportunity to transform this information in authentic ways.

At Washington International School in Washington, D.C., principal Clayton Lewis has led international collaboration among schools and the creation of "News Action" (Student News Action Network, 2011), which is

> created and is maintained by students and teachers at Washington International School in collaboration with TakingITGlobal and bureau schools worldwide. The Network takes the concept of the school newspaper beyond school walls and the confines of print media, allowing students to

work collaboratively on a global level to create an interactive, multimedia-rich student-driven online newspaper. It brings together a network of students in an online peer-driven environment to address issues of local and global significance, such as poverty, the environment, and human rights, in a creative and constructive format that culminates in meaningful efforts to make a positive impact on their world. Contributors bring their unique voices to the discussion, representing their regions and their cultural histories. (Network website)

Commentators on the significance of this program include Daniel Pink, author of *A Whole New Mind* (2006) and *Drive: The Surprising Truth about What Motivates Us* (2009), who notes that "News Action is one of the most exciting new ventures I've seen in a long while. It will help students sharpen some of the 21st century's most important skills—communication, collaboration, and conceptual thinking. But equally important, it offers young people a meaningful way to engage with the world, direct their own work, and shape the public conversation. This one-of-a-kind program has the potential to remake journalism and reinvigorate education" (Student News Action Network, 2011). Doug Jehl, foreign editor of the *Washington Post*, notes, "I am a huge supporter of this approach. It offers a remarkable opportunity to help young people make sense of the world in an era of information overload. A global audience offers students an extra incentive to discern what is important from what is not, and then to deliver clear, confident, sound judgments, tools that will serve them in whatever career they choose." Jean Vahey, executive director/CEO of the European Council of International Schools, agrees that

> New media in the form of blogs, Twitter, Facebook, YouTube and a plethora of other online forums, has dramatically changed how news and issues are accessed and analyzed. What NewsAction gives students is an opportunity to examine critically current issues and to communicate with their international student peers. By providing a forum for both reporting and learning, NewsAction allows students to apply what they learn in school to authentic, contemporary situations. It elevates the opinions of international students, putting them at the forefront of addressing and understanding the most important global issues. Services like NewsAction are crucial for helping shape the opinions of the next-generation of global leadership. (Student News Action Network, 2011)

The mantra continues; teacher education programs must ensure that PSTs continue to lead these kinds of international initiatives.

It is now unavoidable for teacher education to recognize the power of new technologies. Many beginning teachers have information and communication technology (ICT) skills far superior to many of their teacher educators.

Their skills directly connect young people to the knowledge world and to learning. They are surfing the Internet, networking, collaborating, accessing vast levels of information, taking risks in their learning, and exploring and manipulating information technologies. However, these skills must be further incorporated into school and teacher education. ICT can be used in the more collaborative approaches to teaching and learning, where the skills of students and teachers are complementary: students can access a world of information, but their teachers can guide them in its use, in creating knowledge from it, and can help them to deal with the wide range of ethical questions that arise.

THE FUTURE OF INTERNATIONALIZED TEACHER EDUCATION PROGRAMS

Securing a commitment to the internationalization of teacher education is a complex and multifaceted undertaking that includes complex considerations including individual characteristics of students, the location and resources of universities, and the purpose and goals of different aspects of courses, right through to how academics should respond to international obligations that should inform global programs. At the microlevel, we need to be aware of who our students are, their previous education experiences, and their areas of expertise, as well as who and where they might teach. Teacher education programs require new enabling tools if we are to adequately prepare beginning teachers for schools of the twenty-first century. We can't "tell" preservice teachers all that they need to know, or predict the changes they may encounter, and there is no one-size-fits-all for our students, who may teach in diverse contexts all over the world and will continue to face new challenges. Lortie (1975) put forward his now famous notion of the "apprenticeship of observation" and his view that "the average student has spent 13,000 hours in direct contact with classroom teachers by the time he graduates from high school" (p. 61). Mewborn and Tyminski (2006) note that "the catchphrase 'apprenticeship of observation' has become synonymous with the claim that teachers teach as they were taught, and has been widely used to explain the apparent lack of influence of teacher education programs" (p. 71). They argue that "Lortie's work is also used to support the assumption that there is a cycle of intellectual poverty in teaching because future teachers cannot be expected to break away from the traditional teaching they have experienced as students" (p. 71). But Mewborn and Tyminski (2006) agree that "teacher education programs and those who enter them have changed." While we still have much to do to optimize teacher education experiences, PSTs bring to their courses international experiences and competencies, and awareness and skills in new technologies that have evolved markedly since their own school education. It is our challenge to ensure that we offer internationalized models, giving attention to new imperatives and innovations such as the network program discussed previously. However, some perennial aspects of effective teacher education retain their importance, for example, the continuing importance of teachers building strong, respectful, and collegial relationships with students, and some focus on subject specialism. But as Quisumbing and de Leo (2002) argued, specialization is proving to be less useful in our changing world, where multiskilling and integration of knowledge are essential. Beginning teachers require skills as innovative curriculum planners and the capacity to make judgments about what should be learned, how and why.

In Abowitz and Harnish's (2006) framework of the "meaning of transnational and global citizenship," they argue that educational programs that are "global/transnational or international should move from a national/region-centered perspective to a more trans-regional or global perspective" (p. 653). They urge the view that students must learn about their own country as interdependent with other communities and nations, and students should learn to analyze problems of interdependence, inequality, and conflict between different groups, communities, and nations, and be aware of the existence of multiple perspectives on the world. This has synergy with Nussbaum's views (1994, 1996) that students should address global issues and recognize humanity in its diversity, creating a climate beneficial to local and international democratic processes.

In many parts of the world, internationalized dimensions are expected in schools; for example, Cappelle, Crippin, and Lundgren (2009) note that

> the Swedish national curriculum requires all teachers in all subjects to adhere to four overriding perspectives that permeate education at all levels—the historical, the international, the environmental and the ethical. The last three of these apply to intercultural and multicultural education, and to global education. Education is not "about" citizenship, but "for" global citizenship, and thus it is an ideological and normative project. It aims to provide young Europeans and teachers with the necessary competences to navigate a multicultural and globalised world.... Citizenship education is not only about transmitting collective values and attitudes by means of the school system, but also about transforming them so that they harmonize with political and ideological goals. (p. 11)

In Spain, education for citizenship and human rights includes citizenship competences to be developed by students, to understand the features of today's societies, its growing diversity, and its evolutionary character, in addition to demonstrating an understanding of the contribution that different cultures have made to the evolution and progress of mankind, and to have a sense of belonging to the society in which they live. In short, students should develop a sense of global citizenship compatible with the local identity (Trotta Tuomi, Jacott, & Lundgren, 2008). In Finland, the current National Core Curriculum for Basic Education (2004) states that

> the underlying values of basic education are human rights, equality, democracy, natural diversity, preservation of environmental viability, and the endorsement of multiculturalism. Basic education should promote responsibility, a sense of community, and respect for the rights and freedoms of the individual, and help to support the formation of the pupil's own cultural identity and his or her own part in Finnish society and a globalizing world. The instruction also helps to promote tolerance and intercultural understanding. (Trotta Tuomi, Jacott, & Lundgren, 2008, p. 13)

A decade ago, Beare (2001) argued that schools have a responsibility to ensure the systematic development of children's worldviews and belief systems, as well as helping them to acquire useful knowledge and skills. But do teacher education programs sufficiently emphasize these concerns, and within what "subjects" or aspects of courses? Teachers need to be role models for knowledge-era skills, including collaboration and teamwork, shared learning, self-direction and negotiation, shared expectations, knowledge management rather than knowledge imparting, and knowledge creation rather than information finding. Programs need to shift their focus from more traditional transmission of information to supporting young people to learn more independently, a greater emphasis on inquiry-based teaching and learning, and investigations of contemporary global issues within moral and ethical dimensions.

If we are to successfully prepare beginning teachers to provide the knowledge, skills, and capacities required in Sophie's world, we must provide opportunities for consideration of global issues across learning areas, and an explicit focus on how preservice teachers can ensure that school students can be internationally minded and interculturally competent. Teacher educators need to embrace change, and in Australia and elsewhere they need to be receptive to and empathetic toward diverse cultures and ideas. This requires understanding of broader philosophical and pedagogical issues involved in the development of cultural understanding. When successful practice is identified, it must be documented and shared.

CONCLUSION

Kemmis (1990) argued that "curricula reveal how nations and states interpret themselves and how they want to be interpreted. Equally, debates about curriculum reveal the fundamental concerns, uncertainties and tensions which preoccupy nations and states as they struggle to adapt to changing circumstances" (p. 81). In this chapter it has been asserted that internationalization of teacher education in Australia is no longer an optional extra because of a complex range of factors, including flows of students and ideas, strong policy imperatives for change, the impact of new technologies, increasing global interdependency, and shared international concerns. Singh (2002) urges educators to provide opportunities for all students to be able to know how they relate to the nation-state in a changing world of relationships, how they relate to transnational and supranational organizations, how they relate to humanity and to the global/local ecology. He further argued that "through an internationalized curriculum, young people can be assisted to develop a more critical understanding of their own identity; who they are; where they belong; and how they might position themselves and their views in relation to dominant views" (p. 5). Singh (2002) speaks of the "new internationalist worker, citizen and learner" as someone who "is supported by a university education based on innovative approaches to teaching and learning to meet the demands of the global economy" (p. 1). Our beginning teachers need to cultivate a belief in cooperation, collaboration, respect, and a desire for mutual understanding. A great deal of educational literature today reflects common themes articulating a vision for a more just, peaceful, and sustainable world, emphasizing the importance of relationships and interdependence and the need to develop clear values, qualities, and dispositions that support preferred futures. Beare (2007) commented that "after half a century of experience in their midst, I know that the educator profession is by nature future-oriented and almost incurably hopeful. It comes from being daily with the rising generation and with discharging the responsibility of preparing them for their futures" (p. 16). In another of his landmark papers, Beare quoted his joint work with Rick Slaughter in *Education for the Twenty-First Century* (1993), a forecast which has been proven over and over again to be accurate:

> If you want to change the world, then tell the kids first, a teacher once said to us. . . . Children can help to bring about change in the wider community. Generating new ideas about the world and propagating them are tasks, which can be entrusted to the young. If educators are persistent, systematic and consistent, the process can be achieved largely through schools . . . (for) no one is more effective at educating parents than children. So one way to transform prevailing world-views is to help young people teach adults [about it]! (pp. 18–19)

Another way to internationalize is to ensure that teacher education programs empower new teachers in meaningful ways. Preservice teachers are entitled to an internationalized curriculum that gives them the capacity to understand their local, national, and global identity, leading to an appreciation of their future role as leaders of learning in the global world. It is teacher educators' responsibility to ensure that they experience that curriculum.

REFERENCES

Abowitz, K. K., & Harnish, J. (2006). Contemporary discourses of citizenship. *Review of Educational Research, 76*(4), 653–90.

Altbach, P. (2004). Globalization and the university: Myths and realities in an unequal world. *Tertiary education and management, 10*(1), 3.

Australian Curriculum and Reporting Authority. (2010). *Shape of the Australian Curriculum Version 2* (ACARA, 2010).

Beare, H. (2001) *Creating a future school*. Abingdon: Routledge, Falmer.

———. (2007). If this is humanity's final century, then . . . don't just stand there. Do something! *Learning Matters, 12*(1), 3–9, Catholic Education Office Melbourne.

———. (2008). Introduction to *Teaching for uncertain futures*: The Open Book Scenarios Project. Retrieved from www.educationreview.com.au.

Beare, H., & Slaughter, R. (1993). *Education for the twenty-first century*. London: Routledge.

Bremer, L., & van der Wende, M. (1995). *Internationalizing the curriculum in higher education: Experiences in the Netherlands*. The Hague: The Netherlands Organization for International Cooperation in Higher Education.

Cambridge, J., & Thompson, J. (2004). Internationalism and globalization as contexts for international education. *Compare, 34*(2), 161.

Cappelle, G., Crippin, G., & Lundgren, U. (2009) *Emerging global dimensions in education: Preparing students to be agents of social change*. CiCe Guidelines on Citizenship Education in a Global Context.

Chandler, J. (2007, January 1). Scientists in unison: We're ruining earth. *The Age* (Melbourne), p. 1.

Cosgrove, P. (2000). *Australia's defense and the lessons of East Timor*. Public lecture.

Curriculum Corporation. (2005). *Engaging young Australians with Asia*. Asia Education Foundation.

Department of Education and Early Childhood Development. (2009). *Education for global and multicultural citizenship: A strategy for Victorian government schools, 2009–2013*. (DEECD).

Friedman, T. (2005). *The world is flat: A brief history of the globalised world in the 21st century*. London: Allen Lane.

Henderson, K., & Tilbury, D. (2004). *Whole-school approaches to sustainability: An international review of sustainable school programs*. Report prepared by the Australian Research Institute in Education for Sustainability (ARIES) for the Department of the Environment and Heritage, Australian government.

Jensen, B. B., & Schnack, K. (1997). The action competence approach in environmental education. *Environmental Education Research, 12*, 471–86.

Kemmis, S. (1990). *Curriculum, contestation and change: Essays on education.* Geelong, Victoria, Faculty of Education, Deakin University.

Knight, J. (1999). Internationalisation of higher education. In H. de Wit & J. Knight (Eds.), *Quality and internationalisation in higher education* (pp. 13–28). Paris: Organisation for Economic Co-operation and Development.

———. (2004, March). Internationalization remodeled: Definition, approaches, and rationales. *Journal of Studies in International Education, 8*(1), 5–31.

Lortie, D. (1975). *Schoolteacher.* Chicago: University of Chicago Press.

Lundegard, I., & Wickman, P-O. (2007). Conflicts of Interest: An indispensable element of education for sustainable development. *Environmental Education Research,* 13, (1), 1–15.

Marginson, S. (2011). Higher education and global public good(s). *Dialogue* (published by the Academy of Social Sciences in Australia), *30*(1), 21–29.

Mewborn, D., & Tyminski, A. (2006, November). Lortie's apprenticeship of observation revisited. *For the Learning of Mathematics, 26,* 3. University of Georgia, FLM Publishing Association, Edmonton, Alberta, Canada.

Minchin, L. (2007, January 30). Reef facing extinction. *The Age* (Melbourne), pp. 1, 11.

Ministerial Council on Education, Employment, Training and Youth Affairs. (2008). *Melbourne declaration on educational goals for young Australians,* MCEETYA, Melbourne. http://www.mceetya.edu.au/mceetya/melbourne_declaration,25979.html.

Nixon, J. (2011). *Higher education and the public good: Imagining the university.* London: Continuum International.

Nussbaum, M. (1994). Patriotism and cosmopolitanism. *Boston Review, 19*(5).

———. (1996). Patriotism and cosmopolitanism. In J. Cohen (Ed.), *For love of country: Debating the limits of patriotism.* Boston, MA: Beacon Press.

Palavestra, S. (2005). Speech delivered at the Asia Education National forum, Canberra, Australia.

Petocz, P., & Reid, A. (2008). Evaluating the internationalised curriculum. In M. Hellsten & A. Reid (Eds.), *Researching international pedagogies.* New York: Springer.

Pink, D. (2006). *A whole new mind: Why right-brainers will rule the future.* New York: Penguin.

———. (2009). *Drive: The surprising truth about what motivates us.* New York: Penguin.

Quisumbing, L., & de Leo, J. (2002). Values education in a changing world: Some UNESCO perspectives and initiatives. *Australian College of Education College Year Book 2002.* Canberra: Australian College of Education.

Rauch, F. (2002). The potential of education for sustainable development for reform in schools. *Environmental Education Research, 8,* 43–51.

Sanderson, G. (2009, June 19). *The secret lives of internationalised lecturers: A detective's story.* Paper presentation, CICIN conference, Internationalising the Home Student, Oxford Brookes University, UK.

Singh, M. (2002, 6–8 December). *Aligning university curricula to the global economy: Making opportunities for new teaching/learning through the internationalisation of education.* Paper presented at the 2002 Australian and New Zealand Comparative and International Education Society Conference (Internationalizing Education in the Asia-Pacific Region: Critical Reflections, Critical Times), Armidale.

Student News Action Network. (2011). *About us.* Retrieved from http://newsaction.tigweb.org/about.

Trotta Tuomi, M., Jacott, L., & Lundgren, L. (2008). *Education for world citizenship: Preparing students to be agents of social change; CiCe Thematic Network Project (Guidelines on citizenship education in a global context).* Institute for Policy Studies in Education, London Metropolitan University.

Tudball, L. (2005). Grappling with internationalisation of the curriculum at the secondary school level: Issues and tensions for educators. *Australian Journal of Education, 49*, 2005.

United Nations Foundation, Sigma Xi Scientific Expert Group. (2007). *Confronting climate change: Avoiding the unmanageable and managing the unavoidable.* Retrieved May 1, 2011, from http://www.carbontax.org/blogarchives/2007/02/28/united-nations-foundation-and-sigma-xi-on-confronting-climate-change.

Van der Wende, D. (1996). Internationalising the curriculum in higher education. In *Internationalisation of higher education.* Paris: Organisation for Economic Cooperation and Development (OECD).

Webb, G. (2005). Internationalisation of the curriculum: An institutional approach. In J. Carroll & J. Ryan (Eds.), *Teaching international students: Improving learning for all* (pp. 109–18). London: Routledge.

Section 2

AREAS OF COMPLEXITY AND CONFLUENCE

Questions Still to Be Answered in U.S. Schools and Teacher Education

In designing teacher education programs that embrace international learning, the previous section focused on the knowledge, skills, and attitudes that support teacher educators as they prepare teachers for the shifting populations that are the hallmarks of a new world. Such dispositions lead to natural engagements with other critical issues influencing education but also give rise to greater complexity. Schools are cultural, social, economic, political, and technological microcosms, where the challenges and injustices of the broader society affect the individual student in profound ways. Thinking about internationalizing teacher education means that there are areas of complexity and confluence leading to further questions. What does this mean for families? How do children process different experiences and different systems? What roles do different learning styles and technology play in internationalizing teacher education? These questions require flexibility on the part of teacher educators to fine-tune their curricula or open space up to debate how the different influences might be determined by the contexts, not only of their local region where teachers might go to work, but also the global community, in which teachers and students are moving.

These questions offer a challenge to teacher educators. The task of teacher educators is not just to prepare teachers for a more global world, but to engage teachers to then assist their students in developing a deeper understanding of what it means to learn, work, and live in a shifting global environment. It has often been considered enough to offer some readings and encourage opportunities for pre-service teachers to work with "diverse" groups of children to allow teacher educators to feel like they are doing their part. Yet that still does not prepare teachers to better understand the global scope of knowledge, movement, cultures, and allegiances that are permeating through schools in the United States today. Teachers that we have worked with speak of discomfort and lack of preparation when they work in classrooms with students from multiple corners of the globe. Uncertainty over political, cultural, religious, and social knowledge, which might allow them to build relationships with students, dominates their concerns. Beyond that, there is also a sense that there is a difference while being unsure of how to approach such difference.

These are the areas of confluence and complexity. It is a confluence in that education is now seen as a universal right. Children come from rich and poor countries with the expectation that education will offer them opportunities and open doors to greater stability and success. It is complexity in that many of the students coming into the United States have emerged out of different educational systems, with experiences that are unfamiliar to American teachers. To reach these students, teachers need to be better prepared to understand the roles that family, language, conflict, and educational styles have to play in learning. Teacher educators will have to develop curricula that can enhance the ways in which teachers understand such issues.

So how do teacher educators build their own knowledge base to deepen their students' knowledge? What issues and patterns of movement will influence how teacher educators make sense of the global shifts that will impact the classrooms their students will be entering in the next one, three, five, or ten years? Teacher educators have enormous influence in preparing thousands of teachers every year, yet their own knowledge base on this issue requires systematic updating as well. As a result, this next section addresses some of the areas that we believe are areas of confluence and complexity. Going back to teacher educators and teachers who have worked in international settings and with an international disposition of working in internationally minded ways, we sought to ask them some of these same questions. How do international families respond to teachers in American schools? What role do international crises play on children in the teaching and learning process? In what ways do models such as Advanced Placement and the International Baccalaureate have an impact in American schools? What relationships develop between content and pedagogy and international learning and teaching styles? And where does technology fit in internationalizing teacher education? These questions provide perspectives on the issues of confluence and raise thoughts on the complexity of working with teacher educators to internationalize teacher education. They also offer lessons learned and best practices for others who are seeking to address similar challenges in their own curricula. We hope that it is a sampling of the ways in which teacher-educators and practicing teachers are approaching the task of preparing teachers for a more international student body.

· 6 ·

Engaging Teachers in Building Relationships with International Families

Monimalika Day

$\mathcal{T}$he family has been the most critical social setting for educating a child since prehistoric times (Barbour, Barbour, & Scully, 2008). According to Bornstein (2001), children learn from family members through participation in various routine activities and through direct instruction of important skills by their elders. Children gain knowledge about important historical events, the rules of survival, and cultural values of a society through interactions with family members. The various tasks that families perform to meet the needs of the children and adult members are referred to as family functions (Turnbull, Turnbull, Erwin, Soodak, & Shogren, 2011). The authors identify eight categories of family functions: affection, self-esteem, spirituality, economics, daily care, socialization, recreation, and education. It is sometimes assumed that family members who are not literate play a marginal or limited role in the education of their children. Contrary to this belief, research suggests that parents and other elders in the family can play an important role in the education of the children (Heath, 1983). However, schools have traditionally failed to acknowledge the importance of developing partnerships with families to optimize children's learning.

COLLABORATION BETWEEN SCHOOLS AND INTERNATIONAL FAMILIES IN THE UNITED STATES

Collaboration between schools and families is a relatively new trend in the history of the United States, which has gained momentum since the 1980s, following the civil rights movement (Barbour, Barbour, & Scully, 2008). The civil rights movement forced schools to become more inclusive and develop more responsive curricula (Edwards, Derman-Sparks, & Ramsey, 2006). Faced with diversity in the student population, educators began to realize that children's cultural background influences how they learn; therefore it became important to develop approaches that accommodated these differences. During the 1980s and 1990s, globalization and rapid technological advances created further pressures on schools to serve children from diverse families (Eitzen & Zinn, 2005). To develop inclusive schools it is imperative that families become an integral part of the school team.

It is important to note that simultaneously the nationalities of the population immigrating to the United States changed during the 1960s. The U.S. Immigration and Nationality Act of 1965 (Daniels, 2008) eliminated the quota system that had been put into place since 1924 to restrict the entry of individuals from non-European background. As a result of this landmark decision, families from Asia, Latin America, and Africa began to immigrate to the United States, which resulted in a dramatic shift in the diversity of the school population in this country over the past five decades.

Educators in the United States must be prepared to develop collaborative relationship with families from different cultural backgrounds. The discussion in chapter 1 on teacher and student demographics in the United States clearly suggests that the cultural background of teachers will not always be reflected in the student population. Rather, it is fair to assume that with globalization most teachers will be challenged to work with students and families whose background is different from their own (Sleeter, 2008). Teaching, learning, and parenting are cultural processes, strongly influenced by the cultural frameworks that individuals bring to these interactions (Rogoff, 2002). As the society becomes increasingly diverse, educators need to become more adept at communicating across cultures.

THE CHALLENGE OF COLLABORATION BETWEEN U.S. SCHOOLS AND INTERNATIONAL FAMILIES

According to Barrera, Corso, and MacPherson (2005), the challenges related to collaboration between schools and families can be clustered into three groups: challenges of information, challenges of interpretation, and challenges of relationships. When educators do not have adequate information regarding the cultural experiences of students and their families, it can result in cultural dissonance. Teachers may view students from a deficit perspective and may not understand how to connect the classroom curriculum to the students' experiences. It may be difficult for teachers to explain the cultural underpinnings of their curriculum to a parent who was not schooled in the

United States. In addition, we must take into account that the meaning of many literacy practices is grounded in cultural scripts and may be misinterpreted easily by members of other cultures. For example, some families view educators as experts and defer to them for decision making. This action often puzzles educators, and they begin to view the family from a deficit perspective. As educators strive to develop relationships with families from other cultures, they must deal with issues of power and social positioning which influence their interactions. For example, the norms and curriculum of the schools in the United States are based on the values and experiences of the European American population and may not be shared or understood by cultures belonging to minority groups (Delpit, 1995; Nieto, 1999).

According to Turnbull and colleagues (2011), the history of the different roles assigned to parents over the past century helps us to understand the challenges that educators and families now face as they try to form collaborative relationships. Over the past one hundred years, parents have been assigned many roles in the school system that prompted educators to view parents from a deficit perspective. For example parents may be viewed as (1) the cause of a child's disability or poor academic performance, (2) members of organizations that demand certain services from the school systems, and (3) recipients of teachers' decisions.

Over the past few decades there has been a shift in paradigm as reflected in the legislation related to education in the United States. Under IDEA (Individuals with Disabilities Education Act) originally enacted in 1975 and reauthorized in 2004, the role of families as partners in the education system is emphasized. According to Congress, "almost 30 years of research and experience has demonstrated that the education of children with disabilities can be made more effective by strengthening the roles and responsibilities of parents" (Disabilities Education Improvement Act, 2004).

More recently the No Child Left Behind Act (NCLB) of 2001, which is an amendment of the Elementary and Secondary Education Act of 1965, grants parents the right to transfer their child from a failing or unsafe school to a better one. Schools are required to inform parents not just about the progress of the child but the overall performance of the students in the school. As a result of such legislation, the roles ascribed to parents have shifted; they are now viewed as individuals who play an important role in their children's learning, as partners in decision-making processes, and as political advocates (Turnbull et al., 2011).

However, teachers are not adequately prepared to partner with parents, especially with those who do not belong to the mainstream in the United States (Nieto, 1999; Turnbull et al., 2011). Teacher education programs have to train the candidates to learn the culture of their students and families, engage in critical reflection to develop self-awareness, explain the curriculum of the schools in the United States to parents from other countries, and develop collaborative relationships with parents to identify educational goals and strategies for children.

APPROACHES TO DEVELOPING RELATIONSHIPS WITH INTERNATIONAL FAMILIES

Wink (2005) identifies two models of parent involvement in schools in United States: (1) "We Are Going to Do This to You" and (2) "We Are Going to Do This with You" (p. 154). The first model is based on a transmission model of pedagogy and views parents as recipients of information. The second model is grounded in democratic principles and emphasizes the importance of collaboration. It is also the second model of parental involvement that resonates with the cultural reciprocity process and the principles of this model that are extended in the section below.

Barrera, Corso, and MacPherson (2005) argue that respect, reciprocity, and responsiveness are the three key elements in the process of building successful relationships with families. Educators can demonstrate their respect for families by acknowledging and accepting the cultural practices of families. For example, some Muslim families may require their daughters to wear a headscarf. By allowing girls to wear a headscarf in schools, educators can demonstrate respect for the families. Reciprocity involves recognizing that values and experiences of both the families and the educators play an important role in children's learning. Educators can generate a list of options for curricula or educational placement through discussion with families. However, reciprocity does not mean that educators need to deny their expertise in their field, but they need to authentically relate their experiences to develop a shared understanding of a situation. Finally, responsiveness requires educators to turn their assumptions into loosely held hypothesis so they can remain curious regarding the families. It is not possible to completely eliminate preconceived ideas about families; however, by consciously remaining in a state of wondering, educators can learn about other perspectives.

The process of cultural reciprocity is a two-way information-sharing process initiated by the educator to exchange information with families and engage them in a meaningful dialogue (Harry, Kalyapur, & Day, 1999). This involves sharing information about one's culture and negotiating cultural differences to develop shared understanding and to develop common goals for educating the children. Cultural reciprocity is a relationship-based process that is grounded in the principles of mutual respect, collaboration, and reciprocity (Day & Parlakian, 2004). The cultural reciprocity process involves four steps that are clearly rooted in the above principles. The process outlines the kind of approach and actions that are needed to engage in fruitful communication across cultural groups and to develop a cohesive learning community. While the initial framework for cultural reciprocity was developed based on interactions with special educators, Day, Demulder, and Stribling (2010) have modified the steps slightly without changing the actual essence of the process to extend the application of the process to educators in general classrooms. The four steps are as follows:

> Step 1: Self-awareness: exploring the values, beliefs, assumptions and cultural experiences educators bring to an interaction.
>
> Step 2: Learning about students and families from other cultures through participation, observation, and dialogue.
>
> Step3: Clearly explaining the cultural basis of educational practices and recommendations from the school.
>
> Step 4: Collaborating with students and families to develop common goals. (p. 240)

A CASE STUDY ON DEVELOPING RELATIONSHIPS WITH INTERNATIONAL FAMILIES: THE SKILLS NEEDED FOR COLLABORATION

This chapter presents the case study of a teacher who was committed to improving family involvement in her classroom and was enrolled in a graduate program for K–12 teachers. The graduate program encouraged collaboration with families through several assignments but specifically through a case study and an action research project. As a collaborative faculty, we purposefully created several curricular experiences that provided opportunities for teachers to engage in dialogues with families. The assignments required teachers to observe, interact, reflect, and write about children whose cultural backgrounds are different from their own. We encouraged them to engage in dialogues with students and their family members to seek information about their experiences outside the school system. Our research (Day, Demulder, & Stribling, 2010) suggests that teachers gain valuable insights from learning about the cultural framework and experiences of the students and their family members.

While most of the teachers enrolled in the master's program used some of the approaches discussed in the previous section, there are a few who were strongly dedicated to improving family involvement and use a variety of approaches. Amy, a kindergarten teacher, who consciously applied the cultural reciprocity process to develop collaborative relationships with families from various nations, demonstrates the power of engaging in all four steps of the process. In this section, the four steps of cultural reciprocity have been used as a framework to analyze her assignments, specifically the case study and the action research projects. Her assignment was coded (Miles & Huberman, 1999) based on concepts related to each step of the cultural reciprocity process. The excerpts from her assignments provide insight into her teaching dilemmas that emerged from working with families from other cultures and the ways in which she tried to resolve them. Further, examples have been used from other teachers where appropriate to supplement the data from the case study on Amy, and also to demonstrate the application of the cultural reciprocity process in different grade levels.

Amy is of European American decent, but the majority of the children in her classroom were recent immigrants from various countries. She described the population in her classroom in the following words: "My classroom this year consists of students from various cultures: Peruvian, Korean, Chinese, Saudi Arabian, Indian, Afghanistan, Pakistani, Cambodian, Polish, and African and European descents." In other words, her classroom was a microcosm of the larger world, a small international community. In addition, the families whose children enter kindergarten class are least familiar with the school culture unless they have older children who have been through the school system.

Although the information under the four steps is organized in a sequence, it is important to note that this is not a linear process divided into four mutually exclusive steps. Rather, it is a complex process where the steps are interconnected and represent an effective approach to interacting with families. The steps have been discussed separately to capture the essence of each step in sufficient detail and to explore the relationships between the different steps.

SELF-AWARENESS: EXPLORING THE VALUES, BELIEFS, ASSUMPTIONS, AND CULTURAL EXPERIENCES EDUCATORS BRING TO AN INTERACTION

Self-awareness is the most critical step in building relationships with families (Harry, 1992). However, it is also the most difficult step in the process. Like fish in water, educators find it difficult to recognize the cultural underpinnings of their own practices. Awareness of one's own culture emerges from seeking interactions with people whose cultural background is different from one's own and simultaneously reflecting on one's own thoughts, reactions, and cultural experiences. "Understanding one's own cultural heritage, as well as other cultural communities, requires taking the perspective of people of contrasting backgrounds" (Rogoff, 2003, p. 11). Exercising the mind in this way allows one to develop a more flexible of way of being and explore multiple perspectives, a quality that is essential to become a culturally responsive educator.

Kalyanpur and Harry (1999) propose three levels of cultural awareness: overt, covert, and subtle. The overt level refers to differences that are easily noticed such as language, dress, food, and daily rituals. To some extent teachers can anticipate these differences and make some effort to bridge these cultural differences by providing an interpreter or asking about preferences in food. However, in doing so they may or may not consider more complex issues such as the degree of acculturation of the family or a family's views of education.

Below is an example of overt awareness. Here the teacher focuses only on the need to translate information into Spanish but does not consider any differences in values, beliefs, or assumptions that might influence her interaction with families. She also does not demonstrate an awareness of how her cultural perspectives might influence the interactions:

> Especially in my school, which is 80 percent Latino, I need to not be afraid to communicate and conference with my students' parents. I need to seek out interactions with their families, using a translator if needed to speak to them. There are translators readily available including the students themselves. I need to get past my own awkwardness to fully begin building cultural reciprocity.

The covert level involves an awareness of the differences in the invisible aspects of culture such as status in a group, communication styles, or the concept of time. While teachers at this level demonstrate greater sensitivity and tolerance, the overall effect is still somewhat limited as they do not seek to understand the meaning of the behaviors. We created experiences to help teachers identify some of the assumptions they bring to their work. Members of the mainstream culture often assume that they have no culture (Nieto, 1999; Banks & Banks, 2007). Many educators simply assume that education should be the priority for all children and families and do not realize the cultural biases that alienate families from school culture and processes. They are often surprised when they find that others may value education differently and that differing definitions of what constitutes "an educated person" exist. At the covert level, educators often are able to understand the complexity of studying another culture and anticipate that they need to put more effort into this area. Teachers' reflections below illustrate this point. Katherine shares,

> *I never had really thought about my culture; actually I never really thought that I had one.* It is funny how all of my personal values, beliefs, and assumptions play out in my classroom on a daily basis. . . . This has been a real struggle for me this year especially with both my parents and their students. *My assumption is that school is important and they should be the number one priority for my students.* . . . I think I need to remember that not every parent and child view the school the same way I do. *I need to take the time to talk with them and learn from them so I know where they are starting from* (emphasis added).

To reach the subtle level of cultural awareness, educators must be willing to explore the reasons for the behavior from the person's perspective and ask critical questions about their own practices, such as, "Why do I want students to sit quietly?" Day, Demulder, and Stribling (2010) noticed that there were differences in the degree to which awareness of their own perspective motivated teachers to seek further cultural information about their students or families and the degree to which they were willing to question their own practices. The examples of teachers demonstrating the first two levels are from the class feedback we received after presenting the cultural reciprocity model to the students. The example demonstrating the third level is from Amy as she reflects on her assumptions while planning her action research to improve parent involvement:

> One of the assumptions I continue to have is that parents feel it is their responsibility to be a partner in the education of their children. . . . I have not yet asked parents what they feel their role is in the education of their children. Where do the parents in my classroom fall in the spectrum of parental involvement? How do I support them where they are on this spectrum?

Here Amy is cognizant of her own cultural expectations regarding parents' role in the school system but simultaneously demonstrates that there may be a variety of perspectives among the parents in her class. Furthermore, she is interested in responding and connecting to parents who have different perspectives.

As educators read and begin to internalize concepts presented in critical pedagogy texts such as Freire (1998) and Wink (2005), they begin to pose questions from a more critical perspective and develop higher levels of self-awareness and agency. Educators who remain in the overt level of cultural awareness are rarely able to engage in perspective taking and have difficulty establishing relationships with families. Teacher educators have to scaffold their learning through dialogues and written interactions to promote higher levels of self-awareness.

LEARNING ABOUT STUDENTS AND FAMILIES FROM OTHER CULTURES THROUGH PARTICIPATION, OBSERVATION, AND DIALOGUE

The next step in the process requires educators to find out families' views on child development, parenting goals, and education. Educators have to learn to participate in cultural activities of other communities, to engage in dialogues with families to learn about their experiences and perspectives, and to observe children participating in various social settings.

Educators must also explore the underlying cultural values and beliefs of the families from which these perspectives emerge (Harry, Kalyanpur, & Day, 1999). Teacher education candidates have the opportunity to practice these skills when completing the case study assignment.

Understanding parents' priorities through dialogue. "Key to moving beyond one's own system of assumptions is recognizing that the goals of human development—what is regarded as mature or desirable—vary considerably according to the cultural traditions and circumstances of different communities" (Rogoff, 2003, p. 18). The goals and expectations of significant adults such as parents and grandparents are embedded in their values, which are further situated within a larger cultural context and the historical events of the community. Parents' expectations are grounded in the cultural norms of their society. Parents set long-range goals for their children based on their own experiences, to prepare children for the world as they know it (Super & Harkness, 1986; Whiting & Edwards, 1988). These goals evolve from individuals' life experiences, beliefs, and assumptions about children and the process of development, and from the style of parenting they experienced as a child. Adults use these goals to guide their participation in various activities and as a standard against which they assess their own success and the success of their child. The case study assignment required teacher education candidates to find out about families' views of child development and their goals for their children through interviews with significant adult family members. Amy decided to choose a child who had recently moved from India to the United States. The following excerpt from her case study illustrates the parent's value of interdependence and his feeling of bewilderment as he tries to integrate in a society that primarily values independence:

> He explained to me that in India, children are very dependent upon their parents. They often inherit property from their parents. Children rely on their parents and learn to respect them very early. . . . Here, parents work for their children's attention. Children (teens) are able to get a job and be on their own much easier and earlier than in India. He thinks that this

early independence isolates children from their families. He stated, "Living like a stranger doesn't require much effort."

While Amy grew up in the United States and primarily values independence, she was able to learn that this parent values interdependence. Furthermore, the dialogue allowed her to learn and explore the cultural experiences that motivate parents to value interdependence. Such parental dilemmas are common in immigrant families who draw on different cultural frameworks and explore ways to maintain their culture of origin while supporting their children to become a part of the new society. Educators are more likely to be empathic when they understand the sociocultural reasons behind a parenting style.

LeVine (1980) identified a hierarchy of parental goals, based on research in various countries and emphasized the fact that priorities and childrearing practices in each community are tied to the status of health and economic well-being of a community. Parents consider intellectual goals only after they are assured that the above two goals have been addressed. Families who have been through serious crises such as war and famine may not value formal education as middle-class families in the United States do. Many teachers assume that formal education is a priority for all families and children.

Dialogues with parents also provide opportunities to explore parents' struggles and concerns. These may be directly connected to the child's education or may appear to have no direct relevance to the child's learning. However, learning about these concerns allows teachers to respond in a more comprehensive way to the needs of the family and to strengthen the family unit, which in turn provides a strong base for the child. During her conversation with the parent from India, Amy learned that he was feeling isolated in their new community. She related his experience in the case study in the following words:

> We do not know our neighbors. In other countries (like India), doors are open. Neighbors here live like strangers . . . maybe because of the climate. In India, you are helped by your neighbor first.

Amy was deeply moved by the last sentence and was genuinely concerned about the family's experience of isolation. She had several conversations with me and wondered how she could support the family in her current role as a kindergarten teacher. I encouraged her to use the action research project to address the issue. Following her literature search, she was able to design her action research project to help this parent and others like him to form connections with the school and other parents. Knowing the parents cultural framework allows a teacher to address the parents' priorities and respond in a way that is easily understood by them.

Learning about Cultures through Observation

Several scholars engaged in cultural research have emphasized the need to view children's development from a cultural perspective. Whiting and Whiting (1975) present a psychocultural model that emphasizes the need to gain a detailed understanding of children's participation in cultural processes; this understanding must take into account the recent and historical events of the community. What is considered meaningful and adaptive in one context may not generalize to another context. Weisner (2002) proposes that "every cultural community provides developmental pathways for children within some ecological-cultural (ecocultural) context. Cultural pathways are made up of everyday routines of life, and routines are made up of cultural activities [in which] children engage" (p. 275). He proposes that activities are useful units through which to explore children's culture as they reflect the influence of values, goals, relationships, and the scripts for what is considered normal. Based on this notion, teachers in the master's program have to systematically observe children participating in activities in different cultural settings including the school and the community. Lauren, a fifth-grade teacher, chose to study a student who had recently arrived from Peru. She observed the student in the art room:

> The teacher asked for volunteers to recall what they had done the previous week. A bunch of students raised their hands, including Lizeth, which surprised me. Because of her limited vocabulary, I knew she didn't know what the teacher was asking, so I wonder if she did this to participate and fit in.

During the observations she noticed that many of Lizeth's actions suggested that she was trying to be part of the classroom community. This intrigued Lauren, and she tried to find out more information through her dialogues. Both Lizeth and her parents stated that academics were not their priority; they were more concerned about whether she develops friendships in the new country.

To form relationships with students and to develop meaningful curricula for them, it is essential for teachers to understand students' actions and behaviors from a cultural perspective. This allows teachers to relate to children intellectually and emotionally and to develop a sense of empathy. By engaging in this step, teachers are able to understand the cultural meaning of parental goals, community expectations, and children's behaviors. It is clear from the examples presented in this section that the effort to know people of other cultures is central to the process of developing cultural awareness. The experiences teachers gain from this step motivate them to shift their perspective and create a third space where they can consider others' perspectives (Barrera,

Corso, & MacPherson, 2003). The information gained from this step can be used effectively to develop culturally responsive actions discussed in the next two sections.

CLEARLY EXPLAINING THE CULTURAL BASIS OF EDUCATIONAL PRACTICES AND RECOMMENDATIONS FROM THE SCHOOL

According to Nieto (1999), "The role of the teacher as a cultural accommodator and mediator is fundamental in promoting student learning" (p. 70). In her book, Nieto explores in-depth the cultural discontinuities experienced by students from diverse backgrounds within the school environment. Harry and Kalyanpur (1999) propose that explicit explanations of the cultural values and expectations of schools facilitate family involvement in school activities. As discussed in the previous section, people learn about other cultures through participation in cultural activities. It is fair to assume that parents learn about the school culture through participation in school events. Parents probably find it easier to participate in informal events where they can choose their level of participation rather than formal events such as parent-teacher conferences where the stakes are high. Teachers in the master's program used different strategies to explain the school culture to parents. Two of these strategies were clearly very effective in addressing the issue. They were hosting informal events to give families the opportunity to get a taste of the school curriculum and communicating information about class activities regularly through written communication.

Informal Family Events

Some teachers in the program creatively organized events to reach out to families from diverse backgrounds, drawing them into the school community. Amy was one of them, deciding to host an event she called "family fun nights" every month. She clearly recognized that the ways of teaching in American schools may be unfamiliar to the parents in her class who came from many different nations. She made a genuine effort to provide a glimpse of what goes on in the kindergarten classroom through the family fun nights, as illustrated below:

> The children perform some of the class-building songs we do each day. . . . After the children perform the song, they get their parents on the floor and we all do the song together. I am proud of the number of parents who take risks and participate in these songs with us. . . . I understand that many parents are very new to the *"American" ways of teaching*. Many of them have

come from schools that are more traditional and structured. I think it is important for them to see some of the ways their children are being taught to interact with each other and how they learn. . . . *Much of our learning is kinesthetic in nature and utilizes song and movement. This may be very different from how these parents were taught.* (Emphasis added)

In the above example, Amy demonstrated the "American way of teaching" during the family gatherings and invited parents to participate in the activities. Thus parents had an opportunity to learn through watching and participating in the lessons. Although the original intent was to address the sense of isolation experienced by immigrant families in her class, she found out that such events benefit all parents. On a survey that Amy conducted to learn the impact of these events, a European American parent explained her experience in the following words:

> The Family Nights have been invaluable to me in terms of getting to know other families. Until the Family Nights I had not been comfortable in the school—due to our status at [the school] as racial and ethnic minorities. We are not Asian Americans; were [sic] Americans. We are not used to minority status. Takes time to adapt. . . . The cultural diversity was overwhelming. . . . We view diversity as a good thing; however, I as a parent haven't been comfortable approaching other families due to language and cultural barriers.

Similarly, Mary, a sixth-grade ESOL (English for speakers of second language) teacher, invited the students and families to join "game night" once a month. During these gatherings, children and families had the opportunity to participate in different games based on math, history, or language. Although of European American descent, Mary spoke Spanish, and most of the children in her class were recent immigrants from Latin America. Her experience suggests that students may participate in school activities differently in the presence of their families. She wrote:

> I have also witnessed my students feeling empowered when they are with their families. Selena and Dominic come to mind. Selena gives very little in class. She finishes her work and tends to hide it under the work of others. She is fairly quiet and unsure of herself. Dominic is quiet. Both of these children are different children when their families are with them. They look forward to family nights and come enthusiastically. They are the first to come and the last to leave.

This quote along with other evidence suggests that such informal gatherings can be an important mechanism for helping parents to connect with other parents and build a community. This is especially important in geographic locations where the demographics change rapidly and a sense of community may not have developed. Such events lead to parent and student empowerment. Other teachers who used similar strategies also reported the same outcome.

EXPLAINING SCHOOL CURRICULUM THROUGH WRITTEN COMMUNICATION

Some teachers used written communication to familiarize parents with classroom activities and maintain regular contact. Bonnie, a fifth-grade teacher began to send e-mails to parents every day explaining the main activities of the class using digital pictures and brief descriptions of the lessons conducted in class. Following the descriptions, she provided some prompts that parents could use to discuss the topics presented in class. She also included information about the homework for the day. When she surveyed parents to understand the impact of these e-mails, she received many positive responses. She quoted the following e-mail in her action research project to demonstrate the effect of her strategy. The parent wrote:

> I am amazed how involved I feel in Jesse's learning this year! And what is even more amazing is that my husband is as well. He comes home from work and he asks Jesse about whatever he saw posted. . . . We feel so much a part of the whole learning process.

Parents' responses, including the one above, suggest that as parents became more informed about the curriculum in the class, they took a greater interest in supporting the child's learning. Teachers often complain about the lack of parental involvement in school activities, and it is clear that such initiatives to communicate with parents motivate them to engage in their child's learning and strengthen home-school relationships. By providing information about the curriculum, she helped parents to connect with the activities at school and also provided them the choice to decide how they would like to use that information. This approach may have empowered the parents as is suggested by the response of another parent who wrote, "I feel very connected to what Stacey is doing in school and I feel empowered to help her."

This strategy has some limitations. A parent in Bonnie's class pointed out that although she appreciated the daily e-mails, they were not enough, and more was needed through phone conversations and face-to-face interactions. Bonnie had made an arrangement with the ESOL teacher to call the parents of her only Spanish-speaking student each day in order to communicate the daily e-mail message. Electronic communication is not an effective way of reaching families who may not speak English or who may have adult members who are not literate.

In all of these examples, educators have used different strategies to share information about the school curriculum and school culture with families. They have also given families the opportunity to choose to what extent they wish to participate. It is important to note that in some of the examples teachers do not just rely on verbal communication to explain the curriculum. Schools in the United States tend to rely heavily on words to communicate with parents and children. Hall (1977) identified different communication styles based on his research in different countries. He described mainstream cultures in United States as low-context cultures, where meaning is communicated primarily through spoken or written words. In high-context cultures, such as different parts of Asia and South America, people rely primarily on shared knowledge in the group and contextual cues and do not give as much importance to words. Families from high-context cultures may be reluctant to express their concerns and disagreements in words. Informal events provide them with the opportunity to develop relationships and also to learn about the culture of the classrooms. We know from the literature on human development mentioned in the previous section that people learn about new cultures through participation and observation in cultural activities. Here teachers created opportunities to provide a taste of the curriculum and participate in the school culture. Very clearly, engaging families through such activities helps them to better understand the school approach to teaching and learning.

COLLABORATING WITH STUDENTS AND FAMILIES TO DEVELOP COMMON GOALS

Schools in the United States have made some attempts to work in partnership with parents but have a long way yet to go (Turnbull et al., 2011). From a cultural perspective, collaboration requires people to engage in several cross-cultural exchanges to creatively work toward a common endeavor. It is a recursive process where educators have to be willing to share their power with others and develop a trusting relationship. Traditionally, teachers have been regarded as experts in the school system, and students or parents are regarded as the beneficiaries of their expertise.

Since collaboration is such a complex process, Turnbull et al. (2011) suggest that educators carefully consider promoting a climate for collaboration. The first three steps of this process help to establish a climate of collaboration. The experience of engaging in the first two steps makes educators more knowledgeable about themselves and the families they serve. Moreover, their efforts to explain the curriculum explicitly in the third step allow families to interact and become familiar with the curriculum. The exchanges in these steps help to establish a secure base; both educators and parents feel more comfortable engaging in a genuine dialogue when problems emerge.

For example, Amy was concerned about a Latino child in her class and felt he should be retained in kindergarten. As she was wondering how she could share this information with the family, the mother approached her and requested her help. In an e-mail titled "HELP," the mother wrote:

> I am trying, but nobody at home can help him on this. I understand how the currency works but I am not able to teaching my child. I try my best, but this is no [sic] my language, when I write to you please understand that you can interpret [sic] what I wanna [sic] say.

Clearly this parent is not fluent in English but felt comfortable approaching Amy. This communication might have resulted from the fact that the parent had an opportunity to get to know the teacher during the family fun nights. Amy offered to meet with her but found out through her e-mail exchanges that the parent had a new job and was unable to meet during school hours. She implemented step 4 of the cultural reciprocity process by letting the parent know that she was willing to meet the parent after hours at a place of her choice. The parent invited her to come to her home. This gave Amy further opportunity to find out about the family's culture (step 2). She discussed ways the parent could teach currency to her child. During the discussion, Amy explained that Mario was a young kindergartener, and while she felt he made great progress, he was still considerably behind. Together they agreed to retain him in kindergarten.

This is an excellent example of the trust and partnership Amy had developed by implementing the cultural reciprocity process. The critical elements of parent-teacher collaboration are clearly illustrated in this example. Amy had created a climate of collaboration by implementing the first three steps of the process. When the parent requested help, she was very responsive and did not just send an e-mail on how to teach currency. Furthermore, she acknowledged the parent's inability to meet during school hours and gave her the option to choose the time and place, thus creating an empowering experience. In doing so, she demonstrated the ability to be flexible and a willingness to share decision making with the parent. An essential component of collaboration is the ability to share power.

It is important to note that Amy's efforts to reach out to international families influenced her relationship with one parent but improved overall parent involvement in her class. During the final family gathering, Amy reported, "In my journal dated May 15th, I counted eight different conversations I could describe in detail that told me new things about my students and their families." Moreover, at the end of the year parents in the six kindergarten classrooms received a survey from the school. While the response rate from other classrooms ranged between five and eleven, a total of twenty-one parents responded from Amy's classroom. Very clearly the relationship she had developed with them encouraged them to participate more fully in the school activities.

INTERNATIONALIZING TEACHER EDUCATION PROGRAMS: PREPARING EDUCATORS TO WORK COLLABORATIVELY WITH FAMILIES FROM DIVERSE CULTURES

Given the powerful role of culture in educators' interactions with children and families from various nations, it is important to prepare them to critically examine educational practices through a cultural lens. To prepare candidates to work effectively with families, education programs need to focus on three components: (1) family stories, (2) qualitative methodologies, and (3) critical pedagogy. The examples discussed in the previous section illustrate the results of weaving these three components in an integrated curriculum for a graduate program in teacher education. The discussion below provides details on each component.

The Power of Family Stories

Families often use stories to transmit their knowledge and skills to younger generations and develop collective memories through these narratives (Sanchez, 1999). Through stories, families convey the social problems that they encountered, the ways they resolved the problems, and knowledge they gained through these experiences (Heath, 1983). Families play an important role in socializing their children for the world as they understand it. These stories are an important medium for understanding cultural experiences for families from various countries. By carefully listening to the family stories, educators can begin to make sense of the language and cultural practices of diverse families by exploring their sociohistorical and cultural reality. Through stories families have an opportunity to express themselves more authentically compared to structured questionnaires and formal interviews.

It is important to note that such stories can also be an important tool for diversifying the curriculum in a classroom. Families can be invited to share their stories in class or during informal school gatherings. Moreover, educators can encourage children to engage in dialogues with family members to find out their family stories. For example, children can ask their parents how they were named and the significance of their name. The stories that children learn through such an assignment enrich their cultural identity and strengthen their relationship with their parents. Moreover, the content of these stories gives the educator an opportunity to discuss the diversity of cultural and religious practices across the world. Also, in this way families can contribute to the education of their child even if they are not formally literate.

Qualitative Methodologies: Tools for Crossing Cultural Boundaries

Educators need adequate training in qualitative methodologies to begin to understand the cultural practices of families from their perspective and to develop culturally responsive services. Learning to engage in ethnographic interviews, participant observations, and action research methodology prepares teachers to develop culturally responsive services for families. The case study in the previous section clearly demonstrates the importance of training in qualitative methodologies. It is important to note that learning about these methodologies does not imply that educators will conduct detailed ethnographic interviews with each family. They can, however, apply the principles of this technique during their conversation with families. In addition, when faced with a problem, they can use both ethnographic interviews and participant observation to study the situation from various perspectives. It is beneficial for teacher educator candidates to learn about these methodologies by conducting a case study. Such assignments often help candidates to change their perspective of the problem they encountered.

Learning about ethnographic interviews helps educators to engage in authentic dialogue with families and begin to know the family stories. Spradley (1979) described ethnographic interviews as "a strategy for getting people to talk about what they know" (p. 9). Such interviews typically begin with open-ended "grand tour" questions, and subsequent questions often emerge based on the responses of the participants (Lincoln & Guba, 1985). The goal is to understand and interpret the worldview of the participants by engaging in an ongoing exchange of dialogue (O'Donnell, Tharp, & Wilson, 1993).

Participant observation is another tool that helps educators to observe and understand the cultural scripts of families and children from diverse backgrounds. It is a process through which the educator can observe the routine activities of students and families and make detailed observations of people, interactions, and events (Glesne & Peshkin, 1992). It differs from ordinary observation because the researcher simultaneously reflects on his or her own reaction to what is observed. By doing so the researcher addresses the issue of objectivity, not by maintaining an objective stand but by understanding how he or she is influenced and in turn has influenced the situation.

Traditionally, parents have not been viewed as partners but as recipients of the decisions made by educators and school administrators (Turnbull et al., 2011). Teacher education candidates need the tools that they can apply to question undemocratic practices and change the power dynamics between schools and families. Ethnographic interviews and participant observations can prepare teachers to learn about the views and lives of families from other cultures. However, simply learning about the cultural perspectives of families is not enough; educators have to change current practices in schools to include families from various nations in the school community.

To promote change in school settings, educators must be trained in the action research methodology, which can be used effectively to facilitate a change in educational settings (Bogdan & Biklen, 1992). The effectiveness of this methodology in developing strategies that promote parent involvement in schools is clearly demonstrated in the examples discussed in the previous section. Through action research, educators can identify points in the system that can be challenged either legally or through community action and examine them from multiple perspectives (students, families, administrators). Such research raises people's consciousness and helps them to gain better insight into the problem and thus initiate change in educational practices and policies.

Critical Pedagogy

The curriculum in teacher education programs must be based on literacy approaches that enable teachers to "read the word" and "read the world" (Shor & Freire, 1987, p. 135) in order to critically explore the ways in which issues of diversity such as race, class, nationality, and gender play out in school communities. In their interaction with families, educators are bound to encounter challenges related to these issues. Critical pedagogy enables teachers to use their existing knowledge to examine the surrounding power structures and deconstruct them to create a new social order (Freire, 1998). Therefore, it is essential for teachers to become familiar with the key principles of critical pedagogy during their training in universities, as they strive to develop more inclusive school communities.

Critical pedagogy inspires teachers to name, reflect, and act (Wink, 2005). The process of naming and problem posing is essential in understanding the choices that families make and the ways in which they participate in the school. The information that educators glean through informal dialogues and ethnographic interviews must be understood from a sociopolitical perspective. For example, one of the forces influencing the lives of culturally and linguistically diverse families is the status assigned to their native language in the mainstream society. "For example, American families in South West suffered under laws punishing them for speaking Spanish" (Sanchez, 1999, p. 352). Such experiences may influence the ways families interact with educators and the educational placements they choose for their children.

Brookfield (1995) argues that two types of mental activities are essential for teachers to engage in critical thinking: identifying and challenging assumptions and exploring and creating alternatives. Assignments that require candidates to interact with students and families whose cultural background is different from their own give them an opportunity to explore their cultural beliefs and assumptions as they encounter different perspectives. Training in qualitative methodologies prepares candidates to address the issue of objectivity by engaging in the process of reflection. Finally, action research methodology allows educators to explore alternative approaches to family involvement and move into the action phase of critical pedagogy.

SUMMARY AND IMPLICATIONS

Teachers can successfully form relationships with families from different nations and develop inclusive school communities. Many families feel isolated as they move into new communities. Educators can address this sense of isolation by initiating efforts to build relationships with families and by hosting events that promote interaction between families. To do so, education programs have to prepare teachers to learn about the children and the families in their classroom using ethnographic approaches, reflect on their own cultural values, explain the cultural underpinnings of their classroom curriculum, negotiate differences, and develop collaborative relationships. The evidence presented in this chapter suggests that students from various cultural backgrounds participate in school activities with greater enthusiasm when their families become more involved in school activities.

The concept of developing partnerships with families is still new to many educators. Following the civil rights movement in the United States, there has been a shift in paradigm, and much of the current legislation in education provides more decision-making power to parents and requires educators to work collaboratively with families. Such relationships form the foundation for developing pluralistic schools, communities, and societies.

Faculty in colleges of education can prepare educators for such cross-cultural interactions by helping candidates to understand the importance of stories as a powerful medium of communication, and by training them to apply participant observations and ethnographic interviews to learn about cultural practices of children and families. It is also essential to familiarize candidates with the key principles of critical pedagogy so they are able to analyze the information they find out from families through a critical lens, examine the power dynamics, and question undemocratic practices in schools. To be an effective educator in a democratic society, teachers need to give voice to the students and families in the school community, which requires a shift in the power dynamics of the traditional school system. Finally the opportunity to conduct action research in education programs gives candidates the opportunity to name, reflect, and act to try different approaches to develop relationships with families. Faculty members can carefully scaffold the experiences of the candidates by requiring them to engage in a series of assignments that require cross-cultural work with families so they become familiar with the process involved in developing relationships across cultures. Such assignments move individuals from identifying a problem to becoming agents of change.

REFERENCES

Banks, J. A., & Banks, C. A. (2007). *Multicultural education: Issues and perspectives.* Hoboken, NJ: Wiley.

Barbour, C., Barbour, N. H., & Scully, P. A. (2008). *Families, schools, and communities: Building partnerships for educating children.* Upper Saddle River, NJ: Pearson.

Barrera, I., Corso, R. M., & MacPherson, D. (2003). *Skilled dialogue: Strategies for responding to cultural diversity in early childhood.* Baltimore, MD: Paul H. Brookes.

Bogdan, R. C., & Biklen, S. K. (1992). *Qualitative research for education: An introduction to theory and methods.* Boston, MA: Allyn & Bacon.

Bornstein, M. H. (2001). Refocusing on parenthood. In J. C. Westman (Ed.), *Parenthood in America: Undervalued, Underpaid, Under Siege* (pp. 5–20). Madison: University of Wisconsin Press.

Brookfield, S. (1995). *Becoming a reflective teacher.* San Francisco: Jossey-Bass.

Darling-Hammond, L. (2002). *Learning to teach for social justice.* New York: Teacher's College Press.

Daniels, R. (2008). *The Immigration Act of 1965: Intended and unintended consequences.* Retrieved from the U.S. Department of State Publication Archive website, http://www.america.gov/st/educ-english/2008/April/20080423214226eaifas0.9637982.html.

Day, M., Demulder, E. K., & Stribling, S. M. (2010). Using the process of cultural reciprocity to create multicultural, democratic classrooms. In F. Salili & R. Hoosain (Eds.), *Democracy and multicultural education.* Charlotte, NC: Information Age Publishing.

Day, M., & Parlakian, R. (2004). *How culture shapes social-emotional development: Implications for practice in infant-family programs.* Washington, DC: Zero to Three.

Edwards, J. O., Derman-Sparks, L., & Ramsey, P. G. (2006). *What if all the kids are white? Anti-bias multicultural education with young children and families*. New York: Teacher's College Press.

Eitzen, D. S., & Zinn, M. B. (2005). *Globalization: The transformation of social worlds*. Belmont, CA: Wadsworth.

Freire, P. (1998). *Pedagogy of the oppressed*. New York: Continuum International.

Glesne, C., & Peshkin, A. (1992). *Becoming qualitative researchers*. New York: Longman.

Hall, E. T. (1977). *Beyond culture*. New York: Anchor Books.

Harry, B. (1992). Developing cultural self-awareness: The first step in values clarification for early interventionist. *Topics in Early Childhood Special Education, 12*, 333–50.

Harry, B., Kalyanpur, M., & Day, M. (1999). *Building cultural reciprocity with families: Case studies in special education*. Baltimore, MD: Paul H. Brookes.

Heath, S. B. (1983). *Ways with words*. Cambridge, England: Cambridge University Press.

Individuals with Disabilities Education Improvement Act of 2004, Pub. L. No. 108–446, 118 Stat. 2647 (2004).

Kalyanpur, M., & Harry, B. (1999). *Culture in special education: Building reciprocal family-professional relationships*. Baltimore, MD: Paul H. Brookes.

LeVine, R. A. (1980). A cross-cultural perspective on parenting. In M. D. Fantini & R. Cardenas (Eds.), *Parenting in a multicultural society*. New York: Longman.

Lincoln, Y. S., & Guba, E. G. (1985). *Naturalistic inquiry*. Newbury Park, CA: Sage.

Miles, M. B., & Huberman, A. M. (1999). *Qualitative data analysis*. Thousand Oaks, CA: Sage.

Nieto, S. (1999). *The light in their eyes: Creating multicultural learning communities*. New York: Teachers College Press.

O'Donnell, C. R., Tharp, R. G., & Wilson, K. (1993). Activity settings as the unit of analysis: A theoretical basis for community intervention and development. *American Journal of Community Psychology, 21*(4), 501–19.

Rogoff, B. (2003). *The cultural nature of human development*. New York: Oxford University Press.

Sanchez, S. (1999). Learning from the stories of culturally and linguistically diverse families and communities. *Remedial and Special Education, 20*(6), 351–59.

Sleeter, C. E. (2008). Preparing white teachers for diverse students. In M. Cochran-Smith, S. Feiman-Nemser, D. J. McIntyre, & K. E. Demers (Eds.), *Handbook of research on teacher education: Enduring questions in changing contexts* (pp. 94–106). New York: Routledge.

Shor, I., & Freire, P. (1987). *A pedagogy for liberation: Dialogues on transforming education*. Westport, CT: Bergin & Garvey.

Spradley, J. P. (1979). *The ethnographic interview*. Fort Worth, TX: Harcourt Brace Jovanovich.

Super, C. M., & Harkness, S. (1986). The developmental niche: A conceptualization at the interface of child and culture. *International Journal of Behavior Development, 9*(4), 545–69.

Turnbull, A., Turnbull, R., Erwin, E., Soodak, L., & Shogren, K. A. (2011). *Families, professionals, and exceptionality: Positive outcomes through partnerships and trust.* New Jersey: Pearson.

Weisner, T. S. (2002). Ecocultural understanding of children's developmental pathways. *Human Development, 45,* 275–81.

Whiting, B. B., & Edwards, C. P. (1988). *Children of different worlds: The formation of social behavior.* Cambridge, MA: Harvard University Press.

Whiting, B. B., & Whiting, J. W. M. (1975). *Children of six cultures: A psycho-cultural analysis.* Cambridge, MA: Harvard University Press.

Wink, J. (2005). *Critical pedagogy: Notes from the real world.* New York: Pearson.

• 7 •

Redefining Vulnerability in American Schools

Reaching and Teaching Students after International Crises

Supriya Baily

The latest disaster trifecta has been a powerful testimony regarding the fragility of humankind. The Japanese earthquake, tsunami, and subsequent nuclear catastrophe remind us that Mother Nature knows very little about national borders or boundaries, and that there often is nothing to distinguish between the developed and the developing worlds. Such natural disasters lead to the upheaval of people and communities. At other times, there are disasters that are created by people through war and conflict, leading to the unmitigated and chaotic movement of people. Finally, economic turmoil leads to the passage of people in search of opportunities to provide basic needs for their families. Whether they are refugees, internally displaced people, or migrant workers/economic refugees, such movements of people are often under the shadow of turmoil and confusion. The agency that comes with immigrant decisions to relocate from one country to another is relatively absent in such situations. Individuals and families are learning to cope with the loss of home and country, while also adapting to new cultures, languages, and livelihoods.

Children, oftentimes students enrolled in schools, are dealing with not just acclimation and adjustment, but are also trying to move beyond devastating events that shake their very foundations of security and trust. Teachers, who may be used to dealing with trauma at the local level (homelessness, abuse, and/or broken families, all of which take a terrible toll on children), are often adrift when it comes to understanding the international dimensions related to vulnerable children. This chapter seeks to do two things: create a voice for those students who study in American schools but have faced violence and trauma in their home countries, and offer teacher educators and teachers a chance to better understand the nuances of working with such populations.

Having worked with refugee students in India, I have seen firsthand the complexities that arise when teachers are unable, unwilling, or unprepared to work with such students. There are three primary reasons teachers are unprepared to work with such students. The first lies with the lack of resources to help teachers accommodate the needs of these students, affecting the potential for these students to adjust and be successful. The second reason is the fear on the part of the teacher to reopen recollections of trauma, leading to the teacher avoiding the student, continuing to marginalize and make invisible someone who is vulnerable and disaffected. Finally, a lack of awareness on the part of teacher educators omits any formal learning opportunities for teachers to come prepared to work with such students.

Teacher educators may argue that there is far too much to do to prepare teachers for classrooms, and that preparing teachers specifically for vulnerable children may be an unnecessary "extra." Based on the continued high numbers of refugees coming to the United States, the fluid nature of resettlement (as mentioned in the opening chapter, people do not settle in conclaves as much anymore), and the fact that teachers are traveling and increasingly teaching in other parts of the world, where they may be working with larger numbers of refugee children, teacher educators have to be aware and willing to address this to the best extent that they can. This chapter seeks to offer teacher educators background, rationale, and strategies for helping teachers work with students who come with a new range of international vulnerabilities.

SETTING THE STAGE

In the context of the United States, vulnerable children have frequently meant those children who come from fragile homes, unsecured living conditions, or poor or unsafe neighborhoods (Zimmerman & Arunkumar, 1994). Outside the United States and in international situations, vulnerable children could be defined as those children who are facing crises far wider in scope than those of family or community. Leaving war-torn regions, escaping natural disasters, or migrations on a large scale due to political, social, and economic upheavals have been limited in nature in the United States, in part due to its geographic isolation and strict entry and exit requirements. Yet it does not mean that such children do not live in and go to school in the United States. They do, but oftentimes those experiences can hinder their success and development due in part to the limited understanding teachers have of the complexities of their situations and their experiences.

What makes for vulnerability in the context of international students today? As discussed in the opening chapter of this book, the large numbers of international students come from almost every country in the world and can be the children of everyone from the diplomat to the day laborer. Within this subset are those children who are coming from an environment that has been defined by trauma, either natural or man-made, and are trying to adjust to a new life while also dealing with other complicated dynamics resulting from their trauma. What makes a refugee or asylum seeker different from an immigrant is that immigrant children are coming with their families and are leaving under relatively peaceful terms without the threat of violence or fear over the movement from country to country. "The experience of the . . . refugee is distinct from that of the immigrant. Immigrants plan their migration. They choose to leave home, and choose to go to the United States, usually to improve their standard of living. Refugees simply flee. By legal definition, they are running from 'a well-founded fear of persecution.' They cannot go home again" (Sontag, 1992). The initiation of these journeys is very different, and the destination is not a clear goal as it may be for an immigrant child.

A Snapshot of Refugee Migration to the United States

There are two primary categories of refugees: those who are considered anticipatory and those who are considered acute refugees. In the anticipatory status, patterns of migration have primarily been those people who are well educated and "financially solvent," who see signs of oncoming violence, and who make preparations for imminent departure and leave. In the acute status, the sudden onset of violence or natural disaster triggers the flight (McBrien, 2005, pp. 334–35). In the United States, we have seen both types of refugee migration, and schools have absorbed these students into their classrooms.

On average, the United States allows 70,000 to 91,000 refugees into the country every year (Bridging Refugee Youth and Children Services, 2011). Halfway through 2011, the United States has allowed in a little over thirty-three thousand refugees, with the largest percentage coming from the Near East and South Asian region (47 percent), followed by East Asia at 31 percent, Africa at 12 percent, and Latin America and Europe at 6 and 2 percent, respectively (Refugee Council USA, n.d.). Each year the country adds a substantial number of refugees, and the geopolitical nature of conflict has meant that the waves of people have shifted and altered depending on those situations. After World War II, the main region for refugee movement to the United States was from Europe. During the Cold War, the United States saw increased numbers of refugees from the Eastern Bloc countries. Indochinese refugees began to arrive around the same time the United States was involved in wars in Korea and Vietnam (Refugee Council USA, n.d.). In recent times, South Asia and the Middle East have been the regions of origin for the majority of refugees to the United States.

The United States has been able to systematically and methodically address refugee resettlement based on resources and the ability for local communities to absorb the refugees. The estimations of three million refugees in the United States since 1975 (Refugee Council USA, n.d.) are slim compared to the large percentage of refugees in the world today (estimated to be at nearly forty-two million by the United Nations High Commission for Refugees [2011]). Yet the United States "accepts far more refugees for permanent resettlement than any other country in the world" (McBrien, 2005, p. 357). Worldwide, 45 percent of the forty-two million are under the age of eighteen, which mirrors a similar trend in the United States, where between 35 and 40 percent are children (BRYCS, 2011). In 2009, the United States admitted nearly 25 percent of refugees who were considered school age from nearly twenty countries (U.S. Government, 2011).

Getting to the United States: A Long Jump from Community to Community

How do these refugees get to the United States? What experiences do refugee children go through before they are situated in an "American" setting, going to an "American" school? Teachers are often unaware of the lengthy process refugees go through to get to safety and are unfamiliar with the bureaucracy that accompanies refugee resettlement in the United States. Even the U.S. Government Refugee Processing Center—the clearinghouse for all refugee admission to the United States—claims, "resettlement to the United States is a long process that can take months, or even years" (U.S. Department of State, 2010). Arriving in the United States does not discount the fact that many refugees have had to move from location to location and that being in the United States might represent the final leg of a long journey fraught with complications and danger.

The experience of refugees is mixed, but oftentimes moving to the United States is not the first stop in a refugee's journey. A 1992 article in the *New York Times* describes how one refugee felt on his first full day in the United States. In the article, the author describes the refugee movement by saying:

(He escaped) by bus, foot and train, across Vietnam, Cambodia and the border with Thailand. He spent more than a year in three different refugee camps. And then he crossed from one universe to another in the whoosh of a flight, landing at Kennedy International Airport late one night, reporting to his refugee caseworker on Park Avenue early the next morning. (Sontag, 1992)

Complicated and confusing enough for adults, the experience might be magnified exponentially for children.

A critical provision and expectation for refugee children is schooling, and the United States provides refugee children the same free education that is provided to other children living in the United States. Yet the adjustment to a new country, culture, language, and other dimensions of life in the United States requires a strong understanding of refugee experiences by teachers in the American classroom.

FRAMING THE NEEDS OF REFUGEE CHILDREN IN AND AROUND SCHOOLING

It may be unnecessary to say that "refugee children have traumatic experiences that can hinder their learning" (McBrien, 2005, p. 329). Refugees are without both citizenship and privilege. Their inability to align with a nation-state means that they have crossed "a national border and sought protection" (Waters & LeBlanc, 2005, p. 130), leaving them without the privilege of the protection of their nation-state. This lack of legal protection also leaves other dimensions of their personality in a state of flux and is especially cogent when it relates to refugee parents. Due to the lack of a state, there is both an "inherent uncertainty about in which society they should socialize their children as members . . . [and] issues taken for granted in 'normal' societies such as language, choice, history, gender and religion become a focus contention within the community itself" (Waters & LeBlanc, 2005, p. 130). Given the fact that we recognize that the United States has an active refugee student population and that U.S. teachers will need to have some foundation of knowledge as it relates to such students, there are certain important needs that educators will need to consider while working with refugee children. To better understand these needs, the following vignettes attempt to frame the refugee student experience in a way so that both teacher educators and teachers might be able to learn how to respond appropriately. Though these vignettes are not true accounts, the stories are representative of the multiple experiences refugee children face on arriving in the United States.

PSYCHOSOCIAL NEEDS

Mya Than was born in Burma just as the prodemocracy movement began its fledgling efforts to counter the military dictatorship rule that had repressed the people of Burma for over twenty-five years. Her parents campaigned alongside Aung San Suu Kyi, the daughter of Burma's first prime minister and were subsequently arrested and jailed for many months while Mya was only a baby. Soon after they were freed, they made their way to the Thai–Burmese border, where Mya's mother succumbed to malaria and died. Mya and her father made it to the camps on the border from where her father tried to assist in the prodemocracy movement but faced harassment by the Thai police. They moved on and headed to India for a brief period of time, where they filed paperwork to come to the United States. Over a span of three years and multiple interviews at the embassy in New Delhi, they were granted refugee status and came to the United States. Mya was only seven at the time, and her father, who had been a single parent for so long, put Mya up for adoption upon arrival here. A family in Portland, Oregon, adopted Mya but preferred not to tell the school the complete story of her life so that she could start fresh, hoping that time would dull her memories of her journey from Rangoon to Portland.

Students are often placed in classrooms with little regard to the types of traumatic experiences they might have witnessed or been subjected to (Szente, Hoot, & Taylor, 2006). Traumatic experiences include frequent movement and escape, extreme forms of violence, fear of or witness to child abductions, and loss of home, family, and friends. Children who are refugees due to natural disasters also cope with the lack of confidence in their environment, where they might "continue to encounter sights, sounds, smells, sensations, and inner feelings that remind them—even years after—of the [disaster which can] . . . bring on distressing mental images, thoughts, and emotional/physical reactions" (National Child Traumatic Stress Network, 2011). Teachers require strategies that allow them to understand how to help such students, as they can be "a primary resource for healthy psychosocial and cognitive development for children. However, many are poorly trained, unsupported, and unaware of the developmental needs of children" (Omidian & Papadopoulos, 2003). Additionally, teachers need to better understand the complexities that are inherent in refugee situations.

In the hypothetical example above, Mya's situation highlights the transient nature of refugees and the constant movement to safety. The loss of family members, the fear of isolation and danger, as well as the well-intentioned rationale of preferring to hide the prior trauma does little to help teachers work with refugee students. Pryor's (2001) study of refugee student's voices highlights the willingness children have of beginning to talk about their past experiences with "caring adults who will actively listen to them" (p. 278). Additionally, the political backdrop and geopolitical nature of refugee movements are oftentimes unclear to teachers, where research has shown that "many teachers ... lack confidence and feel underprepared in tackling controversial global issues, in terms both of knowledge and methods. They fear children would be anxious if war were discussed, [or] that ethnic tensions in the class would be heightened" (Davies, Haber, & Yamashita, 2004). In a Roper Public Relations poll commissioned by the National Geographic Education Foundation (2006), researchers found that "neither wars nor natural disasters appear to have compelled majorities of young adults to absorb knowledge about international places in the news" (p. 6). Such a lack of understanding is not new information, but it draws attention to the vacuum within which refugee children are attempting to blend and within which teachers are attempting to teach.

Fifteen years ago, Miller (1996) argued that there was a dearth of research on the "experience of children who have fled political violence in their homeland," and this has not changed much over the span of time. There could be many reasons for limited research, including hesitations on the part of researchers to further traumatize refugee children. In spite of that, efforts have been made to provide teachers with key actions or strategies to help refugee students (Szente, Hoot, & Taylor, 2006). McBrien's (2005) excellent review of the needs of refugee students highlights a number of studies that undergird the need for a better understanding of how psychosocial well-being affects refugee children. Additionally, there is a growing body of literature on resilience in children in posttraumatic situations. Actively including such research in teacher preparation course work will provide new teachers an opportunity to better understand the social and emotional difficulties associated with migration and refugee movements.

FAMILY NEEDS

Ayan and Abdi are siblings. As the older sister, Ayan looks after her whole family, Abdi, her younger brother, her two sisters, her mother, and an elderly aunt and uncle. During the height of the violence in Somalia, the family moved constantly for almost a decade. Abdi was born in a refugee camp where his mother was raped by a guard. Moving from camp to camp within the country, Abdi was able to take advantage of some of the makeshift education programs in camp. Discovering that they could apply for refugee status in the United States, the family submitted an application, and eighteen months later, the family headed to Minnesota, which they heard had an active and large Somali population. Ayan was fourteen, and Abdi was eleven when they got off the train in the Twin Cities. Abdi spoke English more fluently than anyone in the family and was quickly enrolled in school. Ayan also enrolled but was often absent from class. Her mother, sisters, aunt, and uncle spoke no English at all, and Ayan was often expected to stay home to help translate for the family. Coming from rural Somalia, the urban environment of St. Paul/Minneapolis presented different forms of fear for the family, and Ayan's support and leadership helped the family. From the landlord to the health clinic staff, Ayan was the family's sole communicator, and the feeling was that as a girl, her need to study was unnecessary.

The family unit in refugee situations depends on the strongest member of the family for survival. In many cases, it is the voice, action, and advocacy of the young adult or adolescent who uses their survival instincts to support the family. Suárez-Orozco and Suárez-Orozco (2002) documents the case of a Vietnamese refugee whose actions highlight the reversal of roles of children as adults, where they have to "become privy to 'family secrets' in their new roles as translators in medical, legal and other social settings . . . turning culturally scripted dynamics of parental authority upside down" (p. 75). In other cases, parents' fear of "losing face" prevents many of them from "asking for help or expressing their frustration" (McBrien, 2005, p. 340). Such parental inhibitions require that their children pick up the slack in negotiating for the family.

In this hypothetical case, Ayan, as a girl in the "in-between" generation (Koch, 2007, p. 3), is expected to be both an adult in terms of her responsibility to her family, and a child, as viewed by the state in which the family has settled. The responsibilities of her family versus the expectations of the state are often at odds, and though this is not unusual for many immigrant children, refugee children bear an especially strong sense of responsibility toward their families. Many refugee adolescents come to the United States with experiences that place them far beyond their biological age, shouldering responsibilities that have supported families in situations that defy understanding.

In a study by Weine and colleagues (2004) on the family consequences of refugee trauma, the authors studied the impact of political violence on family life for Bosnian refugees living in Chicago. Articulating four main themes highlighting the changed nature of family roles and obligations, the authors found that there was an increased dependence on children, a reduction in the time families could spend with each other, challenges to traditional notions of patriarchy, and increased parenting responsibilities for grandparents. The study found that "parents regard children as vitally necessary resources for their own survival . . . [where] the extraordinary intensity that is carried by the parent-child relationship in refugee families is often not matched by existing interventions in refugee trauma" (p. 158). Such trauma on the familial relationship affects multiple aspects of the refugee student's life, including their behavior in school. In Aronowitz's (1984) research on the adjustment of immigrant children to schools and society, he cites earlier studies showing the association of behavior disorders in immigrant children tied to "various kinds of disturbance and disruptions of family relationships" (p. 248). Such broad generalizations may not stand stronger scrutiny in 2011 as research has encompassed additional modalities for disturbances among all children, whether native, immigrant, refugee, or international, but what can be inferred for all students is that familial disturbances do impact learning and socializing in school, and refugee children face a far more difficult road due in part to the complex relationships that are encompassed in the family.

Oftentimes, in my experiences working with teachers, the family becomes an easy target to blame for the inadequacies of the student. The willingness for teachers to disavow the influence of the family comes at a price for refugee children who are often expected to protect their families in traumatic situations. The already demanding task of creating a parent-teacher relationship becomes fraught with tension, and typical school challenges of language and timing of conferences become even more difficult with refugee families.

Educational Needs

Javed hated being called a "rag head." His father told him to take no notice of the teasing, but Javed felt it was worse than teasing—it was anger and hatred and a constant reminder that he was an outsider. The students in his class were careful not to do it too close to the teachers, but they knew that it bothered Javed and kept up a low rumbling during lunch and in the hallways. Javed had grown up in Kabul, and his father had a good job as a linguist. Unfortunately, after the surge, his father had been blacklisted by the local Taliban fighters with a price on his head. Under the cover of darkness, the family escaped over the mountains, with a goal to arrive in Pakistan and immigrate to the United States. Though Javed's father had wired some money ahead of their departure and carried some family heirlooms and jewelry that could be sold to give them a relatively solid start, they still arrived in the United States with very little and for the first time were dependent on public assistance. His mother was embarrassed at their changed economic status and spent much of her time crying. Javed was thirteen, and though he spoke limited English, he was ahead in math and science, although his teachers were unaware of how far advanced he was due to his inability to communicate clearly. Additionally, his parents had asked for him to have additional English classes that required him to be pulled from music and PE classes where he might have actually had a chance to make friends since both music and sports require little translation.

Schools can be the "prime acculturating agents within societies ... (where) the values, norms, and tools of a particular culture are transmitted to its young" (Anderson, 2004, p. 78). Refugee children make adjustments in school on a daily basis and beyond the psychosocial and familial needs; educational needs are a high priority for refugee families. The challenges that refugee children face in school range from language, safety, parent involvement, and developing relationships with peers. Other chapters in this volume speak to language issues in newly arrived immigrants in the United States and the role of parents' culture in schools. Safety and developing relationships with peers might be a universal issue for all international students in the U.S. educational system, but refugee children are rarely here out of choice and therefore find acculturation more burdensome and/or threatening to their own cultural identity (Koch, 2007).

Children from refugee families often face prejudice and discrimination and can be fearful of speaking up to authority figures based on their history of movement and migration (Pryor, 2001). Studies documenting the experiences of various refugee groups highlight such bias and prejudice, where for instance Koch (2007) discusses the alienation a Somali student experienced in school, Fong (2004) articulates how the Christian focus of holiday crafts and projects alienates Muslim children, and Zhou (1997) claims that such alienation might often lead to the "willful refusal to learn" that hinders academic growth and success for immigrant and, I argue, refugee children as well. The American Psychological Association (2010) recognizes that many refugees come from situations that are based on discriminatory practices, but this does preclude them from the more racialized discrimination and prejudice that occurs in the United States, where skin color is also a distinguishing factor for marginalization.

Peer relationships are an important aspect of schooling. Suárez-Orozco and Suárez-Orozco (2010) document the importance of peer relationships for immigrant students while also highlighting the loss for such students when they do not have access to a strong peer network. They say,

> Peers can provide emotional sustenance that supports the development of significant psychosocial competencies in youth. Peers can specifically serve to support or detract from academic engagement. By valuing (or devaluing) certain academic outcomes and by modeling specific academic behaviors, peers establish the norms of academic engagement. Peers can tangibly support academic engagement by clarifying readings or lectures, helping one another in completing school assignments, and by exchanging information (about examinations, helpful tutors, volunteer positions, and college pathway knowledge). However, as immigrant youth often attend segregated schools, they may have limited access to knowledgeable networks of peers. (p. 634)

In the hypothetical situation presented above, Javed highlights his feelings of marginalization in school where teachers are frequently unaware of the hostilities affecting refugee children. Refugee children are often trying to balance their cultural identities while also learning to fit into the new social and cultural structure they belong to. In learning to fit in, they also experience increasing alienation from their families. The more they are able to acculturate, the more the increasing tensions affect the family unit that may not be as adaptable as their children. This type of Americanization doesn't happen as smoothly or fluidly as educators might expect, in spite of the natural inclination for young people to try to adapt and become resilient in times of movement. Feelings of isolation are enhanced due to the fact that "students . . . feel they do not belong anywhere, as they become alienated from their parents, but are not truly accepted by their peers" (McBrien, 2005, p. 352).

An additional note that supports the need for teachers to become more aware of refugee situations and educational needs lies in the controversies surrounding the curriculum in refugee camps and schools. As refugees leave their home countries, they become people without a state, a nationality, a passport, or a history. Aid agencies have quickly recognized that setting schools up in camps is one of the easiest ways to promote some sense of normalcy for children while also preventing restlessness among bored and disenfranchised youth. The problem lies in the nature of schooling itself, where challenges include the nature of the curriculum and pedagogy, the role of "political judgments" around education, and the fact that "schooling is inherently embedded in broader issues of individual and economic development that for refugee populations are inherently unclear and often unimaginable" (Waters & LeBlanc, 2005, p. 132). Such weighted issues around curriculum matters means that education might have been sporadic and inconsistent for the refugee students in their classroom and that what might be expected in other formal systems of education has been held hostage to the "plethora of programs [that] sought to satisfy a wide variety of competing constituencies" (Waters & LeBlanc, 2005, p. 144).

MAKING THE CASE FOR TEACHER EDUCATORS

Patterns of migration, movements of people, and the increasing spread of refugee families in the United States increases the chances that teachers in the United States will work with a refugee child at some point in their career. Though any child could be faced with the types of challenges described in this chapter, it becomes imperative for teacher educators to address the political, economic, social, and cultural reasons leading to refugee movements around the world. The concerns related to trauma, familial needs, and education require teachers to approach refugee children with a different set of tools and awareness. As this book suggests, dispositions including empathy, respect, and social justice ideals are important to foster international mindedness in teachers; this chapter seeks to provide a voice for the experiences of refugee children, while also offering a deeper understanding of how teacher educators might prepare their students to work more specifically with this population.

Tailoring teacher preparation courses to be more international in scope requires systematic understanding of the issues. By offering pedagogical practices, assessments, and learning opportunities to both preservice and in-service teachers in the relative safety of their university or college classroom allows teachers a chance to explore what they might do before potentially facing their first refugee student in schools and classrooms. Szente, Hoot, and Taylor (2006) found that to make the "transition to the new school system and life in the US easier . . . refugee resettlement agencies, colleges/universities and school" (p. 19) would need to work together to ensure the success of refugee students in U.S. classrooms.

Exercises that promote deeper understanding of teacher assumptions about "foreigners" are vitally important to working with refugee populations. In the literature selected for this chapter, researchers focused on many different groups of refugee student experiences in U.S. schools. A common finding across all these books and articles was a lack of awareness of the processes around the bureaucratic nature of refugee resettlement in the United States. Pryor (2001) documented the case of a family that was overwhelmed by medical problems, but a parent needed to work forty hours a week to receive Medicare benefits. With unaccompanied children, single-parent households, physical and mental illnesses, care for multiple members of the family, limited language skills, and few job training programs for adults, some of these obvious "truths" of working forty hours may be a far more difficult task than many teachers initially fathom.

Teachers also seem to have limited opportunities to explore and understand different systems of education. The focus in the United States has been on preparing teachers to teach in U.S. classrooms with students who might "epitomize" the U.S. experience while making some allowances for immigrant or minority students. In a graduate class for in-service teachers, I assigned a project where teachers conducted a study of another country's educational system while also interviewing some of the international students in their school. With nearly sixty different educational systems represented in the class and almost twenty countries represented in the interviewing process, reactions to this assignment were similar. Teachers were surprised at how many different ways countries "did" education, were shocked at the levels of depth in content and curriculum in many countries, and were intrigued by the policies around assessment, evaluation, and movement from grade to grade. One teacher said:

> I have not often thought or ever cared what was happening in other countries when it came to the educational systems. I was always focused on what I was doing or responsible for and didn't think is there another way. I watch the news and also read the paper in which education of other countries rarely makes the headlines unless there is a significant issue.

Another teacher said:

> I think there is so much more to all of our students, so much we don't see and they don't tell us. I can only imagine how hard it would be for me to go into another country and teach. It must be equally as hard, if not harder, for some of our students to come into our country and have to join the masses of students and survive here. I think education varies so much from country to country that we make it hard on students who move globally. Not all education systems in other counties are "bad," but the differences are so big that adjusting from one system to another can be difficult. The more teachers understand these other educational systems the better prepared we are to make this transition easier for our students.

Such insights do not occur without teacher educators taking on an active sense of responsibility for the diverse student population teachers are expected to work with. Recognizing the different systems, the level of adjustment, and engaging in a sense of curiosity about the ways in which other countries address education is important if we are expecting to internationalize teacher education. With refugee children, who have had sporadic and incomplete access to education and have struggled through different systems, teachers will have to recognize that the challenges facing these students are far more rigorous.

Encouraging teachers to better understand some of the psychological issues associated with trauma will help teachers be more confident in preparing to work with refugee children. While adults might prefer to forget or ignore the painful memories of the past (Weine et al., 2004), children can be engaged in ways that both protect their vulnerability while also allowing them to trust their new environment. Mistrusting authority figures, including teachers, is a factor of development of refugee children (McBrien, 2005), and teachers must be prepared to work with case officers, counselors, and other school officials to assist refugee children. The adjustment of refugee children is critical for their future success, and teachers might need to ensure that this happens since family members are often unable to be as resilient to these changes. School performance is a good indicator of refugee children's adjustment (APA, 2010), but teachers should partner with school psychologists to ensure that progress is more than just grades and completed projects and homework. Teacher educators can help by encouraging teachers to learn to work collaboratively with nontraditional partners across the school and community.

CONCLUDING THOUGHTS

The successful settlement of refugee children in the United States depends on multiple factors, including the ways in which they left their homeland, the years and intensity of the conflict they experienced, their own resilience, and the ways in which schools receive and educate these children. Zhou (1997) defines the success of the immigrant child experience as being

> largely contingent upon human and financial capital (brought) along, the social conditions from which their families exit as well as the context that receives them, and their cultural patterns, including values, family relations, and social ties, reconstructed in the process of adaptation. (p. 90)

Refugee children often come with little human or financial capital, negligent and dangerous social conditions, unfamiliarity with the context where they are received, and cultural patterns that might have been dangerous to exhibit or retain. In such an environment, it is important to recognize that there is a responsibility teachers have to work with refugee students, and teacher educators can play a critical role in developing an awareness of refugee situations among teachers. Teacher educators might manifest similar concerns that teachers speak to—limited resources, fear of the unknown, and lack of training—but such a passing of the buck belies the need for such students and disavows the safe harbor that schools are expected to be for all students. Speaking to the refugee experience, offering opportunities in course work to look beyond the traditional immigrant experience, and encouraging new teachers to actively voice their fears and present ideas on how to reach and teach this population of students is vitally important and should be a strong element of internationalizing teacher education in the United States.

REFERENCES

American Psychological Association, Resilience and Recovery after War: Refugee Children and Families in the United States. (2010). *Report of the APA task force on the psychosocial effects of war on children and families who are refugees from armed conflict residing in the United States.* Retrieved from http://www.apa.org/pubs/info/reports/refugees-full-report.pdf.

Anderson, A. (2004). Issues of immigration. In R. Hamilton & D. Moore (Eds.), *Educational Interventions for Refugee Children: Theoretical Perspectives and Implementing Best Practice* (pp. 64–82). London: Routledge.

Aronowitz, M. (1984). The social and emotional adjustment of immigrant children: A review of the literature. *International Migration Review, 18*(2), 237–57.

Bridging Refugee Youth and Children Services, Refugee Children in U.S. Schools: A Toolkit for Teachers and School Personnel. (2011). *Tool 3: Refugee child welfare; guidance for schools.* Retrieved from http://www.brycs.org/documents/upload/ChildWelfare-FAQ.pdf.

Davies, L., Haber, C., & Yamashita, H. (2004). *Global citizenship: The needs of teachers and learners* (key findings from the DFID project). Retrieved from Centre for International Education and Research website, http://www.education2.bham.ac.uk/documents/research/CIER/Global_Citizenship_Report_key_findings.pdf.

Fong, R. (2004). *Culturally competent practice with immigrant and refugee children and families.* New York: Guilford Press.

Koch, J. M. (2007). How schools can best support Somali students and their families. *International Journal of Multicultural Education, 9*(2), 1–15.

McBrien, J. L. (2005). Educational needs and barriers for refugee students in the United States: A review of the literature. *Review of Educational Research, 75*(3), 329–64.

Miller, K. (1996). The effects of state terrorism and exile on indigenous Guatemalan refugee children: A mental health assessment and an analysis of children's narratives. *Child Development, 67,* 89–106.

National Child Traumatic Stress Network. (2011). *Earthquakes: What you should know about earthquakes.* Retrieved from http://www.nctsn.org/trauma-types/natural-disasters/earthquakes.

National Geographic Education Foundation, Final Report. (2006). *National Geographic-Roper Public Affairs: Geographic literacy study.* Retrieved from http://www.nationalgeographic.com/roper2006/pdf/FINALReport2006GeogLitsurvey.pdf.

Omidian, P., & Papadopoulos, N. (2003). *Addressing Afghan children's psychosocial needs in the classroom: A case study of a training for trainers* (based on the experiences of IRC in Pakistan). Retrieved from http://www.healingclassrooms.com/downloads/Addressing_Afg_Childrens_Psychosocial_Needs.pdf.

Pryor, C. (2001). New immigrants and refugees in American schools: Multiple voices. *Childhood Education, 75*(5), 275–83.

Refugee Council USA. (n.d.). History of the U.S. refugee resettlement program. Retrieved from http://www.rcusa.org/index.php?page=history.

Sontag, D. (1992, September 27). Making "refugee experience" less daunting. *New York Times.* Retrieved from http://www.nytimes.com/1992/09/27/us/making-refugee-experience-less-daunting.html?src=pm.

Suárez-Orozco, C., & Suárez-Orozco, M. (2002). *Children of immigration.* Cambridge, MA: Harvard University Press.

———. (2010). Children of migrant populations. In E. Baker, B. McGraw, & P. Peterson (Eds.), *International Encyclopedia of Education* (8 Vols., 3rd ed., pp. 629–35). Oxford: Elsevier.

Szente, J., Hoot, J., & Taylor, D. (2006). Responding to the special needs of refugee children: Practical ideas for teachers. *Early Childhood Education Journal*, 34(1), 15–20. doi: 10.1007/s10643-006-0082-2.

UNHCR. (2009, June 16). UNHCR annual report shows 42 million people uprooted worldwide. *UNHCR*. http://www.unhcr.org/4a2fd52412d.html.

U.S. Department of State, Bureau of Population, Refugees, and Migration, Office of Admissions Refugee Processing Center. (2011). *FY 2011 Arrivals Sorted by Region by Month*. Retrieved from http://webcache.googleusercontent.com/search?q=cache:8eWNSU4fNWMJ:www.wrapsnet.org/LinkClick.aspx%3Ffileticket%3DFL%252FQC8nJURk%253D%26tabid%3D211%26mid%3D1192%26language%3Den-US+FY+2011+Arrivals+Sorted+by+Region+by+Month&cd=1&hl=en&ct=clnk&gl=us&source=www.google.com.

U.S. Government, Office of the President of the United States. (2011). Proposed refugee admission for fiscal year 2011: Report to congress. Retrieved from http://www.state.gov/documents/organization/148671.pdf.

Waters, T., & LeBlanc, K. (2005). Refugees and education: Mass public schooling without nation-state. *Comparative Education Review*, 49(2), 129–47.

Weine, S., Muzurovic, N., Kulauzovic, Y., Besic, S., Lezic, A., Mujagic, A., Muzurovic, J., et al. (2004). Family consequences of refugee trauma. *Family Process*, 43(2), 147–60. doi:10.1111/j.1545-5300.2004.04302002.x.

Zhou, M. (1997). Growing up American: The challenge confronting immigrant children and children of immigrants. *Annual Review of Sociology*, 23, 63–95. Retrieved from http://www.jstor.org/stable/2952544.

Zimmerman, M., & Arunkumar, R. (1994). *Resiliency research: Implications for schools and policy*. Social Policy Report, Society for Research in Child Development (Research Report Volume 8, No. 4). Ann Arbor, MI: SRCD Executive Office.

• 8 •

Understanding Secondary Models for Advanced Programs in the United States

Kimberley Daly

INTRODUCTION

For secondary students in the United States with the goal of attending a four-year college or university, taking advanced academic course work is no longer an option (Geiser & Santelices, 2006). College admissions officers want to see that students have been successful in rigorous academic programs, taking challenging courses and examinations while still in high school. Higher education relies on test scores from advanced academic course work as a potential measure of college readiness (Conley, 2007), and some admissions offices use examination scores as a tool to select those students who might be the best matches for their particular programs and institutions. The pressure on educators to prepare students for these examinations is sometimes overwhelming, as American attitudes toward testing and standards require teachers to not only convey curricula but also increase minority participation and improve overall achievement (Mayer, 2008; Clemmit, 2006). With these demands, educators who teach these advanced courses often undergo professional development to accommodate curricula and assessment changes that occur within the program as well as those of the districts within which they operate.

This chapter will focus on the two main advanced academic programs in the United States, the Advanced Placement (AP) program and the International Baccalaureate Diploma Programme (IBDP), discussing the history and aims of each program, the role of teachers who are integral to teaching curricula and preparing students for assessments, and the options available for professional development. Finally, because the two programs differ in their approaches to professional development, especially as it relates to internationalism, this chapter will discuss the differences and suggest ways that teachers might be better supported.

THE ADVANCED PLACEMENT PROGRAM

The Advanced Placement (AP) program is currently overseen by the College Board, which has its main offices in New York City; Washington, D.C.; and Reston, Virginia, but maintains several other regional offices throughout the United States. Founded in 1900, the College Board is a nonprofit organization that oversees several other programs, including the SAT. In recent years, the College Board has started providing students and parents with college planning information as well as services for those in higher education and educational policy.

Before the AP program was created in the early 1950s, universities had engaged in advanced placement efforts on their own if a student's credentials warranted it (Lacy, 2010). Although the AP program is now part of the College Board, it originated as a result of five different advanced placement efforts. Despite five having contributed, the Kenyon Plan and a joint series of meetings on the East Coast of the United States are more cited than others, and because of their strong connections to the AP program, they will be included in this discussion.

History and Program Structure

The first advanced placement effort, called the Kenyon Plan of 1950, was developed based on the philosophy that gifted students could successfully do college-level work in a high school setting as taught by trained high school teachers (Lacy, 2010). It was led by Kenyon College president Gordon Keith Chalmers and was also officially called the School and College Study of Admission with Advanced Standing (SCSAAS). The Kenyon Plan maintained that high school and not early admission to college was the best social setting for adolescents.

The structure of the Kenyon Plan was similar to the organization of the AP program today. Early participants included advisors from the College Board as well as representatives from about a dozen colleges (including Kenyon College in Ohio and the Massachusetts Institute of Technology), as well as seven pilot high schools from the northeastern and midwestern United States. By 1952, the Kenyon Plan had spread across the United States, and committees were exploring advanced placement examinations in history, chemistry, Latin, French, German, biology, physics, and English

(Lacy, 2010). While each pilot school's experience was different, there were some distinct commonalities: the plan had to be introduced, course offerings decided, students selected for participation, and faculty engaged (Rothschild, 1999). College students were tested as a control group as the College Board formally took control of the Kenyon Plan for the 1955–1956 academic years.

The other advanced placement effort that contributed to the development of the current AP program was a joint series of meetings and a subsequent final report completed in 1952 by several elite secondary schools and prestigious universities on the East Coast of the United States. The committee consisted of professors from Harvard, Yale, and Princeton universities along with faculty from elite schools Andover, Phillips Academy, Lawrenceville School, and Phillip Exeter Academy. The committee members were concerned that advanced students were not being challenged enough. Discussions of the committee were largely philosophical, centering on the idea of "connecting a liberal education to the proper development of a democracy" (Lacy, 2010, p. 27). Another part of the group's report recommended that secondary schools recruit "imaginative teachers, that they encourage seniors to engage in independent study and college-level work, and that achievement exams be used to allow students to enter college with advanced standing" (College Board, 2011d).

From these efforts came the current iteration of the AP program, a series of courses and tests currently offered in thirty-four subjects (College Board, 2011b). Although originally designed as a college placement incentive, taking AP courses and the subsequent examinations has become a significant factor in the American college admissions process. The College Board generates a subject curriculum for each course that is used to guide teachers as they prepare students for national examinations each May (Klopfenstein, 2003). Schools may offer as many AP courses as they would like, but in order to label a course "AP" on a student transcript or in school materials, including on a website, an individual school or district must annually submit a course syllabus for each teacher of an AP course to the College Board for review, a process called AP course audit. This process came about as a response to secondary educators and members of the higher education community who wanted to ensure that uniform standards were being met throughout AP course work (College Board, 2010a). Besides providing teachers and administrators with clear guidelines for what materials should be in AP courses, the AP course audit provides college and university admissions officials with the assurance that seeing an "AP" designation on a student's transcript ensures a rigorous course of study.

Students may take as many AP courses as their secondary schedules allow within a school. AP courses typically duplicate general education classes that students would take during the first two years of college. In addition, the AP program has endeavored to add what would traditionally be considered elective courses such as comparative government and politics and statistics, which might satisfy either a general education requirement or perhaps a prerequisite for a specific major (Thompson, 2007).

Students are scored by external examiners, called AP readers, for individual AP examinations. Although individual colleges and universities set their own credit recognition policies, students who score between a three and five on an AP examination may receive varying degrees of placement and/or credit at the university level. Although AP courses and examinations are available outside of the United States, AP continues to be influential in American college admissions and in discussions of closing achievement gaps (Santoli, 2002). Federal initiatives have played an increasingly important role in the adoption of AP courses as a way of introducing rigorous curricula for secondary schools, and in 2002 the AP incentives program was established to provide funds to help districts increase the number of students who take advanced academic programs (Kyburg, Hertberg-Davis, & Callahan, 2007).

In 2010, there were 3,213,225 AP examinations given to 1,845,006 students around the world, with the top three AP examinations being English Language and Composition, English Literature and Composition, and U.S. History, respectively. These numbers represent a 10 percent growth rate over 2009, when just over 2.9 million students worldwide took various AP examinations (College Board, 2010b). As the AP program grows, more teachers will be called upon to teach these challenging courses and prepare students for examinations.

Professional Development and Training of AP Teachers

Despite the number of students taking AP courses and AP examinations, the College Board does not require teachers to be specially trained in any way before teaching an AP course. In addition, as is often the case in education, AP teachers, like many other educators, do not necessarily have a major in the subject in which they teach. According to the College Board (2011e), "There is no rigidly defined selection criteria for who can serve as an AP teacher." State licensure as well as local school autonomy in choosing who will teach an AP course can cause situations where teachers might be teaching an AP subject outside of their area of expertise and thus learning the material for the first time along with their students (Klopfenstein, 2003). Further, the College Board does not mandate how AP courses are structured and taught to students, although in some courses there would be a logical order for curriculum items (Byrd, 2007). With the exception of the AP course audit, all professional development for an AP teacher is at the discretion of the teacher and possibly the school or district they might be working in, as many professional development opportunities involve cost. Teachers of AP courses have a variety of voluntary options for professional development, from AP institutes and workshops, to course outlines and teachers guides, to discussion boards to network with other AP teachers. Each of these options as well as how AP has responded to globalization and internationalized teacher professional development will be discussed in the next few paragraphs and the next section.

AP workshops and institutes are offered for every subject and provide participants with an overview of the general requirements of the specific AP course. There are AP workshops and summer institutes for new and experienced AP teachers as well as for administrators and pre-AP teachers. Many of the weeklong AP summer institutes meet on college campuses when teachers are on summer recess, and several state incentive programs fund AP teacher training. The summer institutes and even the shorter AP workshops provide an invaluable avenue for introducing new teachers to what is expected in AP course work, acquiring new ideas, planning syllabi, and networking with other AP teachers (Klopfenstein, 2003; Milewski & Gillie, 2002). Additionally, the College Board holds an AP national conference, another outlet for teachers and administrators that provides several days of sessions targeted at AP curriculum and assessments as well as program updates.

In the same way that an AP teacher or administrator can attend a workshop and receive professional development support, course outlines and teacher guides for every AP subject are available online. For any of the thirty-four AP subjects, a teacher can download a course description, teacher's guide, sample syllabi, AP course audit information, and classroom resources. There is also information about pre-AP teaching strategies. Another part of the AP Central website offers searchable resources with a way for AP teachers to add additional reviews of textbooks, articles, websites, and other teaching resources via a link to a suggestion form (College Board, 2011c).

Finally, AP has discussion boards, called electronic discussion groups, so that teachers can both network with other AP teachers and find answers to questions. Each subject has a board led by a moderator, and there are also discussion groups for AP coordinators, small schools, and issue-oriented discussions on equity and access to AP programs. These boards provide an opportunity for teachers to ask questions, share materials, and network with other teachers.

Despite the above options for professional development, one option that is often not available to many AP teachers is the opportunity to take college courses in the subjects in which they teach. The level of courses taken should be commensurate with a teacher's previous experience and should not be confined to the upper-level courses or graduate level as many states require for teacher license renewal. Another suggestion would be for new AP teachers to audit the college-level equivalent of their AP course, even if they took the course as a student (Klopfenstein, 2003). These ideas might widen the options for professional development of AP teachers, even if the College Board does not require AP teachers to be specifically trained.

The Internationalization of AP

For some organizations, internationalization might simply mean transferring goods and services to another country along with staff that has expertise with the culture of the country or countries that business would like to gain a foothold in. But for an educational program such as the AP program, internationalization is a larger issue, requiring relationships with multiple stakeholders in many countries, including schools, universities, administrators, teachers, and accrediting bodies. These partnerships are all worthwhile, but all require time and effort on the part of those involved.

The goals of the AP program have not really changed in the last sixty years, in that the College Board provides standardized course materials and examinations so that secondary students would be able to pursue a rigorous course of study potentially culminating in college credit. After the end of AP's original founding period, the College Board introduced the program as widely and as quickly as possible to public and private schools throughout the United States. Concern about American education in light of the Soviet Union launching Sputnik in 1957 spurred American growth of both the College Board and the AP program until the early 1970s (Lacy, 2010). From the mid-1970s to the early 1990s, the populations and locations of students taking AP examinations started to change, requiring the College Board and the AP program to adapt.

Always seen as an American creation, the AP program has also been adopted by international schools outside of the United States, although in much smaller numbers. This forced the College Board to consider professional development for international teachers, although unfortunately the College Board really separates its AP international program from the American program. The first move to internationalize AP came in 1981 when about 2,700 students in countries beyond the United States took AP exams. At that time, the College Board began approaching international universities to accept AP credit; soon after, the U.S. Department of Defense Dependent Schools began recognizing examination results as well as teaching some AP courses (Lacy, 2010). With the expansion of AP programs abroad, the College Board began to offer professional development for AP teachers through conference presentations as well as AP summer institutes offered at international school sites or in conjunction with American universities that had international campuses (DiYanni, 2003).

Another way that the AP program moved to internationalize was through curriculum. As a response to globalization, the College Board introduced three courses into the AP program that are notable for "global reach and their international inclusiveness" (DiYanni, 2008, p. 159). These three courses—AP Comparative Government and Politics, AP Human Geography, and AP World History—provide students with course work on different aspects of globalization. AP Comparative Government and Politics, first offered in 1986–1987, studies cultural effects and backlashes of globalization as subjects (DiYanni, 2008; College Board, 2010c). AP Human Geography, first offered in academic year 2000–2001, has globalization and regionalization as core concepts, and AP World History studies global processes and the nature of changes of international frameworks, among other topics. The AP World History course, first offered in 2001–2002, has been the most popular of the three courses (DiYanni, 2008).

The recognition of the AP program by international universities coupled with the development of three individual global courses as well as an AP world language initiative helped to internationalize the AP program, although the benefit to American teachers is only extended as far as the curriculum for those that teach those particular courses. Because the subject matter of those courses is about globalization and international topics, teachers who voluntarily attend professional development for those subjects learn about the international subject matter. Unfortunately, there is no overarching idea of internationalism or global mindedness in the AP program, as the courses are not woven together in a cohesive, single program.

As stated earlier, students can take as few or as many AP courses as they choose; nor is there an AP diploma available in the United States. An AP international diploma (APID) is available for students only outside of the United States or going to universities abroad and requires students to take five AP examinations in four specific content divisions, including two selected from English and world language; one from mathematics or science; one examination in history, social sciences, or arts; and one exam designated with a global perspective, either AP World History, AP Human Geography, or AP Comparative Government and Politics (DiYanni, 2008). Students must obtain no lower than scores of three on all five examinations to qualify for the APID. Additionally, students who have language proficiency in a language not offered as an AP subject can submit a letter from a school administrator substituting that language for the world language requirement but must take another AP examination in another subject area so that they are still taking five tests (College Board, 2011a).

The existence of the APID creates a kind of split personality for the AP program as there are conditions abroad that are not applicable in the United

States. As AP has chosen to internationalize through curriculum rather than through a total program, some additional courses have chosen to broaden their focus such as the case of AP Art History, which now includes non-Western art and architecture, and AP Spanish Literature, which has modified their required texts to include works written in countries other than Spain. New courses include the AP World Language Initiative, which created AP courses in Italian, Chinese, and Japanese.

In terms of teacher professional development, AP is only internationalizing this insomuch that potentially American teachers might be able to connect with teachers abroad through the electronic discussion groups. AP has chosen to internationalize their programs through curriculum updates and new courses; it appears this trend will continue, sparking conversations to broaden other current courses and ideas for new ones. It would also be nice to see interdisciplinary presentations at something like the annual AP conference so that AP teachers perhaps from related disciplines could discuss topics of mutual interest. This could only augment an already successful program and provide new and experienced AP teachers with additional support and fresh perspectives in their subject areas.

Regarding research on the effectiveness of AP teacher professional development, there seems to be a lack of substantial research, and perhaps more attention is needed. As the College Board does not require AP teachers to be trained before teaching AP courses, it is very possible that some AP teachers are in the classroom without having attended an AP institute or workshop, especially in difficult economic times. Although a couple of studies concerning the characteristics of AP teachers have been completed, they have focused on the relationship between the characteristics of the teachers and student achievement. One study about AP biology teacher characteristics and practices found that although the AP biology teachers had a high degree of academic preparation for the classroom, more than half of the 667-person sample had not attended an AP institute (Paek, Braun, Ponte, Trapani, & Powers, 2010). A 2005 study by Paek and colleagues noted AP teachers' critical training needs as practical concerns, including getting course content covered in the class time available and suggestions about content that could be modified or dropped altogether. Still, another study did focus on teachers at Florida AP institutes during 2006 and 2007 and investigated impressions of AP summer institutes as well as classroom change as a result of attendance at those same professional development opportunities. In that study,

> Several new teachers reported discomfort with attending the same APSI as experienced teachers, because the content covered may have been too advanced for a new teacher's needs. Several experienced teachers noted the same issue. (Godfrey, 2009, p. 4)

An additional survey of AP teachers completed in 2002 asked the teachers to rank a series of twelve issues facing high schools. Included among the choices were access to good professional development, school safety, lack of family involvement, new technology, and providing good advice regarding college to students as well as others. The AP teachers surveyed (over 32,000) said that issues related to professional development, "including training in new trends within one's discipline, training in new teaching methods, increasing test preparation skills, and increasing access to professional development" (Milewski & Gillie, 2002, p. 16), were major concerns.

Research regarding how the AP program has successfully or unsuccessfully internationalized teacher professional development does not seem to be available. Given the fact that the AP program runs its teacher professional development model with attention to giving teachers an outline for conveying the subject matter of the various AP courses, the only courses that might have an internationalized teacher professional development program would be those courses in the World Languages Initiative, designated global studies courses, or the few courses mentioned that have expanded to include a broader study of the world such as AP Art History and AP Spanish Literature. These courses might be considered ripe areas for research concerning teacher professional development. Perhaps these are areas where multidisciplinary AP forum presentations or some other professional development opportunities might be beneficial for teachers, as students may overlap in these courses, and teachers might benefit from professional development opportunities where, for instance, the history studied in AP Art History for a particular international region might intersect with the intellectual history studied in AP World History. Further, this also might be a way for the College Board to link AP programs in the United States with AP programs in other countries, creating partnerships for teachers in places that could stimulate discussion, facilitate exchange of ideas, and create a dialogue that could open the door for professional development opportunities across nations. An initiative such as this used in a broader sense than the existing electronic discussion boards could produce a truly international teacher professional development community.

THE INTERNATIONAL BACCALAUREATE DIPLOMA PROGRAMME

The IBDP today is slightly different from its beginnings in the 1960s, especially in the United States. The advanced academic program grew from the development of a course in contemporary history, sponsored by teachers of social studies in international schools and organized by the International Schools Association (ISA) based in Geneva. This first curriculum sparked the creation of a culminating examination and, later, uniform standards for grading (Hill, 2002). The common standards and examinations led to the development of the International Baccalaureate Diploma Programme because teachers wanted to address the problem of national bias in classes while developing student appreciation of the range of cultural perceptions of events (Hill, 2008; Peterson, 2003). This concept, called international mindedness, later became one of the core values of all IB Programmes as well as the entire IB organization and will be discussed in more detail later.

In addition to developing curriculum and assessments, an internationally recognized diploma was a guiding force for international school parents and teachers, as it would enable students to go anywhere for higher education. Further, as the IBDP was developed:

> Learning about other cultures and world issues, and being able to speak other languages, were important pragmatic elements. It was clear to the teachers that a new pedagogical approach was needed to promote international understanding, an approach that would cut through stereotypes and prejudices: critical inquiry coupled with an open mind willing to question established beliefs, willing to withdraw from conventional positions in light of new evidence and experiences, willing to accept that being different does not mean being wrong. (Hill, 2002, p. 19)

This focus on international mindedness and critical inquiry is woven throughout every IB diploma course as well as the Primary Years Programme (PYP) and Middle Years Programme (MYP) in IB.

History and Program Structure

Established in 1969, the International Baccalaureate maintains three separate curricular programs, the IBDP for students in the final two years of secondary school, a Middle Years Programme established in 1994 for students eleven to sixteen years old, and finally a Primary Years Programme (PYP) started in 1997 for students three to eleven or twelve years of age. School districts do not have to offer all three programs and often do not have the facilities or resources to offer the entire continuum (all three programs) to students. Each program (PYP, MYP, and DP) is authorized by IB separately for a school or district, and teachers are trained in the methodology of each IB program according to specific program guidelines and uniform world requirements, including international mindedness and reflection (Hill, 2008).

For students in their last two years of schooling, the IBDP requires students to study material in six course areas culminating in a series of international assessments. Schools that offer the IBDP are permitted to allow students to pursue individual subjects (called IB Diploma Programme Courses) or to require students to complete the entire diploma sequence—an undertaking during which a student completes study and examination in six subject areas, including foreign languages and the arts. In addition to this requirement, students are also required to complete three additional obligations that are unique to IB—a critical thinking and philosophy course called Theory of Knowledge (TOK), the development and writing of a four-thousand-word piece of original research known as the extended essay, and the completion of 150 hours of Community, Action, and Service, also known as CAS (Sjogren & Campbell, 2003). Schools choose which subjects to offer depending on resources but must cover all six general subject areas. The idea of a cohesive diploma is one way that the IB is philosophically different from the AP program; where the AP program only offers single courses and examinations, IB gives students the option to pursue the entire diploma or to pursue individual courses.

Students are awarded an IB diploma if they achieve a total score of twenty-four points or more on their exams, do not fail more than one exam, and do not receive an "E" (elementary) grade on either their extended essay or their TOK essay. Exceptional TOK or extended essays can also help a student's total score by awarding up to an additional three points for particularly insightful work. Students in the United States, located in the northern hemisphere, take their exams in May each year. IB examinations are internationally assessed by examiners from across the world.

The TOK course is at the heart of every other IBDP course, as students in IB courses are continually asked to consider "how they know what they know." The course examines different ways of knowing, the role of knowledge in culture, and the role of the knower or the learner to the outside world (Schachter, 2008). That is one of the cornerstones of IB theory—the knower is in the center of all instruction. As teachers are trained in their individual subjects, they are also trained in how TOK fits into their given subject area.

Course work for IB examinations officially begins in the junior year, but many schools typically have a preparatory program of some kind to build skills that will be needed in IB classes. The International Baccalaureate does provide training programs for teachers, both those teaching the DP courses and those teaching in preparatory programs. Teachers of IB classes are required to be trained in IB teaching methodologies, and before schools can offer any IB program, schools must complete "a rigorous self-study and other accreditation-type measures" (Byrd, 2007, p. 10). The organization maintains consistency through oversight of instructors and a regular five-year review of IB programs.

Currently, the IBDP is offered in 2,302 schools across the world with 751 schools located in the United States (International Baccalaureate, 2011b). Although the IB and the IBDP began in Europe, in the 1980s, IB programs began to grow quickly in the United States and Canada, surprising many of the European founders (Peterson, 2003). Currently, the United States has the largest number of IBDP schools with 751, representing nearly one-third of the total Diploma Programme schools in the world. This number is always growing as new schools choose to become IB world schools. In addition, for the May 2010 examination session, there were 55,779 American candidates registered for various assessments (International Baccalaureate, 2010); as student numbers rise, the number of teachers that will be required to teach IB courses will also increase.

Unlike in Europe, where many IBDP schools are located in private international schools, over 90 percent of IB schools in the United States are public. Another thing that sets IB programs in the United States apart from IB programs abroad is the large number of students enrolled in IB Diploma Programme courses rather than the entire diploma sequence. In the United States, where each state has autonomy over its own educational system, IB was seen by some policy makers as a way to offer rigorous curriculum options that would not only open the door to higher education but also meet the requirements of federal initiatives, including No Child Left Behind as well as reduce the achievement gap (Kyburg et al., 2007). Some states, including Florida, Minnesota, Oregon, Texas, and others also provide financial incentives to implement IB, and still others provide financial assistance for IB teacher training, although in recent years financial support for both AP and IB has been subject to state budget cutbacks.

IB Teacher Professional Development and Training

For teachers who teach IB courses, training and ongoing professional development are crucial and required by International Baccalaureate. It is suggested that IB teachers and coordinators receive training every five years. In addition to providing workshops and training opportunities at various locations regarding individual courses, IB-sponsored training is also focused on various objectives that center on program philosophy, learning theory, pedagogy, leadership, and assessment. In 2009, IB developed a plan for professional development called the Global Workshop Architecture. In addition to training contained under the Global Workshop Architecture, the organization has developed an advanced program for IB teachers in partnership with selected universities, called the IB teacher awards. This program recognizes further commitment by IB teachers and administrators to professional learning and development and allows them to gain additional knowledge about IB topics while pursuing higher education options.

The first professional development requirement for a potential IB world school is that the school needs to send one teacher in each subject group area to be trained, plus the coordinator, plus, optimally, a school administrator (S. Richards, personal communication, January 28, 2011). There are three types of workshops in the Global Workshop Architecture, labeled by categories. Each category has different objectives and is designed to target different levels of IB teachers and leaders. The various categories can be attended by teachers in any of the three IB programs but would be specific to each program and possibly subject area.

Category 1 workshops are for teachers new to IB programs, and during these workshops, which may be face to face or online, participants will learn IB philosophy, the mission statement, the learner profile, and a basic outline of assessment (International Baccalaureate, 2009b). One of the cornerstones of the IB, international mindedness, is discussed through the organization's current mission statement:

> The International Baccalaureate aims to develop inquiring, knowledgeable and caring young people who help to create a better and more peaceful world through intercultural understanding and respect. (International Baccalaureate Organization, 2011a)

There should be no doubt that in order to prepare students to be successful and productive citizens they should understand, respect, and be prepared to communicate with other cultures. In one instant, students can be connected to other individuals and groups in faraway places, learning and sharing information. Again, central to IB's philosophy is the idea that students should be "compassionate and lifelong learners who understand that other people, with their differences, can also be right" (International Baccalaureate Organization, 2011a). The IB's first official mission statement, written in 1996, also stressed the importance of international mindedness to the organization, calling for students to be:

> Informed participants in local and world affairs, conscious of the shared humanity that binds all people together while respecting the variety of cultures and attitudes that makes for the richness of life. (Hill, 2008, p. 33)

While teachers learn about their individual courses in Category 1 workshops, they also learn about IB's learner profile, "the IB Mission Statement translated into a set of learning outcomes for the 21st century" (International Baccalaureate, 2009a, p. 1). These ten attributes for IB learners encourage students to strive for open-mindedness for one, making students and teachers aware again of other cultures and perspectives:

> They understand and appreciate their own cultures and personal histories, and are open to the perspectives, values and traditions, of other individuals and communities. They are accustomed to seeking and evaluating a range of points of view, and are willing to grow from the experience. (International Baccalaureate, 2009a, p. 5)

The concept of international mindedness, although said in different ways, is embedded in various parts of the IB philosophy and framework. No course can be taught without understanding these ideals, as they are essential to any IB program.

The overall purpose of Category 2 workshops is to build on knowledge learned in previous workshops and "enhance the understanding of the IB philosophy and programme model" (International Baccalaureate, 2009b, p. 2). In these workshops, participants might engage in more detailed study of a subject, discuss best practices in the classroom, and evaluate, share, and/or develop resources, but the focus moves from basic learning about IB programs to improving the quality of program delivery. Again, these workshops may be face to face or online. Globally, online professional development has grown immensely for IB. In 2010, there were two hundred new online professional development programs available for teachers (S. Richards, personal communication, January 28, 2011).

Category 3 workshops are concept specific and may be any topic related to IB practice. These workshops both provide opportunities for specific investigations as well as a venue for exploring educational ideas. Anyone can apply to develop a Category 3 workshop, but IB approves all offerings. The most popular sessions have been on international mindedness and assessment, across all levels.

IB teachers who attend workshops sponsored by IB through the Global Workshop Architecture can obtain graduate credit upon completing a reflective paper tailored to their individual program level (PYP, MYP, or DP) through Kent State University in Kent, Ohio (K. Brown, personal communication, June 16, 2011).

In conjunction with the various workshops offered through the Global Workshop Architecture, IB teachers, coordinators, and administrators have access to the Online Curriculum Centre (OCC). This online site provides IB teachers and others with discussion forums for each subject in the IBDP (as well as the MYP and PYP). There is also a searchable resource area and many other areas containing information about IB programs, assessment, academic honesty, special education needs, language, and learning, as well as the general subject information. Workshop and events calendars are also posted on the OCC. Teachers can get access from the IB school coordinators.

The IB teacher awards are the connection between IB and universities to recognize those educators who successfully complete postgraduate work developed by universities in conjunction with IB. In the United States, three universities have been authorized by IB to offer the IB teacher awards—George Mason University in Fairfax, Virginia; Oakland University in Rochester, Michigan; and Bethel University in St. Paul, Minnesota. Only George Mason University is authorized to offer both the Level 1 and Level 2 teacher awards. In addition, ECIS based in the United Kingdom offers the Cambridge International Teacher Certificate, a twelve-to-fourteen-month program culminating in a portfolio submitted and assessed according to five standards for internationally minded teachers. This credential has also been recognized for Level 1 of the IB teacher award and is another option open to American teachers. ECIS uses a blended/onsite model for instruction and holds institutes in various locations (S. Richards, personal communication, June 16, 2011). The Level 1 award is designed to meet the needs of teachers with little or no IB experience who would like to work in IB schools. Courses designed for this program are intended to develop understanding of the basic curriculum, pedagogical issues, and knowledge of IB philosophy and assessment (International Baccalaureate, 2008). The Level 2 award is aimed at experienced IB teachers who wish to build upon established knowledge. This award requires completing a graduate degree or similar program and in-depth work in the areas of IB education and active research engagement presumably in the teacher's subject or IB program area (S. Richards, personal communication, January 28, 2011).

As IB has an extremely organized structure of workshops and teacher professional development in place for their programs, the question remains whether or not all teachers take advantage of the training options offered to them. The resources available on the Online Curriculum Centre can connect American IB teachers with the rest of the world, and this can only make teachers more proficient, benefiting students in the long run. The creation of the IB teacher award scheme should be expanded so that more teachers might take advantage of this option, as some states and districts subsidize professional development, including university course work. Tight economic times may also limit sending some teachers to faraway training opportunities, especially for less familiar subjects.

The Internationalization of IB

As the IBDP started in Europe and had at its core an understanding of international mindedness and the idea of an internationally recognized credential, the IB organization was always internationalized because the founders realized the importance of cultivating relationships with several European countries and European universities to which diploma students eventually matriculated. The growth of IB programs in North America, particularly in the United States, has forced the IB organization to rethink its original idea of an internationally recognized diploma in regards to the United States, not because it was a faulty idea but because the market which accepted the IBDP (mainly public schools instead of private, international schools) had a mixture of students completing the diploma and single IBDP courses. In addition, since the IB diploma is not recognized as a school-leaving certificate in the United States and a state secondary school diploma usually signals the graduation of an American student from high school, university recognition needs to be handled differently in the United States.

These things notwithstanding, the IBDP has grown and flourished in the United States, maintaining the core values it holds dear. In terms of teacher education, since international mindedness, the learner profile, and the mission statement are so crucial to all IB programs, American and global, IB has maintained a truly international teacher professional development program, with various options for multiple audiences and linking both the American and global educational community together though the Online Curriculum Centre.

As far as research concerning the effectiveness of IB teacher professional development, the Global Architecture developed by IB has only completed one full year of operation. IB obtains feedback data from all workshops, from not only participants but from workshop leaders as well. In addition, IB has workshop observers who audit workshops and report to researchers at IB on their findings. Because IB is at such an early stage in their teacher education framework, the organization is only "at the benchmarking stage and only starting to interpret the data" (S. Richards, personal communication, April 7, 2011). In addition, as each institution which offers the IB teacher award scheme has a different setup and course structure, there is no overarching research available evaluating that program. This topic, like AP teacher professional development programs, is also ideal as a potential research area.

CONCLUSIONS AND FURTHER THOUGHTS

In today's global world, internationalizing teacher education for programs like the AP program and the International Baccalaureate Diploma Programme is important. Not only are these two programs considered advanced academic programs in the United States, but they are constantly looked to by policy makers as not only a way to prepare students for university, but to improve American education, close the achievement gap, and make American students competitive with the rest of the world. Both programs are considered rigorous, and both are highly prized by college admissions officials. The AP program is firmly entrenched in the American educational system as it had originally reached out to universities and colleges seeking credit for its programs and is backed by the massive organization of the College Board. IB, on the other hand, is gaining ground but is still dwarfed by the number of AP schools nationwide. If American students are to compete with the rest of the world, programs taught in the United States must be internationalized, and that means that the professional development delivered to the educators providing the programs must be internationalized.

For both programs, educators are crucial as they have the job of delivering curriculum and the philosophy of the program to the students they are entrusted with. For AP teachers, the message is to teach the curriculum, and if they are teaching one of the subjects affected in recent years by the AP program's efforts to expand abroad and internationalize the AP program, then teachers and students are possibly being internationalized. To what degree teacher education may or not be internationalized for an individual teacher is debatable, as the College Board does not specifically require AP teachers to be trained. The AP course audit is one step toward maintaining a standard, but for a task so critical and with such high stakes, perhaps the College Board might rethink a teacher training policy. Another thing that might be considered to help teacher professional development would be some changes to the structure of AP institutes, where there can be different levels of workshops, including those for separating new teachers and specialized in-depth discussions of course topics, perhaps even interdisciplinary workshops. Districts and schools that require AP teachers to be trained before they teach the comparable AP course should be commended as it can only be better for the students sitting in those courses and eventually taking those examinations. The AP international diploma is another example of AP's split personality between treatment of the United States and abroad that could be addressed.

For teachers of IB diploma courses, the core values of international mindedness and critical inquiry are woven through every course. Each course in an IB program is built around the principles of the learner profile and the mission statement. The objectives of IB teacher education programs are the same whether a teacher is in the United States, Europe, or Asia; depending on the level or category of the professional development program, IB teachers across the world follow a continuum of professional education that guides instruction and creates lifelong global learners, whether it be through workshops, the Online Curriculum Centre, or the IB teacher awards. In the case of IB, it is imperative that research about IB teacher professional development be completed and disseminated, as the global architecture is still new. IB teachers should be encouraged to use the resources available to them via the Online Curriculum Centre, as this resource and newer online resources like IB Answers and Global Engage provide excellent, instant professional development materials which teachers can access at any time.

Globalization touches every country and every individual. Because of the continuous contact of people through trade and immigration, nation-states and different cultures of people have learned to interact with one another and thus have started to value the importance of learning the other's cultural, political, and economic structures (Sampatkumar, 2008). The IBDP understood that concept from inception, while the AP program chooses to be more nationalistic in its approach. Of the two programs, the IBDP has internationalized teacher education and made teachers global educators, while the AP program struggles with two separate identities—a distinctly American one of courses, credit, and exams where teachers may or may not be trained, and an international one that has revised curriculum to propagate abroad but again doesn't require training to give it substance.

REFERENCES

Byrd, S. (2007, November). *Advanced placement and international baccalaureate: Do they deserve gold star status?* Washington, DC: Thomas B. Fordham Institute.

Clemmit, M. (2006, March). *AP and IB programs: Can they raise U.S. high school achievement?* (Vol. 16, No. 9). Washington, DC: CQ Press.

College Board. (2010a). The AP course audit. In *AP Course Audit*. Retrieved December 16, 2010, from College Board website, http://www.collegeboard.com/html/apcourseaudit/higher_ed.html.

———. (2010b). *AP Data 2010* [program summary report]. Retrieved February 19, 2011, from College Board website, http://professionals.collegeboard.com/profdownload/AP-Program-Summary-Report-2010.pdf.

———. (2010c). Comparative curriculum outline. In *Government and politics: United States, comparative* [course description]. Retrieved February 6, 2011, from College Board website, http://apcentral.collegeboard.com/apc/public/repository/ap-govt-politics-course-description.pdf.

———. (2011a). *Advanced placement international diploma (APID)*. Retrieved April 2, 2011, from College Board website, http://www.collegeboard.com/student/testing/ap/exgrd_intl.html.

———. (2011b). Course home page index. In *AP central* [course home pages]. Retrieved December 19, 2010, from College Board website, http://apcentral.collegeboard.com/apc/public/courses/teachers_corner/index.html.

———. (2011c). Teachers' resources search. In *AP central*. Retrieved January 21, 2011, from College Board website, http://apcentral.collegeboard.com/apc/PageFlows/TeachersResource/TeachersResourceController.jpf.

———. (2011d). The 1950s: A pilot program is born. In *AP central* [The history of the AP program]. Retrieved January 12, 2011, from College Board website, http://apcentral.collegeboard.com/apc/public/program/history/8019.html.

———. (2011e). *Training AP teachers*. Retrieved June 16, 2011, from College Board website, http://professionals.collegeboard.com/k-12/assessment/ap/plan/training.

Conley, D. T. (2007). *Toward a more comprehensive conception of college readiness*. Eugene, OR: Educational Policy Improvement Center.

DiYanni, R. (2003, April). The internationalization of the Advanced Placement Program. *International Schools Journal, 22*(2), 25–33.

———. (2008). Internationalizing the US secondary and university curriculum. In M. Hayden, J. Levy, & J. Thompson (Eds.). *The Sage handbook of research in international education* (pp. 152–63). London: Sage. (Original work published 2007.)

Geiser, S., & Santelices, V. (2006). The role of advanced placement and honors courses in college admissions. In P. Gándara, G. Orfield, & C. Horn (Eds.), *Expanding Opportunity in Higher Education: Leveraging Promise* (pp. 75–114). Albany: State University of New York Press.

Godfrey, K. E. (2009, April). *Advanced Placement Summer Institute: A survey of Florida AP teachers* (Rep. No. 39). Retrieved January 15, 2011, from College Board website, http://professionals.collegeboard.com/profdownload/pdf/09_0949_AP_RN_SummerInst_WEB_090515.pdf.

Hill, I. (2002). The history of international education: An international baccalaureate perspective. In M. Hayden, J. Thompson, & G. Walker (Eds.), *International Education in Practice: Dimensions for National and International Schools*. London: Routledge Falmer.

———. (2008) International education as developed by the international baccalaureate organization. In M. Hayden, J. Levy, & J. Thompson (Eds.), *The Sage Handbook of Research in International Education* (pp. 25–37). London: Sage. (Original work published 2007.)

International Baccalaureate. (2008). *The IB teacher awards* [Brochure]. Cardiff, Wales: Author.

———. (2009a). *IB learner profile booklet* (Updated ed.). (Original work published 2008.)

———. (2009b, July). *IB professional development global workshop architecture: Goals and objectives*. Retrieved February 2, 2011, from International Baccalaureate website, http://www.ibo.org/events/documents/IBPDGlobalArchitecture.pdf.

———. (2010, November). Nationalities of candidates registered May 2010. In *The IB diploma programme statistical bulletin* (sec. 9) [Brochure]. Retrieved January 18, 2011, from International Baccalaureate website, http://www.ibo.org/facts/statbulletin/dpstats/documents/May2010Statisticalbulletin.pdf.

———. (2011a). *Mission and strategy*. Retrieved January 4, 2011, from International Baccalaureate website, http://www.ibo.org/mission.

———. (2011b, February). IB world schools statistics. In *IB fast facts: One page of key information about the IB*. Retrieved June 16, 2011, from International Baccalaureate website, http://www.ibo.org/facts/fastfacts/index.cfm.

Klopfenstein, K. (2003, Fall). Recommendations for maintaining the quality of advanced placement programs. *American Secondary Education, 32*(1), 39–48.

Kyburg, R. M., Hertberg-Davis, H., & Callahan, C. M. (2007, Winter). Advanced placement and international baccalaureate programs: Optimal learning environments for talented minorities? *Journal of Advanced Academics, 18*(2), 172–215.

Lacy, T. (2010). Examining AP: Access, rigor, and revenue in the history of the advanced placement program. In P. M. Sadler, G. Sonnert, R. H. Tai, & K. Klopfenstein (Eds.), *AP: A Critical Examination of the Advanced Placement Program* (pp. 17–48). Cambridge, MA: Harvard Education Press.

Mayer, A. P. (2008, Winter). Expanding opportunities for high academic achievement: An international baccalaureate diploma programme in an urban high school. *Journal of Advanced Academics, 19*(2), 202–35.

Milewski, G. B., & Gillie, J. M. (2002). *What are the characteristics of AP teachers? An examination of survey research* (Rep. No. 2002-10). Retrieved January 15, 2011, from College Board website, http://professionals.collegeboard.com/profdownload/pdf/200210_20717.pdf.

Paek, P. L., Braun, H., Ponte, E., Trapani, C., & Powers, D. E. (2010). AP biology teacher characteristics and practices and their relationship to student AP exam performance. In *AP: A Critical Examination of the Advanced Placement Program* (pp. 63–84). Cambridge, MA: Harvard Education Press.

Paek, P. L., Ponte, E., Sigel, I., Braun, H., & Powers, D. (2005). *A portrait of advanced placement teacher practices* (Rep. No. 2005–2007). Retrieved February 8, 2011, from College Board website, http://professionals.collegeboard.com/profdownload/pdf/051388_RD_CBR05-7.pdf.

Peterson, A. D. (2003). *Schools across frontiers: The story of the international baccalaureate and the united world colleges* (2nd ed.). Chicago: Carus Publishing. (Original work published 1987.)

Rothschild, E. (1999, February). Four decades of the advanced placement program. *The History Teacher, 32*(2), 175–206.

Sampatkumar, R. (2008). Global citizenship and the role of human values. In M. Hayden, J. Levy, & J. Thompson (Eds.), *The Sage handbook of research in international education* (pp. 70–78). London: Sage. (Original work published 2007.)

Santoli, S. P. (2002, Summer). Is there an advanced placement advantage? *American Secondary Education, 30*(3), 23–35.

Schachter, R. (2008, February). The "other" advanced program. *District Administration, 44*(2), 26–30.

Sjogren, C., & Campbell, P. (2003, Fall). The international baccalaureate: A diploma of quality, depth, and breadth. *College and University Journal, 79*(2), 55–58.

Thompson, K. S. (2007). *The open enrollment of advanced placement classes as a means for increasing student achievement at the high school level*. Doctoral dissertation, University of Southern California, Los Angeles, CA. Retrieved from ProQuest Dissertations and Theses database (AAT 3278336).

· 9 ·

STEM Disciplines and World Languages

Influences from an International Teacher Exchange[*]

Wendy M. Frazier, Rebecca K. Fox, and Margret A. Hjalmarson

Standards for the professional development of teachers have been designed to provide guidance in the most effective educational approaches for the continuing development of teacher leaders that are consistent with education reform. With attention to the continuing professional development of internationally minded, experienced educators and the preparation of our future generations of teachers to be internationally minded educators, this chapter focuses particularly on the application of the standards in two areas—the fields of science, technology, engineering, and mathematics (the STEM disciplines) at the secondary level (grades six through twelve in the United States and five through eleven internationally) and the field of world languages (WL)—to the development and implementation of a teacher exchange program. In the context of the rapidly changing global demographics of the twenty-first century, there is an increasing need for educators who know the world and are able to prepare students to be effective world citizens. We, as U.S. teacher educators, must remain mindful of the global context and the role that language, particularly English as a world language, plays in

---

[*] This material is based upon work funded by the U.S. Department of State's Bureau of Educational and Cultural Affairs. Any opinions, findings, and conclusions or recommendations expressed in this material are those of the author(s) and do not necessarily reflect the views of the U.S. Government or any agency thereof.

the teaching and learning processes in the STEM disciplines in the United States and abroad.

Students today will need to be capable of working and living in a changing world (National Center on Education and the Economy, 2007; National Research Council, 2007). Many of the jobs students need to be prepared for have not yet been created, particularly in the fields of science, technology, engineering, and mathematics (O'Connor, 2008). In addition to knowing the content of their work, future citizens will also need to be internationally minded and know how to communicate important information across cultures and languages. To that end, the immediate relevance of preparing a citizenry that can meet such rapid global changes calls for new opportunities in teacher professional learning that include knowledge building in the content areas they teach, as well as in cross-cultural capacity, so that up-to-date global skills and new concepts might be actively incorporated in schools and classrooms around the world.

BACKGROUND AND CONTEXT

Aligned with professional development standards and the call for educators who have increasing knowledge of global contexts and a rapidly changing student demographic, this case offered opportunities to engage secondary school teachers, in STEM and WL, to develop internationally minded dispositions. Further, we examined how such efforts can be extended to our preservice teacher preparation programs. In the U.S.-Russia Teacher Professional Development Program (USRTPD), we have used the term *world languages* (WL) to encompass English as a foreign language (EFL) in Russia and Russian as a foreign language (FL) in the United States. The program created opportunities for authentic language learning through STEM content areas, while also providing teachers a dual context within which they might expand their understanding of the world. Through an international exchange of ideas regarding content, pedagogy, and language, the program encouraged the use of reflective and systematic practice with the goal of supporting lifelong learning and providing leadership development. Aligned with the book's focus on internationalizing teacher education in the United States, key questions explored potential implications for U.S. teacher education efforts:

1. How can teacher educators design meaningful professional development experiences for STEM and WL teachers that will encourage intercultural understanding and a mutually respectful exchange of ideas about

STEM Disciplines and World Languages 177

   the nature of teaching to foster professional growth and systematic reflection focused on enhanced teaching practice?
2. How can the realities of far-reaching geography, language, and cultural differences among a group of international teachers become positive enhancements rather than be viewed as barriers to intercultural exchange?
3. What essential elements must be present to extend participant engagement beyond the exchange period to encourage continued sharing of ideas, intercultural understanding, systematic reflection, and professional growth for STEM and WL teachers?

In addition, a fourth question serves to refocus our attention on the future generations of teachers and what these understandings may mean for this population:

4. In what ways can teacher educators draw on international cross-disciplinary work to inform the design of meaningful preservice experiences for future teachers that will support the development of internationally minded perspectives that translate into K–12 classrooms that incorporate internationally focused learning experiences?

With these key questions in mind, we share important elements from the program, funded by the U.S. Department of State's Bureau of Educational and Cultural Affairs. The exchange program was designed to allow in-country opportunities for both Russian and U.S. secondary school teachers of mathematics, sciences, technology (STEM), and foreign/world languages (WL) to spend time in one another's schools, learn from one another, compare effective teaching practices, and foster intercultural communication and excellence in the classroom through sharing of ideas and pedagogical expertise over a four-week period in the United States with a follow-on of two additional weeks in Russia (see the following).

Overview of Program Components

Spring: Recruitment and selection of Russian participants

Late Summer: Predeparture orientation in Primorsky Krai, Far East Russia, for participants traveling to the United States

Russian participants apply for visa to travel to the United States

Mid-Fall:	Russian participants travel to Washington, D.C., for four weeks
	Professional learning seminars and cultural experiences
	Field experience at partner school with an assigned partner teacher
	Daily debriefing facilitated by program codirectors
	Creation of electronic portfolio, digital PhotoStory, and follow-on teacher research plans
Late Fall:	Recruitment and selection of U.S. participants
Winter:	Collaboration between U.S. and Russian participants on collaborative, follow-on teacher research via portfolio, Blackboard, VK.com, Facebook, e-mail, and Skype
Early Spring:	Predeparture orientation in United States for participants traveling to Russia
Mid-Spring:	Five U.S. participants travel to Primorsky Krai, Russia, for two weeks
	Professional learning seminars and cultural experiences
	Field experience with debriefing
	Continuing portfolios, PhotoStories, and follow-on teacher research
	Follow-on conference: Teacher Researcher Day
	Panel discussion on U.S. and Russian education systems
	Description of follow-on projects
	Teacher research findings
	Debriefing
	Next steps for continuing collaboration
	(Additional U.S. participants attend via videoconferencing)
Late Spring:	Dissemination seminar in United States
	Panel discussion on U.S. and Russian education systems
	Description of follow-on projects
	Teacher research findings

                Debriefing
                Next steps for continuing collaboration
                (Russian participants attend via videoconferencing)

Summer: Collaboration between U.S. and Russian participants on collaborative, follow-on teacher research via Blackboard, VK.com, Facebook, e-mail, and Skype

Academic Year: Implementation of collaborative teacher research with documentation via electronic portfolio

Research findings demonstrate that in order to effectively meet the needs of teachers, professional development must be situated in the work of teaching and must focus on student learning (Whitcomb, Borko, & Liston, 2009). Teachers must have access to professional learning opportunities that cater to their unique backgrounds and content-specific professional knowledge base. It has become critical that professional development for experienced teachers use both content-specific knowledge development and the research on teaching and learning to guide the professional learning experiences in order to determine the overall impact on teachers and their classroom practice (Zeichner, 2006). We believe that this expectation should be upheld for teacher educators' work with preservice teachers as well.

BUILDING THE USRTPD PROGRAM

The program theme was "teacher leaders think systematically about their practice and learn from experience" (Frazier, Fox, & Shaklee, 2009, p. 1). During the Russian teachers' four-week visit to the United States in the fall of 2010, both Russian and U.S. participants attended professional development seminars, experienced practical classroom-learning opportunities, and engaged in reflection on teaching and education. Participants from the United States made a two-week reciprocal visit to Russia several months later, where they also experienced practical classroom-learning opportunities and continued their collaboration on joint projects anchored to their classrooms and educational settings to build on the professional experiences established during the Russian participants' visit. Russian and U.S. teacher participants also worked to conduct a teacher research conference in Far East Russia focused on the implementation of these new projects and to share the results of investigations in their classrooms in the United States and Russia. Teachers also began to consider content for postprogram professional development workshops for colleagues in the United States and Russia. In the following sections, we share the program's components that were designed and implemented in a manner consistent with professional development standards to positively impact teachers, students, schools, and communities through intercultural exchange and critical reflection.

Professional Standards in the United States

Standards for professional development in science (National Research Council [NRC], 1996) and mathematics (National Council of Teachers of Mathematics [NCTM], 2000) are focused on supporting teachers to portray their discipline in the classroom in a manner consistent with the nature of the two disciplines as professional fields of study (American Association for the Advancement of Science [AAAS], 1993; Lederman, 1999; NCTM, 2000; Paulos, 1992; Peters, 2009). For mathematics, reform has driven instructional trends toward classroom practices that support students' development of reasoning, problem solving, proof, and communication in mathematics as well as procedural knowledge (NCTM, 2000). Science education reform has driven instructional trends toward classroom practices that support student-driven investigation and discovery (NRC, 1996). With respect to engineering, core ideas are suggested for infusion into existing mathematics, science, and technology curriculum to provide engaging contexts for learning engineering ideas and to augment learning in the other STEM disciplines (National Academy of Engineering, 2010). In technology, defined standards support the introduction of technology as a content field of study in the classroom, as well as a vehicle to support creative inquiry and innovation in the other STEM disciplines via face-to-face and online opportunities (International Society for Technology in Education, 2008).

In the United States, standards for teachers of WL define what teachers should know and be able to do. The *Standards for Foreign Language Learning in the 21st Century* (National Standards in Foreign Language Education Project, 2006) describe content and pedagogical knowledge for teachers of world languages and include in the area of professionalism the importance of ongoing professional development through reflection and classroom inquiry. Encompassing interactive pedagogical practices that focus on consistent application of the target language, experiential learning, and communicative competence, the standards for our FL/WL teachers are overseen by the American Council on the Teaching of Foreign Languages (ACTFL). These standards also place a strong emphasis on the acquisition of knowledge about the target language's culture(s).

Cultural understanding extends beyond an individual's ability to state facts or know about a country's cultural celebrations; it means that individuals should be able to engage in culturally relevant and sensitive dialogue. Thus, teachers need deep cultural knowledge in order to extend classroom learning beyond the mere surface-level understanding of any culture in order to engender in their students the growth of a deeper understanding of cultural knowledge, one that will foster sensitivity and cultural competence. "Linguistic and cross-cultural competence is both a pathway and a goal that seeks to facilitate learning at all levels by all participants" (Osterling & Fox, 2004, p. 490) and be actively and consciously incorporated in our classrooms to support deep learning. As our world becomes increasingly connected across cultures, speakers of many languages are students in U.S. classrooms and around the world, and English is more and more present as the language of both communication and instruction in world classrooms.

In all disciplines and content areas, teachers are encouraged to be facilitators of students' learning rather than directors. Consequently, according to U.S. practices, professional learning experiences for teachers should employ many of the practices and experiences that K–12 students should have in the classroom in order to model reform-based instruction and help teachers learn through engagement in inquiry-based, authentic activities in the disciplines (Loucks-Horsley, Stiles, Mundry, Love, & Hewson, 2010). Research on effective professional development supports the nurturing of teacher leaders via professional development components that focus on establishing a community of practice (Wenger, 1998), of critical friends (Bambino, 2002; Hole & McEntee, 1999) focused on continuous improvement (Schmoker, 1996) via action research (Lewin, 1946), which is consistent with the recommendations from the STEM disciplines (Loucks-Horsley et al., 2010). To this end, teacher participants in this international program were provided the context to be empowered to authentically explore, creatively problem solve, and use evidence to drive future professional decisions in a systematic, reflective process (Lewin, 1946; Miller & Pine, 1990; Wei, Darling-Hammond, Andree, Richardson, & Orphanos, 2009).

Professional Standards in Russia

Similar to the U.S. standards, federal Russian standards have been established for the preparation of teachers through university-level teacher education programs (Ministry of Education and Science of the Russian Federation [MESRF], 2009). Also, similar to the United States, federal Russian content standards for STEM and WL exist to identify the content that teachers should teach across the country in each of the STEM and WL disciplines spanning primary through the secondary grades. Last published in 2004, *The*

Federal Component of State Standard of General Education in Parts One and Two (MESRF, 2004a, 2004b) is now under review with the most recent draft of standards for secondary grades. Additionally, lists of approved textbooks for required teachers' use in schools mandates the actual content within each course that teachers are to teach at each grade level (MESRF, 2010) and required equipment that teachers must be able to use in their teaching. Also provided are guidelines for the number of clock hours that teachers are to spend covering each topic within a particular course. The federal standards are meant to standardize teachers' efforts in all parts of the country, and special service may visit the school or speak with parents and students at any time to ascertain the extent to which the standards are being addressed. Thus teacher preparation at the university, and continuing professional development offered locally, is focused on supporting teachers to be able to satisfactorily meet these mandates (E. Novikova, Director of Asia Pacific School in Vladivostok, Primorsky Krai, personal communication, June 15, 2011).

Program Context

By exploring research-based practices, teaching and leadership strategies in STEM disciplines, and reciprocal FL/WL education with educational professionals from another culture, participants in the USRTPD program had the opportunity to develop their capacity as leaders through mutual inquiry. Additionally, the program provided an opportunity to consider additional perspectives and aspects of international representation within our own teacher education programs with a more informed and critical lens. The project designers purposefully joined STEM and WL teachers to encourage dialogue across disciplines and to address the role that language plays in the teaching, learning, and professional needs of our field of teacher education. As previously stated, the need for teachers who understand and can teach diverse students in a rapidly changing world provides the global context for this program. Specifically, the program goals were to

- Enable the exchange of knowledge and cross-cultural understanding through systematic inquiry that is anchored in K–12 classrooms;
- Advance professional learning for practicing teachers through dialogue about and inquiry of international and intercultural perspectives;
- Facilitate the ability to integrate technology to achieve instructional and leadership goals with all STEM and FL teachers and students;
- Foster the development of teacher leaders who are critically reflective of their teaching practice and able to conduct systematic research in their educational settings sharable with peers; and

- Support increased mutual visibility, accuracy, and sharing of the U.S. and Russian education systems with colleagues and students in educational settings and beyond.

Overall, faculty commitment to these goals was high since these goals are consistent with our university's strong international focus; with U.S. professional standards in the STEM and WL disciplines; and with our faculty's research and work with experienced teachers through advanced professional programs. Further, through discussions with our project's advisory board, we anticipated that these goals would potentially support both U.S. and Russian teachers to stretch their thinking beyond the scope of their immediate contexts and incorporate a more international focus in their work with students.

Professional Learning for Russian and U.S. Teachers

The program's professional learning component, *taught by faculty with expertise in STEM and WL,* was implemented in two phases: first, during the Russian participants' four-week visit to the United States, and second, during the U.S. teachers' two-week visit to the Primorsky Krai Region of Far East Russia. Professional learning consisted of intensive seminars encompassing primary areas essential to supporting participants' professional development and leadership capacity, and integrating experience, research, and practice during a systematic inquiry into their teaching practice and the U.S. and Russian education systems. Both Russian and U.S. participants were invited to attend seminars to support cross-cultural learning.

The seminars included combined sessions for Russian and U.S. STEM and WL teachers and sessions for each discipline independently, with breakout sessions tailored to STEM or WL content as needed. Specifically, STEM participants spent seminar time on developing reflective practice and integration of experience, educational technology, and research-based STEM teaching practices with attention to cross-cultural exploration and appreciation. Similarly, WL participants' seminar time focused on deepening reflective practice and integration of student-centered classroom practices that promote communicative competence in the language, educational technology, and WL teaching practices that are research based with attention to authentic cross-cultural exploration and integration. STEM and WL seminars for participants were enriched through participation of representatives from national/international agencies and organizations with central offices in the Washington, D.C., region.

Seminar Content for Russian and U.S. Teachers

In all of the seminars, an essential goal was to bridge research-based recommendations for teaching and professional development with classroom needs. Teachers were engaged in learning activities that could later be used with their students, and projects were focused on long-term needs. Follow-up and continuation activities (e.g., the professional portfolio) were deliberately infused throughout the program. In the following sections we provide an overview of each seminar and findings from our experiences.

Reflective Practice This seminar for participating teachers was designed to develop the teachers' capacity in critical reflection in and on their teaching practice (Brookfield, 1995). It included an examination of participant professional identity and culture, grew to include cross-cultural articulation of similarities and differences in teaching approaches across countries, and called on them to draw on deeper understandings about the salient aspects of teaching and learning for all learners. Through a dialogic approach and interactive learning, teachers experienced the development of a learning community of critical friends (Bambino, 2002; Hole & McEntee, 1999).

Technology Integration Development of technology skills was differentiated for the specific needs of Russian teachers as dictated by their content areas and structured to respond to their emergent needs. Free and low-cost software programs and easily accessible technology resources were used throughout the project whenever possible to accommodate the diversity of access that participants had to technology. This allowed Russian teachers to learn programs and technology that would be more easily accessible to them in their educational settings, such as VK.com (a Russian social network site). Teachers also engaged in ongoing dialogue with their U.S. colleagues and seminar faculty regarding viable ways that technology is currently being implemented to support their professional learning, as well as instruction for K–12 learners. Through audiovisual media, public and private areas of VK.com for social networking, and a private course page developed through an online educational service (Blackboard) to support mutual sharing of ideas when participants are in their respective home locations, technology was integrated throughout all aspects of the program. In this way, teachers had the opportunity to develop new understandings about technology's application for their own professional development and to consider the ways that they might build on its use upon return to Russia. Important for both Russian and U.S. teachers were discussions about interesting and viable ways to implement technology with their learners, which contributed to greater cross-cultural understanding about K–12 learning, in general, and provided some interesting ideas for potential U.S.-Russia follow-on projects.

Professional Portfolio The USRTPD professional portfolio was implemented as a key learning outcome of the program. To support purposeful examination of practice and continuous improvement, teachers were introduced to critical reflective practice and action research to help them analyze and reflect deeply about their teaching. Additionally, teachers were introduced to and created electronic portfolios to support systematic reflection throughout their participation in the program and beyond. Each teacher who attended the seminars successfully created a portfolio with sections for the areas of culture and teaching, teaching and learning, technology, and professionalism and action research. Reflection was a core element infused throughout the portfolio, and the postings largely stemmed from the seminar curriculum and field experience debriefings.

Teacher Leadership through Action Research This seminar combined the development of teacher leadership, teacher action research, and reflective investigation of teaching approaches that would support continuing implementation of classroom research upon the participants' return to their respective classrooms. The seminar was designed to support teachers as they developed skills in observing, recording, and analyzing the teaching and learning from a deliberative reflective stance. In a supportive collegial community, teachers worked in content teams to conceptualize and author classroom-based inquiries with support of colleagues/critical friends. Activating research and reflection skills developed during the program, participants developed a research plan conceptualized and begun during the Russian teachers' visit in the United States, followed through after their return home, refined during the U.S. teachers' visit to Russia, and continued into the following academic year. The goal was to develop skills that the Russian and U.S. teachers would build upon in subsequent years and share with their colleagues, hopefully forming inquiry groups in Primorsky Krai and in their U.S. region.

Our goal is that participants take a leadership role in creating a sustainable learning community in their respective schools, and engage in and apply reflective practice strategies that were introduced and developed during their participation in the program. Russian teachers have gathered regularly to reflect on teaching and learning and support the development of one another's classroom research, a new concept in this region of Russia. The U.S. teachers have gathered as a group to support their projects and investigate possibilities for cross-disciplinary K–12 projects with their Russian colleagues. Follow-through is important for both U.S. and Russian teachers and is strongly supported through the communication afforded us by technology.

Developing Capacity in Intercultural Understanding Building upon new skills in reflective practice, and with attention to inquiry of one's own teaching through action research, this seminar provided teachers with a framework that helped participants consider ways that culture might be actively applied in their teaching practice. Through readings, dialogue, and examination of cultural dimensions in teaching and learning, teachers considered practical applications of culture to enhance student engagement and performance, with a goal of fostering equity and academic excellence. The joint teams discussed the highly diverse student population at the U.S. host high school and compared it to schools in their region of Russia, which are not so diverse. Ideas about how culture and language affect classroom interactions and curriculum development around the world surfaced to provide the participants rich cross-cultural dialogue. Sessions were planned for both groups to explore cultural perspectives and culture's role specific to their disciplines.

During the seminars, participants came to realize that teaching from a cultural perspective is the responsibility of all educators regardless of background and expertise, and is not limited to the world language classroom. Intercultural competence is something that every STEM and WL educator can and should practice on a daily basis to incorporate new perspectives, increase the visibility of both countries' education systems, and appreciate the strengths and worthiness of others.

Members of the program's advisory board also served as cultural partners to shape the planning and implementation of the cultural program implemented during visits to the United States and Russia. A wide variety of opportunities that included important historical sites, museums, and events were used to promote cultural understanding among participants.

Special Professional Learning Topics for STEM Teachers Additional seminars addressing classroom-, community-, and policy-level issues and best practices in STEM curriculum involved a variety of partners. Sessions for teachers included design mode, modeling, and engineering education (Bereiter & Scardamalia, 2003, 2006); problem-based learning as a curriculum model for STEM teaching (Chin & Chia, 2005; Delisle, 1997; Frazier & Sterling, 2008; Hmelo-Silver, 2004; Krynock & Krynock, 1999; Stepien & Gallagher, 1993; Sterling, Matkins, Frazier, & Logerwell, 2007); curriculum trends in STEM teaching in grades nine through twelve, such as increased attention on the nature of the STEM disciplines as a driving force for STEM teaching and learning (AAAS, 1993; Lederman, 1999; NCTM, 2000; Paulos, 1992; Peters, 2009); and interdisciplinary trends in STEM teaching (Delisle, 1997; Jacobs, 1989, 2010; Krajcik, Czerniak, & Berger,1999). Relying on the existing relationships established among faculty in our university's secondary teacher preparation program, sessions were collaboratively planned with secondary education faculty from science, mathematics, and technology along with local science coordinators from school districts local to the university. Additionally, professional development in STEM continued with visits to the Smithsonian Institute and the USA Science and Engineering Festival held on the Washington, D.C., National Mall. Finally, led by the program's lead STEM teacher, seminars also emphasized the application and implications of these topics with the Russian and U.S. education systems to support intercultural understanding and reflection on best practices.

Special Professional Learning Topics for WL Teachers Special topics sessions were also arranged for WL education. Guest speakers addressed classroom-, community-, and policy-level issues in WL education in the United States and focused on the application of technology in WL classrooms to enhance student-centered classrooms focused on communication in the language. Additionally, in the areas of language acquisition research and the role of culture, faculty sessions focused on interactive language learning in classrooms and new ways to support a culturally responsive pedagogy. Seminar topics addressed research-based approaches to language instruction (Shrum & Glisan, 2010), such as contextualized instruction and the importance of *authentic realia*, as well as ways to integrate the latest technologies to support student learning in K–16 world language classrooms. Drawing on the expertise of the faculty in our university's world language teacher preparation program, sessions were planned in collaboration with education faculty in world languages, such as those focusing on the multiple intelligences and learning styles. Local world language coordinators from school districts in proximity to the university were also able to contribute important context and explain the application of our educational practices in U.S. settings. Further, learning experiences were enhanced by speakers from the American Council on the Teaching of Foreign Languages (ACTFL) and other school district leaders. During their visits, information was shared with the teachers about world language research and its dissemination through professional organizations. As a result of focused WL sessions, world language teachers were able to consider their teaching in a more holistic and global context.

Fieldwork Experiences during Russian Teachers' Visit to the United States

The fieldwork component for project teachers was a critical dimension of participants' professional development, planned, managed, and closely reviewed by the program's codirectors. Field experiences at a partnering high school distributed over the duration of participants' course work allowed both Russian and U.S. teachers to incorporate reflection, research, and theoretical perspectives into their collaborative time in schools. Russian teachers worked with U.S. partner teachers in the same field of specialization (STEM and WL) to develop a deeper appreciation of alternative approaches to their curricular area, through teaching and team teaching hands-on classroom experiences. The Russian teachers worked with a U.S. partner teacher to discuss the process of lesson planning, assessment, instructional goal setting, and other aspects of teaching, with attention to opportunities for collaborative action research. Russian teachers observed, team taught, and discussed important aspects of learner-centered instruction, interactive language application, cooperative learning, thematic approaches to instructional units, learning strategies–based instruction, integration of technology, and other pedagogical methods and approaches.

Care was taken so that Russian teachers were partnered with U.S. teachers in a manner to support collaborative action research during and beyond the length of the teachers' stay. Russian STEM teachers were partnered with U.S. teachers in similar content areas (for example, chemistry, physics, geology, and calculus) so they might mutually share their own content-specific approaches (on personal and country levels) and develop a cross-cultural appreciation and collaborative adoption of alternative approaches. EFL teachers from Russia were partnered with U.S. WL teachers, who share the unique challenge of fostering both language acquisition and cultural understanding of the target language culture.

As part of the leadership and policy component of participant work, opportunities were planned for teachers to meet with administrators from a variety of levels within the school district and policy makers from professional organizations. These opportunities were distributed over the duration of the program to allow teachers to incorporate reflection, research, and theoretical perspectives into their collaborative field experiences. Facilitated by the program codirectors, debriefing sessions were held almost daily with the entire set of Russian participants to encourage systematic reflection and sense making within our community of learners. Additional content-specific debriefing sessions for both groups encouraged systematic reflection and sense making within a larger, developing international community of learners focused on mutual understanding and respect, which this program was designed to foster.

Fieldwork Experiences during U.S. Teachers' Visit to Russia

Fieldwork experiences during the U.S. teachers' visit to Russia were an opportunity for U.S. teachers to observe classroom instruction in the Russian teachers' schools in urban, suburban, and rural areas of the Primorsky Krai region. An agenda of school visits was planned in coordination with the program's Russian in-country partner. Each school planned a welcome event for U.S. teachers to have more interaction with students, teachers, and administrators. To complement the observation of instruction, U.S. teachers reviewed the Russian teachers' classroom materials and textbooks and spoke with students. Designed to support U.S. and Russian teachers' continuing incorporation of reflection, research, and theoretical perspectives into their collaborative time in schools, an opportunity was planned for U.S. teachers and Russian teachers to catch up on the status of their collaborative action research plans and plan for the Teachers as Researchers Conference. To further support U.S. teachers' reflection, teachers wrote a reflective essay on their experience that examined the program's impact on their salient learning as teacher leaders, development of their intercultural competence, and next steps for continuing collaboration and dissemination.

Structures for Ongoing Support in Russia and the United States

The program's efforts toward ongoing support consisted of six components spanning the length of the project:

- a public website for information;
- an ongoing electronic community for Russian and U.S. teacher participants with a common, private web page for teacher participants to share their electronic portfolio as a means of communicating their experiences, reflections, and application activities to project participants and to their colleagues in Russia;
- Russian teachers' digital presentations on the salient aspects of their experiences upon conclusion of their visit to the United States and a tangible means of sharing their experience upon returning to their home schools;
- ongoing support of U.S. and Russian teachers' implementation of action plans through face-to-face meetings and electronic communication, with purposeful staggering of teacher participants' reciprocal visits to the United States and Russia to span an academic year;
- the Teachers as Researchers Conference in Primorsky Krai conducted in person by Russian and visiting U.S. teacher participants for educators in Primorsky Krai, with virtual attendance by education colleagues in the United States and remote regions of Primorsky Krai; and
- dissemination seminars upon U.S. teachers' return home.

To support continuing collaboration and inquiry into teaching practice and both countries' education systems, the project's private page on VK.com and the project's public website will remain active to support continuing collaboration upon the project's end.

OPPORTUNITIES AND CHALLENGES: LESSONS LEARNED

A variety of opportunities arose and challenges occurred during the implementation of the program that have significant implications for U.S. efforts toward internationalizing teacher education. In this section we share lessons learned and share responses to the four questions initially raised in the context of U.S. teacher education's efforts toward internationalizing teacher education at the in-service level. Finally, we reflect on the implications of these findings with respect to promoting international mindedness among our future generations of teachers and informing the work we need to do in the preservice domain to prepare teachers for work with twenty-first-century students.

Mutual Exchange, Professional Growth, and Systematic Reflection

The first question was how to provide meaningful professional learning experiences for STEM and WL teachers to encourage intercultural understanding and a mutually respectful exchange of ideas. Further, we were interested in what such an outcome might mean for future teacher education efforts at the pre- and in-service levels. Throughout all correspondence with participants, the in-country partner, the field placement principal, professional learning instructors, and advisory board members, there was a commitment to maintain explicit communication of the program's expectation that learning during the program be viewed as reciprocal so that no one country was viewed as an expert. Each member of our learning community was perceived as having both knowledge to share and opportunity to grow through a mutual exchange of ideas.

The academic component that took place during the Russian participants' travel to the United States was primarily held at the field placement site to enable U.S. teachers to attend during their planning periods alongside their Russian teacher partners. While having seminars at the field placement site was a positive experience for the U.S. teachers, we found that principal and teacher buy-in are important factors to consider during the scheduling of seminars during the workday. The sessions best attended were those that called for the most active input from the principal and teachers. Further, consultation with individual U.S. teachers' schedules supported more consistent attendance during their school day.

Critical reflective practice and action research can be an effective driving force for the development of internationally minded teachers and classrooms. For example, we documented collaborative projects of study of both cross-cultural and cross-disciplinary natures. Topics included the use of multiple intelligences during instructional planning, language learning in the context of local environmental issues, language study and space science exploration across nations, and effective strategies for language instruction. Results from such studies were intended to be shared at language conferences in both countries.

With respect to our efforts for developing internationally minded teachers, we found that explicit prompts were needed to open up dialogue for both U.S. and international teachers to promote collaboration in the international arena (Sercu, 2006). One such example that appears to be effective is the sharing of a data set accompanied by a request for additional data from an internationally based teacher's location. In this instance, U.S. biology students shared the data from their study of salamanders, an indicator species of environmental conditions that is readily available for study in their locale, and U.S. students requested data from Russian students regarding a similar indicator species in their geographic locale so that they could learn about human impact on the environment in an international context. This work promotes authentic language learning through content and real-life application and communication.

We continue to explore how the electronic portfolio may be able to support teachers' reflections on their findings from these collaborations and systematic sharing of their results and experiences. The teachers' learning community was enhanced by introducing them to VK.com, which served as a means for participants to be able to communicate with each other in text and photographs. Introduction to action research, as a means of taking an inquiry stance and systematically reflecting on one's practice, provided an opportunity for collaboration between teachers, application of experiences, and enhanced teaching practice through new ideas for projects and approaches in each of the settings. Participants' efforts toward planning and implementation of a Teachers as Researchers Conference in Far East Russia and dissemination seminar in the United States provided structured opportunities necessary for participants to fine-tune their collaborative efforts and think purposely about the findings of their action research.

Meaningful messages that emerged from their work to carry forward in their personal practice developed around active exchange of pedagogical ideas during the teachers' discussions. This was followed by research questions that delved into various areas, such as the implementation of multiple intelligences or interactive student activities promoting problem solving. It is hoped that many of these will continue to be shared to the benefit of their colleagues and provide further opportunities to seek input from the larger community of learners.

Teachers from both countries struggled with articulating their prior conceptions of what constituted a typical American viewpoint and a typical Russian viewpoint. Participating teachers from both countries noted that there were more similarities than differences in teaching and learning between nations. They each also noted that there is more variation within each nation than one imagines, especially those nations as large as the United States and Russia. For U.S. teacher educators, the opportunity for dialogue in an international conference provides a meaningful opportunity for experienced teachers to reflect on their learning experiences on a personal and professional level while considering the experiences and perspectives of others from a remote region in a truly reciprocal exchange of ideas.

As teacher educators who work with both pre- and in-service teachers, experiencing both of the in-country experiences in the United States and Russia, it is particularly important to understand the full contexts of our work. There are the obvious cross-cultural considerations regarding areas such as the standards, approaches to teaching, school culture in the United States and Russia, and assessment. As educators must consider these and other important areas, however, there are important areas that are present for us all, such as motivation, curriculum and planning, meeting the needs of all learners, and adapting our teaching style to meet those needs. When we consider the work that we do as teacher educators on a daily basis and the increasingly diverse student population worldwide, international mindedness and intercultural understanding must be present in our teacher education programs at all levels in order to ensure that it is a force in our K–12 classrooms. This will not happen automatically or on its own. In order to make these changes present, we must plan for change and implement strategic opportunities for international experiences and dialogue in order for teachers to build on their experiences and consider the perspectives and practices of others.

Geography and Language

Embarking on a professional development project for local and remote teachers can be a daunting task for everyone. Participants in the program arrived with different years of classroom experience, diverse background experiences, diverse schools, diverse curriculum standards and expectations, diverse leadership roles in the schools, and experiences with diverse students. Background experiences included university degrees in disciplines, research experience, generalized and specific pedagogical training, and many years of teaching experience.

With respect to the U.S. schools, four U.S. participants taught in the partner school selected for the Russian participants' field placement, a magnet-like public high school specializing in STEM, and one U.S. participant taught in a rural middle school with a diverse student population. Russian participants taught in both urban and rural public and private schools of varying size and mission based on their geographic location. Two teachers selected as participants of the program were a teacher of English and the other a STEM teacher of chemistry who taught the subject in both Russian and, to a limited extent, English. As an emerging English speaker herself, this provided a model for ongoing language learning for her students. Another school is in a remote farming community where the project codirectors were the first primary English speakers to ever visit the Russian school. In this case, the principal is one of our program participants since her duties are split between principalship and physics teaching.

With respect to curriculum standards and expectations, the main difference between U.S. and Russian approaches stemmed from the order in which the content areas of each STEM discipline were taught. For both mathematics and science, students in Russia are exposed to the diverse subareas of mathematics and science throughout their secondary years, while U.S. students are exposed to certain subareas of mathematics and science only in particular years so that limited opportunities exist for U.S. students to revisit subareas and visualize how the subareas are interconnected. Both countries tended to negate the importance of engineering in secondary grades five and up, while reform efforts in both regions continue to encourage integration of engineering principles, such as design mode during problem-based learning instruction. Additionally, technology instruction was more likely to be viewed as a topic of study (for example, lessons on hardware specifications) in the upper grades in Russia, while U.S. instruction was more focused on programming and the use of technology to collect data and model phenomena. For U.S. teacher educators, the teachers learned of these similarities and differences through panel discussions during teacher-designed academic seminars and a conference session, designed by the U.S. and Russian teachers.

There was concern that lack of common language would be a barrier to the sort of in-depth discussion necessary to develop a community of learners focused on continuous improvement of learning and teaching practices in the context of cultural exchange. To this end, world language teachers were an invaluable partner in the learning process, providing translation during informal discussions for those who did not speak Russian or English. Russian teachers experienced enhanced English language skills on a personal level, and the language teachers exchanged ideas with the STEM teachers about how their language content instruction could be embedded within a STEM context and thus provide authentic application of the language to real-life topics. While the project enlisted the aid of a team of translators with backgrounds capable of performing simultaneous translation during discussions of problem-based learning in STEM and the nature of the STEM disciplines as a driving force for instruction, the STEM teachers actively partnered with the WL teachers to debrief, reflect, and plan for how project experiences could be applied in their individual school settings in both the United States and across the region of Primorsky Krai, Russia.

Consequently, teachers' follow-on action research projects illustrate a breadth and depth that we believe could not have happened if participation in the project were limited to STEM teachers alone. Translation support in Russian and English via participant peers during more informal exchanges, and a cadre of paid translators for professional learning seminars and more formal exchanges, made it possible for the STEM teachers and seminar instructors to more easily communicate and discuss the essence of their understanding of their particular discipline quickly in another language. This was language in action playing its essential role in communication and classroom learning and exchange (see table 9.1 for an overview of the participants' action research projects). The collaborative nature of the action research projects that are

Table 9.1. Action Research Projects

Collaborators	Locations	Topic(s)
Chemistry teacher and two biology teachers	Three schools in Vlad and Virginia	The formation of subjective experience of the teachers in the professional learning community
Chemistry teacher and English teacher	Two schools in Vlad and Virginia	Developing fluent English through interactive content-based study and critical thinking
Tech teacher and English teacher	Two schools in Vlad and Virginia	Interdisciplinary project "Natural Disasters and Ways of Surviving"
English, Russian, and biology teachers	Two schools in Nakhodka and Virginia	Investigating the results of student-centered learning on students' language fluency, IT knowledge, and leadership skills in the Access Program
Physics teacher and tech teacher	Two schools in Vlad and Virginia	Taking into account the multiple intelligences in teaching physics
English teacher and Russian teacher	Two schools in Vlad and Virginia	1. How to teach students to express their own opinion and ideas and not to be afraid of speaking about serious problems 2. Teaching English lessons through the development of critical thinking

STEM Disciplines and World Languages   195

English teacher and two chemistry teachers	Two schools in Vlad and Virginia	Collaboration of a pupil and a teacher through creating a portfolio
Two chemistry teachers (one also serves as principal)	Two schools in Vlad and Virginia	1. Developing ways to increase interest in the study of chemistry in students by teachers of international integration of the two countries 2. Optimization of the educational process of the school with increased motivation for learning by making local changes in activity from the experience of partner high school
English teacher and Russian teacher	Two schools in Kavalerovo and Virginia	Teaching English to preschool and primary school aged children
Two tech teachers	Two schools in Artyem and Virginia	Developing teachers' knowledge, attitudes, and practices through professional development in new technologies
English teacher and mathematics teacher	Two schools in Fokino and North Carolina	Exploring multiple intelligences, or different ways to learn
Technology teacher, English teacher, and mathematics teacher	Three schools in Ussuriisk, Vlad, and North Carolina	Multiple intelligences, learning styles and strategies
Physics teacher and tech teacher	Two schools in Artyem and Virginia	Effect of the introduction of new technologies/methods in the educational process to develop students' critical thinking
Two biology teachers	Vlad and Virginia	Formation of scientific understanding and interest in nature among schoolchildren; activities and useful outdoor recreation with elements of learning
English teacher and Russian teacher	Vlad and Virginia	Investigating effective ways of teaching vocabulary in English foreign language classes
English teacher and mathematics teacher	Artyem and North Carolina	Investigating the impact of multiple intelligences learning approaches in English language classes (middle school)
Two mathematics teachers	Artyem and North Carolina	1. Practice-oriented projects in the teaching of mathematics as a tool for individual students 2. An integrative approach to learning as a form of competence of students

ongoing across languages and vast geographic distance is consistent with the nature of the STEM and WL disciplines as collaborative and creative human endeavors that span our globe. This is an important area for consideration by teacher educators who work with both pre- and in-service teachers. In a study by Wiseman and Fox (2010), research findings indicated the importance that action research played on in-service teachers' learning. The approach of implementing action research as a collaborative learning tool to examine educational practices adds the dimension of intercultural development for teachers. We call for ongoing research in this area to better understand the saliency of the results of such international projects as this one.

For U.S. teacher educators, we believe it is key for professional development to incorporate opportunity for collaboration across geography and language barriers. While obvious barriers to our implementation included the physical costs and time associated with travel across vast distances, an additional barrier to our implementation included U.S. teachers' preconceptions about an invisible divide between STEM and WL; but we found this was quickly overcome, and teachers were energized by the collaborative possibilities with their colleagues in their own school and abroad. Perhaps the most worrisome barriers stemmed from issues of power and class associated with varied English and Russian language acquisition levels among the teachers. For example, U.S. STEM teachers observed classrooms taught in Russian and participated in discussions that sometimes drifted to Russian only when Russian teachers became overly involved in the discussion or into English only when the discussion was between a U.S. teacher and a Russian teacher more fluent in English.

As teacher educators concerned with creating a supportive, productive environment, we worked to establish norms for our international-level community of practice, which each member had to work to maintain through ample attention to conveying ideas in two languages, honoring our translators from within our teaching community, viewing translation as an opportunity for growth, and being respectful of school norms as visitors of the school, region, and country. Unfamiliar with the use of interpreters, U.S. teachers struggled with feeling out of control in conversations during school visits and during presentations at the conference. Translations were provided by both the school's English teacher and school students to ensure a level of comfort for everyone. As part of their growing international mindedness, U.S. teachers need opportunities where they can learn to develop cultural sensitivity to issues of power surrounding world language acquisition.

Question Three: Maintaining Momentum

Maintaining the productive momentum of the project's community of practice, focusing on continuous improvement, and achieving a level of sustainability was identified as a key goal of the project. This remains an aspect for ongoing inquiry. For U.S. teacher educators, we contend that teacher education efforts for both pre- and in-service teachers should incorporate social media utilized in various regions across the world rather than limited to those with U.S. development roots. While our findings illustrate the now global nature of Facebook as a social media tool, we recognize that many of our Russian STEM teachers continue to collaborate on VK.com, and our American STEM teachers need further encouragement and support in accessing foreign-based social media. In our limited study, we found that more technologically savvy U.S. teachers were willing to go through the multistep registration process and were willing to link their foreign-based registration to their personal cell phone number, but we also noted a distinct pattern of social media usage between those who possessed the commodity of English language proficiency versus those who did not. In this case, Russian teachers with English proficiency were on Facebook collaborating with their U.S. counterparts while those Russian teachers with low English proficiency were left wondering why their U.S. counterparts were not available to collaborate with on VK.com.

We have observed several changes in the teachers' electronic portfolios since the Russian teachers' return home. These included the addition of curriculum guides, lesson plans, and updates to the teachers' professional information. These continue to be a source of pride among the community of practice, and we observed evidence that teachers had shared these with their Russian colleagues. In one instance, a participating teacher led in-services at her school so that each of her teaching colleagues and her principal now have an electronic portfolio that serves as the basis for documenting and sharing their professional ideas. The school's director was proud to share with us during the teacher research conference in Far East Russia her own professional portfolio. Additionally, we received reports that teachers have actively shared their portfolios and their cultural stories via PhotoStory with their Russian colleagues in their schools and regional areas. We continue to monitor and encourage teachers to make additions to their portfolios following their implementation of the Teachers as Researchers Conference and dissemination seminars. While our U.S. in-service teachers had prior experience with electronic portfolios, our findings illustrate the utility of these for communication of ideas locally and abroad, which is applicable for this population as well.

We have also noted that planning for the international conference and seminars provided an impetus for teachers to ramp up their communication within their community of practice. While the U.S. teachers were in Russia, plans were discussed concerning the exchange of student data from joint or parallel research projects, and many students from the U.S. and Russian teachers' classrooms have been in active e-mail exchange with one another.

We believe that these opportunities will focus participants on next steps for collaboration during the following academic year to positively impact teachers through intercultural exchange and reflection. Within the first month of the U.S. teachers' arrival home, there has been international collaboration among the teachers via e-mail on two major interdisciplinary projects so far, in the areas of environmental science and space science, which will involve multiple Russian and U.S. schools and the application of authentic English.

Barriers that need to be addressed included limited time, competition with alternative methods for social media with which the U.S. teachers were more familiar, awareness of the importance of reaching out to teacher partners with limited English proficiency on a platform with which they would be comfortable, understanding and sensitivity to issues of social standing and power perceptions among those with more versus less English proficiency, and a willingness to divulge personal information required for registration on a foreign-based social media website. Leaving more questions than answers, a potential solution may be to provide specific tasks for experienced teachers that need to be completed via foreign social media that highlight the benefits of its use over other more readily available social media of domestic origin or alternate communication pathways, such as e-mail.

With respect to future U.S. teacher education efforts at the in-service level, we believe that our findings illustrate the importance of a two-way, physical exchange of teachers. Our participating teachers remarked on multiple occasions how their understanding of their partners' experiences and perspectives, as well as their more specific understanding of the nuanced variations with the Russian and U.S. education systems, was enhanced by observing firsthand their schools, their classroom instruction, their students, and their neighborhoods. We contend that two-way physical exchange of teachers across the globe should continue to be a key factor in supporting the development of an internationally minded cadre of experienced teachers. We believe our findings also illustrate that electronic tools need to be in place for teachers to continue their professional collaborations after the physical exchange has ended so that a virtual exchange can continue.

Teacher Education

A variety of opportunities and challenges occurred during the project implementation phase that have significant implications for U.S. efforts toward internationalizing teacher education. Our experience suggests that several of the program's components could be successfully extended to the preservice teacher domain. With a focus on the development of international mindedness among preservice teachers, our findings suggest that this population should be provided opportunities for professional travel exchange focused on direct observation of classroom instruction and interaction with teachers and children abroad. This has traditionally been the case for preservice teachers of world languages who wish to ensure their language proficiency in the target language; however it has not been a universal practice. We contend that in order to meet the needs of an ever-changing K–12 student population, preservice teachers need a deep understanding of the role that culture and language play in K–12 classrooms and schools, the kind of understanding whose optimum results are only reached with in-person experience in other contexts. Even when a physical travel exchange is not possible, U.S. teacher educators should provide (1) opportunities for preservice and experienced teachers to explore general and content-specific education issues from an international perspective and (2) opportunities for preservice STEM and WL teachers to explore connections between their disciplines and opportunities for coplanning, which could be enhanced via participation of experienced teachers. Additional opportunities should include

- in-person interaction with teachers from abroad through dialogue, panel discussions, and sharing of photos and other visuals from teachers' home schools;
- social media technology to support professional interaction and collaboration with attention to technology originating domestically and abroad;
- e-mail to support professional collaboration across distance;
- videoconferencing to support professional collaboration and/or interaction with children across distance;
- electronic portfolios to organize and support systematic reflection throughout the program and to archive growth and change over time;
- digital stories to support sense making, reflection, and sharing of experiences;
- international sharing of data sets and requests for data in the STEM and WL fields during discipline-specific methods courses;
- introduction to action research to support systematic reflection on practice during preservice teaching internships (student teaching); and
- international conferences on teaching as opportunities for interaction and collaboration, with pre- and post attention to issues of social collaboration, power differentials stemming from commodity differences in discipline-specific knowledge and language proficiency, and development of cultural sensitivity.

Additionally, teacher educators should have a personal foundation of these experiences themselves so that language instruction is embedded within other content areas in a larger real-world context.

NEXT STEPS AND ONGOING LEARNING

At the time of this writing, data collection and analysis regarding program outcomes and sustainability are ongoing. We are also utilizing our experiences to inform our university's teacher education efforts to maximize the potential for producing internationally minded future teachers, as well as how our efforts can best support intercultural competence among our experienced teacher leaders. The reflective practice component for STEM and WL participants has continued to focus on integrating academic and field-learning experiences for Russian and U.S. teacher participants to further develop their intercultural awareness and deepen their understanding of diverse contexts for learning. Now in their home countries and schools, the individual portfolios created by the teachers containing action research plans, reflections, and materials have provided the teachers with a professional space for sharing their growth and learning.

It is hoped that these portfolios, along with the Russian and U.S. teachers' sharing of action research during the Teachers as Researchers Conference in Vladivostok and continued sharing of their experiences in their home countries, will extend the benefits of the project's professional learning opportunities to colleagues and peers throughout their educational settings and regions. They are also anticipated to provide rich evidence for the project principal investigators as we work to identify how to best support experienced teachers in their development as internationally minded educators and what this means for our efforts working with preservice teachers.

This chapter has focused particularly on the application of the standards in two areas: the fields of science, technology, engineering, and mathematics, the STEM disciplines, at the secondary level (grades six through twelve in the United States and five through eleven internationally), and the field of foreign/world languages (FL/WL). In the context of the rapidly changing global demographics of the twenty-first century, there is an increasing need for educators who know the world and are able to prepare students to be effective world citizens. As U.S. teacher educators, we must be cognizant of how world perspectives should be embedded in our teacher education programs if we are to foster this learning in our preservice and experienced teacher populations so that they may incorporate this into their own teaching. It therefore also is important to understand the role that language, particularly English as a world language, plays in the teaching and learning processes in the STEM disciplines in the United States and abroad so that this relationship becomes a focal point of teaching methods course work in the STEM areas. The person-to-person components in the United States and Russia have provided a strong foundation for the relationships that could sustain dialogue and explore teaching practices across cultures. The development of intercultural communication and the full extent of the results of the program in this area with regard to the applicability of such learning to U.S. teacher education efforts will need to be explored further.

Additionally, this chapter highlights the necessity for teachers' professional learning opportunities to be grounded in teachers' classrooms (Whitcomb, Borko, & Liston, 2009) and supported by face-to-face opportunities with teachers abroad in order to build a basis for teachers' intercultural understanding and a mutually respectful exchange of ideas about the nature of teaching to foster professional growth and systematic reflection focused on enhanced teaching practice. Once teachers have forged a foundation for collaboration and have been able to ground their questions about teaching and learning, technology can support the sustainability necessary to fully realize the larger mission of our efforts to positively impact teachers personally and professionally, as well as their students, schools, and communities both in the United States and abroad. For U.S. teacher educators focused on supporting international mindedness among the experienced and preservice teachers with whom they work, this chapter illustrates the power of dialogue within a community of practice and first established face to face when possible. Dialogue that is focused on intercultural understanding and mutual respect has the potential to provide robust opportunities for growth that arise when individuals are asked to view their professional endeavors through another lens introduced via international collaboration.

REFERENCES

American Association for the Advancement of Science. (1993). *Benchmarks for science literacy*. New York: Oxford University Press.

Bambino, D. (2002). Redesigning professional development: Critical friends. *Educational Leadership*, *59*(6), 25–27.

Bereiter, C., & Scardamalia, M. (2003). Learning to work creatively with knowledge. In E. De Corte, L. Verschaffel, N. Entwistle, & J. van Merriënboer (Eds.), *Powerful learning environments: Unravelling basic components and dimensions* (pp. 55–68). Oxford: Elsevier Science.

———. (2006). Education for the knowledge age: Design-centered models of teaching and instruction. In P. A. Alexander & P. H. Winne (Eds.), *Handbook of Educational Psychology* (pp. 695–713). Mahwah, NJ: Erlbaum.

Brookfield, S. D. (1995). *Becoming a critically reflective teacher*. San Francisco: Jossey-Bass.

Chin, C., & Chia, L. (2005). Problem-based learning: Using ill-structured problems in biology project work. *Science Education, 90*(1), 44–67.

Delisle, R. (1997). *How to use problem-based learning in the classroom*. Alexandria, VA: Association for Supervision and Curriculum Development.

Fox, R., Bond, N., van Olphen, M., & Tian, J. (2010, November). *Using technology actively in K–16 world language classrooms!* Research presentation at the Forty-Third Annual Meeting of the American Council on the Teaching of Foreign Languages (ACTFL), Boston, MA.

Frazier, W. M., Fox, R. K., & Shaklee, B. (2009, June). *U.S.-Russia Teacher Professional Development*. Proposal submitted to Teacher Exchange Branch in the Office of Global Educational Programs of the Bureau of Educational and Cultural Affairs (ECA), U.S. Department of State. Federal grant number: S-ECAAS-09-CA-175 (EB); Funded: 9/18/2009–12/31/2011.

Frazier, W. M., & Sterling, D. R. (2008). Problem-based learning for science understanding. *Academic Exchange Quarterly, 12*(2), 111–15.

Hmelo-Silver, C. E. (2004). Problem-based learning: What and how do students learn? *Educational Psychology Review 16*(3), 235–66.

Hole, S., & McEntee, G. (1999). Reflection is at the heart of practice. *Educational Leadership, 56*(8), 34–37.

International Society for Technology in Education. (2008). *National education technology standards for teachers* (2nd ed.). Eugene, OR: Author.

Jacobs, H. H. (1989). Interdisciplinary curriculum: Design and implementation. Alexandria, VA: Association for Supervision and Curriculum Development.

———. (2010). *Curriculum 21: Essential education for a changing world*. Alexandria, VA: Association for Supervision and Curriculum Development.

Krajcik, J. S., Czerniak, C. M., & Berger, C. (1999). *Teaching children science: A project-based approach*. Boston, MA: McGraw-Hill.

Krynock, K., and Krynock, L. (1999). Problem solved: How to coach cognition. *Educational Leadership, 50*(3), 29–32.

Lederman, N. G. (1999). Teachers understanding of the nature of science and classroom practice: Factors that facilitate or impede the relationship. *Journal of Research in Science Teaching, 36*, 916–29.

Lewin, K. (1946). Action research and minority problems. *Journal of Social Issues, 2*(4), 34–46.

Loucks-Horsley, S., Stiles, K. E., Mundry, S., Love, N., & Hewson, P. W. (2010). *Designing professional development for teachers of science and mathematics* (3rd ed.). Thousand Oaks, CA: Corwin Sage.

Miller, D. M., & Pine, G. J. (1990). Advancing professional inquiry for education improvement through action research. *Journal of Staff Development, 11*(3), 56–61.

Ministry of Education and Science of the Russian Federation. (2004a). *The federal component of state standard of general education. Part I. Primary general education. Basic general education.* Retrieved on June 15, 2011, from http://mon.gov.ru/work/obr/dok/obs/1483.

———. (2004b). *The federal component of state standard of general education. Part II. Secondary (complete) general education.* Retrieved on June 15, 2011, from http://mon.gov.ru/work/obr/dok/obs/1487.

———. (2009, December 22). *Federal state educational standard of higher education in the direction of preparation 050 100 Teacher education (qualification (degree) "Bachelor") Number 788*, registered with the Russian Ministry of Justice on February 9, 2010, Registration Number: 16 277. Retrieved on June 20, 2011, from http://www.edu.ru/db-mon/mo/Data/d_09/prm788-1.pdf.

———. (2010, December 14). *Federal list of textbooks recommended (approved) for use in the educational process in educational institutions for the 2011/2012 academic year*, Registered with the Ministry of Justice Russia on February 10, 2011, Registration Number: 19776. Retrieved on June 15, 2011, from http://mon.gov.ru/work/obr/dok/obs/8267.

———. (2011a, January 17). *Federal state educational standard of higher education in the direction of preparation 050 100 Teacher education (qualification (degree) "Bachelor") Number 46*, Registered with the Russian Ministry of Justice on March 22, 2011, Registration Number: 20 228. Retrieved on June 20, 2011, from http://www.edu.ru/db-mon/mo/Data/d_11/prm46-1.pdf.

———. (2011b, April 19, Draft). *The federal component of state standard of general education. Part II. Secondary (complete) general education.* Retrieved on June 15, 2011, from http://mon.gov.ru/files/materials/7956/11.04.19-proekt.10-11.pdf.

National Academy of Engineering. (2010). *Standards for K–12 engineering education?* Washington, DC: National Academies Press.

National Center on Education and the Economy. (2007). *Tough choices or tough times: The report of the new commission on the skills of the American workforce.* Retrieved on November 10, 2010, from http://www.skillscommission.org/wp-content/uploads/2010/05/ToughChoices_EXECSUM.pdf.

National Council of Teachers of Mathematics. (2000). *Principles and standards for school mathematics.* Reston, VA: Author.

National Research Council. (1996). *National science education standards.* Washington, DC: National Academies Press.

———. (2007). *Taking science to school: Learning and teaching science in grades K–8.* Committee on Science Learning, Kindergarten through Eighth Grade. Richard A. Duschl, Heidi A. Schweingruber, and Andrew W. Shouse, editors. Board on Science Education, Center for Education. Division of Behavioral and Social Sciences and Education. Washington, DC: National Academies Press.

National Standards in Foreign Language Education Project (NSFLEP). (2006). *Standards for foreign language learning in the 21st century (SFLL).* Lawrence, KS: Allen Press.

O'Connor, S. (2008, June). *Preparing students to meet tomorrow's challenges in education.* Quality Education for Minorities (QEM) Network: Student Professional

Development Workshop for STEM Faculty at Grantee Institutions in the National Science Foundation's Historically Black Colleges and Universities Undergraduate Program (HBCU-UP). Downloaded on November 10, 2010, from http://www.qem.org/HBCUUP_studentdevJun08/O'ConnorQEMHBCUUPKeynote1.pdf.

Osterling, J. P., & Fox, R. K. (December 2004). The power of perspectives: Building a cross-cultural community of learners. *International Journal of Bilingual Education and Bilingualism 7* (6), pp. 489–505.

Paulos, J. A. (1992). *Beyond numeracy.* New York: Vintage.

Peters, E. E. (2009). Shifting to a student-centered science classroom: An exploration of teacher and student changes in perceptions and practices. *Journal of Science Teacher Education.* Available online: http://www.springerlink.com/content/t1r9620275t82502/fulltext.pdf.

Schmoker, M. (1996). *Results: The key to continuous school improvement.* Alexandria, VA: Association for Supervision and Curriculum Development.

Sercu, L. (2006). Foreign language teachers and the implementation of intercultural education: A comparative investigation of the professional self-concepts and teaching practices of Belgian teachers of English, French, and German. *European Journal of Teacher Education*, 28(1), 87–105.

Shrum, J. L., & Glisan, E. W. (2010). *Teacher's handbook: Contextualized language instruction* (4th ed.). Boston, MA: Cengage.

Stepien, W. & Gallagher, S. (1993). Problem-Based learning: As authentic as it gets, *Educational leadership 50*(7), 25–28.

Sterling, D. R., Matkins, J. J., Frazier, W. M., & Logerwell, M. G. (2007). Science camp as a transformative experience for students, parents, and teachers in the urban setting. *School Science and Mathematics, 107*(4), 134–48.

Wei, R. C., Darling-Hammond, L., Andree, A., Richardson, N., & Orphanos, S. (2009). *Professional learning in the U.S. and abroad.* Oxford, OH: National Staff Development Council.

Wenger, E. (1998). *Communities of practice: Learning, meaning, and identity.* New York: Cambridge University Press.

Whitcomb, J., Borko, H., & Liston, D. 2009. Promising professional development models and practices. *Journal of Teacher Education* 60, no. 3: 207–12.

Wiseman, A., & Fox, R. (2010). Supporting teachers' development of cultural competence through teacher research. *Action in Teacher Education, (32)* 4, pp. 26–37. DOI: 10.1080/01626620.2010.549708.

Zeichner, K. 2006. Reflections of a university-based teacher educator on the future of college- and university-based teacher education. *Journal of Teacher Education* 57, no. 3: 326–41.

• *10* •

Pedagogical Diversity and the Need for Contextually Responsive Teacher Education in the United States

Rachel Grant and Maryam Salahshoor

To prepare language teachers for meeting the diverse needs of today's language learners, teacher education programs in the United States must consider how best to address the needs of teachers whose sociocultural and sociohistorical orientations to teaching and learning differ from English as a second language[1] (ESOL) and English as a foreign language (EFL) teacher preparation in the United States. English is recognized as an international language, and the complexity resulting from the expanding circles of teachers of English is not limited to its linguistic forms and function but also reflects the political and ideological dimensions of who teaches English and where English is taught. As teachers develop the knowledge base and skill sets that qualify them to teach English in ESOL or EFL classrooms, they must confront the challenge of transitioning to contexts where ways of teaching may differ vastly from pedagogies indicated as desirable in their U.S. teacher preparation programs (Haley, Grant, Ferro, & Steeley, 2010). What cultural and ideological differences challenge teacher education programs in preparing English language teachers whose pedagogical orientation is unique to their own contexts? How can we prepare teachers to address the needs of students, that is, immigrant or refugee who possess different cultural and ideological orientations to teaching and learning? This chapter addresses tension among the pedagogical approaches and overall orientation teachers in U.S. ESOL/EFL teacher preparation programs receive as well as the issue of contextual relevance for nonnative English-speaking teachers and native English speakers who will teach English to students from other parts of the world.

We begin by describing the historically situated practice of teaching in contexts where there has been an increasing demand for learning English.

We draw parallels between the countries of the Middle East with those of the Far East where the thirst for English and U.S.-trained teachers is strong. We also provide an overview of the issues in teaching English in the broader educational contexts of those regions. The chapter concludes with implications for reexamining the contextual relevance of U.S. ESOL/EFL teacher education programs and provides recommendations for internationalizing teacher education in order to reduce what we see as a "reality gap" between how teachers are prepared to teach English and where they teach. This is especially critical for teachers who will teach with students whose historical, cultural, religious, social, and political environments reflect beliefs, practices, and realities regarding teaching and learning that may differ sharply from their own. What we argue for here is teacher preparation that is geostrategic and contextually responsive.

HISTORICAL PRACTICES

The popularity of English as an international language has been abundantly clear over the past decade as government and private agencies seeks to train teachers to meet the aspirations of populations demanding to learn English (Liyanage & Bartlett, 2008). The pace and scope of expansion in speaking and teaching English has changed the linguistic ecology of the world and is unmatched in terms of language learning within modern linguistic times. The process of "globalization" and the expanding reach of U.S. military and postindustrial influence, as well as the ongoing search for resources and commercial markets by developing nations, has increased contact across international borders and intensified the need for common systems of communication or "lingua franca" (Zughoul, 2003). Not since the period of extreme European mercantilism (sixteenth to eighteenth century) that spawned European imperialism, colonization, and the transatlantic slave trade have peoples situated in such vastly different contexts desired a common language through which they could interact and communicate.

Due to space limitations, we cannot fully address the impact of the spread of English; however, we would be remiss if we did not consider that growth in speaking and teaching of English has differentiated consequences related to where and upon whom it is imposed. The issue of "linguistic imperialism" or how relations of dominance are entrenched by, and in, language and how such dominance comes to be viewed as part of the natural order has been explored by those concerned with the political, sociological, and economic impact of English on local populations, indigenous languages, and the world stage (e.g., Bailey, 1991; Crystal, 2003; Edge, 2006; McArthur, 1998;

Mesthrie & Bhatt, 2008; Pennycook, 1994; Phillipson, 1996). Further, as terms such as "new Englishes" and "world Englishes" or "English language complex," comprising "all subtypes of English distinguishable according to some combination of their history, status, form and function" (Mesthrie & Bhatt, 2008, p. 3), gain in popularity, we are only now beginning to explore the possibility that English no longer has one single base of authority, prestige, or normativity.

Earliest accounts suggest that English, a West Germanic language, originated from the Anglo-Frisian dialects brought to Britain by Germanic invaders from various parts of what is now Germany. Over time English was shaped by waves of invading armies from Scandinavia, Norman-French dialects, and the spread of Christianity, which introduced Latin and Greek influences. Indeed, a major challenge to those learning and teaching English is the enormous and varied vocabulary that is the result of borrowing from other languages.

The historic role of the British Empire as a colonial power resulted in the spread of English through exploitation and colonization. In modern times the United States assumed the role of "superpower" and through its military forces and global corporations enhanced desire for English. In his many writings about the role of English in India and South Asia, Kachru (1985, 1991, 1992) asserts there are various reasons for which languages are used in society. For example, using a particular language could be motivated by the perceived need for cultural or religious enlightenment, to gain economic advantage, to control domains of knowledge and information, and for deception. Language also can be a vehicle of symbolic violence (Bourdieu & Passeron, 1977) and linguistic terrorism (Grant & Lee, 2009). A case in point is how enslaved Africans, specifically those transported to British colonies in the West Indies and later the United States, came to acquire English. Africans were forced to learn the languages of those who enslaved them because Europeans took measures to reduce the likelihood of plotting escape or rebellion by keeping separate those captives who were capable of communicating through shared languages (Baugh, 1999). As a result, Africans needed to learn European languages in order to perform the labor tasks demanded by their captors. This meant that they were not merely torn from their native communities and transported thousands of miles, but they also suffered linguistic isolation and silencing (Grant & Lee, 2009). Over time, as the sphere of influence of English-speaking countries has intensified, so too has the need to develop facility in English.

Today, the thirst for English reflects the blending of commercial markets, the networks of technology corridors, and the interconnecting economies where the desire for English indicates the growing impact of globalization and the need for individuals to communicate simultaneously across multiple international borders. Once viewed as primarily spoken in what is now known as Great Britain, Australia, New Zealand, and the United States, English has become the official language in over fifty-two countries and is spoken and understood by more than one-third of the world's inhabitants. Focusing on the spread of English in China, Wang (2007) notes, "Of all the foreign languages taught in schools, English undoubtedly enjoys the largest number of learners. By the end of 2002, there were about 66.9 million junior secondary school students and 16.8 million senior secondary school students in the formal educator sector" (p. 87). It is important to note that these numbers did not include those in China who study English at the tertiary level (i.e., college, vocational schools), or through the private sector, thereby increasing these numbers considerably.

REGIONAL ISSUES IN TEACHING ENGLISH

Throughout Asia, the status of English as a global language is undisputed. The impact of globalization especially in Korea and Thailand drives the demand for learning English. Across South Korea the popularity of so-called cram school or private tutoring in English for those with the ability to pay is a growing trend. It is, however, important to point out that the demand for English or any language having been imposed from outside existing linguistic tradition has consequences on local populations. Shin (2007) notes:

> The global spread of English bound up with the spread of capitalism and its dominance in higher education in many parts of the world has made it the language of power and prestige in many countries. Indeed, the global use of English inherently serves the interests of some over those of others and often results in exacerbating the unequal relationship. . . . South Korea definitely belongs to a group of countries where the intimate relationship between language, language teaching, and power is clearly evident. (pp. 76–77)

Even in countries such as China, where there exists a somewhat different geohistoric relationship with the West, there is conflict about the teaching of English, especially the presence of Western EFL teachers and the impact this has on Chinese identity. Simpson (2008) suggests that while the desire to learn English has resulted in the presence of many Western teachers in China, many foreign teachers misinterpret the desire for their linguistic expertise with a call to bring their pedagogical expertise. Simpson states, "This misunderstanding is most evident when Western teacher-trainers come over to give professional support for Chinese EFL teachers. Westerners try to teach methodology, while the Chinese want more English enrichment. . . . When these two expectations are in conflict, the potential results are frustration and accusations of wrongful treatment, ignorance, and laziness of both sides, by both sides" (p. 382). Sensitivity about preserving identities linked to culture, ethnicities, and nationality is especially important for ESOL teachers in U.S. classrooms because demographic trends indicate increasing numbers for students whose ancestries are linked to China and other parts of Asia. Promoting awareness and the development of cross-cultural understandings in teacher education that help teachers establish modes of conduct, attitudes, and beliefs that show respect for diversity is critical to internationalizing teacher education.

The concomitant expansion of English as an international language raises other issues for teachers and students learning English who are from countries having different definitions of teaching and learning emerging from their cultural heritage, including religious and linguistic differences. For example, Muslim populations like those in the Arabian peninsula, South Asia, North Africa, and the Middle East bring forward questions to challenge teacher educators such as: How can we prepare English teachers, many of whom have little knowledge of linguistic structures, social practices, and religious traditions common to students from these areas of the world? How will we prepare language teachers who have experienced different education customs and teacher-centered traditions to teach in U.S. classrooms? To help teacher educators think about what this might mean for teacher preparation, we offer the educational traditions in Saudi Arabia as an example of how the traditional and formal lineages of general education for some teachers and their students might differ.

The educational history of Saudi Arabia reveals that traditional learning took place at home or in the local district mosque in a Qur'anic school where the curriculum was exclusively based on the Qur'an (the sacred writings of Islam revealed by God to the prophet Mohammad during his life at Mecca and Medina) and the Hadith (narrations originating from the words and deeds of the Islamic prophet Mohammad). The main reason schools existed was to ensure oral transmission of religious works from one generation to the next. Prior to 1932, not only was education severely limited, it was largely restricted to males. Occurring primarily in *kuttabs*, the curriculum was limited to instruction in religious studies, the Arabic language, and mathematics. Later, the modern elementary school or madrassa replaced the *kuttab* and offers somewhat broader curricula; however, the method of instruction still reflects the "preacherlike," teacher-centered practice of earlier education tradition (Elyas & Picard, 2010). Even today modern education offered beyond the elementary level, including tertiary and English language teaching classes, are expected to follow this didactic teaching tradition. While not limited solely to Arabic society, it is often the case that practices in classrooms throughout the Muslim and Arab world reflect this tradition and that the ceremonial-like, teacher as primary, students as secondary, framing of instruction is locally situated and contextually appropriate. "This reverence for the teacher/lecturer is deeply rooted in Arabic society. . . . The teacher or lecturer, the conveyor of knowledge is imbued with both ideological and spiritual power" (p. 138).

Two countries with sizable Muslim populations, Pakistan and Malaysia, provide further examples that responses to the spread of English is both historic and contextually situated and reflect geopolitical circumstances for countries in their relationships with westernized countries. The Muslim response to English in Pakistan can be traced to Britain's creation of the modern state of Pakistan in 1947. Throughout Britain's colonial presence in Pakistan and current U.S. military actions within its borders, Pakistani response to English is a case study of ways that English has been used in the domains of power—through government, administration, judiciary, military, higher education, higher commerce, media, and the corporate sector—to create both inequality and intolerance (Rahman, 2005). In his writings on the Muslim response to English, Rahman (e.g., 1996, 2002, 2005) discusses the historical context of English in Pakistan and describes three reactions—resistance and rejection, acceptance and assimilation, and pragmatic utilization—to the imposition of English in this majority Muslim and largely Urdu speaking nation:

> Muslims probably could not articulate clearly exactly what it was which made them oppose English to begin with. It is, indeed, very likely that the opposition came simply as a reaction to their defeat at the hands of the English. It may also have been part of their boundary-marking ("othering") on religious grounds. . . . But, if one goes deep into the polemical diatribes which Muslims wrote against English, it becomes clear that they were extremely anxious about its alienating potential. (2005, p. 122)

In sum, Rahman characterizes the first kind of response to English as resistance and rejection, suggesting this reaction is religious in nature; although not entirely theological, it is also one of identity borne out of fear of "losing their identity in a welter of alien values brought with English" (p. 122).

The second kind of response, acceptance and assimilation, is the modernist or secularist reaction to English, marking the emergence of the elitist and professional middle class in Pakistan. The so-called westernized Muslims saw English as a critical part of modern identity and "became the chief marker . . . separating Muslim society into English-using elite and the traditionally educated proto-elite or the illiterate" (Rahman, 2005, p. 123).

The third Muslim response to the spread of English in Pakistan also indicates the sway of modern times, acknowledging English as a tool for power in areas of information technology, commerce, and education. Those espousing this view of English see that selective adoption of secular features or tools of the West, including languages, as consistent with the teaching of the Prophet Muhammad as a means to access knowledge.

Although Malaysia shares a similar colonial past with Pakistan, the response to the spread of English has been somewhat different. Highlighting the evolution of a Muslim reaction to English in Malaysia as one of recognizing the importance of learning English for the purpose of acquiring contemporary knowledge, Mohd-Asraf states, "More than being just a language of communication, English, by virtue of its influence, has the capacity to empower, just as it has the capacity to divide" (2005, p. 103). Situating English within the Malaysian milieu, Mohd-Asraf notes commonalities and differences in attitudes toward adopting English in the Muslim world. Morocco, for example, has experienced a series of foreign occupiers, the French and Spanish. Morocco's response, for the most part, tends to separate the instrumental linguistic value of English as a lingua franca from any real threat to Moroccan identity and culture. However, Mohd-Asraf notes this has not been the attitude widely adopted in the countries of Kuwait or Saudi Arabia.

Malaysia offers a rich multilingual, multiethnic, multiracial, and multireligious landscape for study of the spread of English in the Muslim world. Interestingly English has experienced a "reversal of fortune" with respect to its use as a second language in Malaysia. Since gaining independence as a British colony in 1952 and until 1972, due to its sociopolitical status, English was used in English medium schools as the language of instruction. However, for purposes of nation building and to create a Malaysian national identity, use of English as a medium of instruction has been gradually phased out and replaced by the official language, Bahasa Melayu, or Malay. Quoting Asmah Haji Omar (1992), Mohd-Asraf notes that English "came as a colonial and remained, until after Independence, a prestige language accessible only to the privileged few. It was one of the factors that assisted in drawing the line between the haves and the have-nots, the urban and the rural, the modern and the traditionally educated, and so on" (p. 121). In the fifty years since independence, Mohd-Asraf suggested there are changes in the Malay/Muslim attitude toward English and notes that although some negative attitude may still exist toward English, increasingly the situation is changing, and many Malay "see need to learn, and want to learn English" (p. 113).

The status of English on the world stage is also associated with increased immigration to the United States and other countries where English is the official language. Families and their children settle throughout

English-speaking countries, dramatically increasing the need for ESOL teachers at every level and subject area. In the United States it is well documented that individuals whose first language is Spanish represent the largest and fastest-growing segment of the population, 48.4 million or 16 percent. In fact, U.S. Census data project that by 2050 the Hispanic population will be 132.8 million, or 30 percent of the population. U.S. Census data also indicate the growing presence of individuals from Asian/Pacific Island nations. In 1990, 6.9 million Asians[2] were counted. Census 2000 reported an increase of 3.3 million, or 48 percent. The need for more English language teachers also reflects the presence of more students whose first languages are Arabic, Persian or Farsi, and Hindi, who often are refugees or immigrants because of mounting political unrest and war in South Asia, the Middle East, and countries throughout Africa. Such movements lead to the question, how are U.S. teacher preparation programs evolving to meet the needs of the changing populations of students and parents?

IMPLICATIONS FOR TEACHER EDUCATION

Education practices based in didactic instruction are in sharp contrast to current pedagogical competencies expected, such as teacher as facilitator, dialogic approaches, inquiry-based learning, and critical thinking emphasized in many teacher preparation programs in the United States. This means that ESOL and other teachers who work with English learners should be aware of strategies to help so that students become more comfortable with the teacher-as-facilitator role emphasized in today's classrooms. Teachers need to know how to engage modeling and scaffolding frameworks to assist students in redefining their expectations for teaching and learning. English learners with lineages in education similar to countries like Saudi Arabia also must be supported as they come to understand the social network of the classroom that could appear to be at odds with their cultural traditions.

In the post-9/11 era, English language teaching and beliefs about the potential for English as a lingua franca may require different sensitivities and knowledge when working with students from different cultural traditions. A recent poll conducted by the Council on American-Islamic Relations (2006) revealed that 40 percent of Muslims living in the United States come from the Arab world, 33 percent from South Asia (Pakistani, Indian, and Bangladeshi), 6 percent from Africa, 5 percent from Iran, and 3 percent from Europe (CARI, 2006). It is against this political backdrop that U.S. teacher preparation programs must address the sociopedagogic context of teacher development and contextual relevance for those who will teach English to students from vastly different educational and cultural orientations in the United States and elsewhere.

Internationalizing teacher education is necessary for meeting growing demand for English in the United States and throughout the world. Worldwide estimates suggest that there are roughly three nonnative speakers of English for every native speaker (Crystal, 2003). With the globalization of English and recognition of world Englishes, the number of English learners around the world has drastically increased and will continue to grow in the coming decades (Rao, 2010; Block & Cameron, 2002; Nunan, 2001). As demand for learning English increases at home and elsewhere, the internationalization of teacher education in the United States must take place in two different arenas. First, we need to prepare teachers to work with students from diverse linguistic and cultural backgrounds in order to help children and youth meet the language and academic demands for learning in today's classrooms. Second, teacher education programs must take into account the large numbers of nonnative English speakers who are admitted to TESOL (teachers of English to speakers of other languages) programs in the United States each year (Kamhi-Stein, 2004; Liu, 1998, 1999; Braine, 1999, 2010). The growing presence of students and teachers from outside the United States presents new challenges for teacher education programs in addressing the sociopedagogic preparation of teachers who represent uniquely different education histories and who will work with students from varied linguistic, cultural, and social backgrounds.

Currently, there is no single template that integrates TESOL curricula and the perceived needs and concerns of English language learners. Ongoing discussion in the field recognizes the growing demand for English language teachers who are capable of teaching in different school cultures and who are prepared to provide contextually responsive instruction in support of students' language development and academic success. Calls for change in teacher preparation range from special seminars for prospective teachers to professional development and ongoing support for teachers during initial years of teaching (Carrier, 2003; Ramanathan, Davies, & Schleppegrell, 2001; Liyanage & Bartlett, 2008).

RECOMMENDATIONS FOR TEACHER EDUCATION

In the absence of specific guidelines for preparing to teach in the contexts highlighted in this chapter, we offer a broad range of ideas that are based on our own experiences in ESL/EFL English and reviews of work by scholars in the field of English language teaching and research. Our suggestions in this section are organized into three broad categories: course design, pedagogy and methods, and research. We see these as minimally essential in addressing the ongoing needs described in this chapter.

Course Design

Reflecting the needs of teachers for English language learners, teacher educators might enhance second language acquisition (SLA) curriculum to include the following:

1. Research results obtained from other contexts where there are English learners rather than only focusing on Western English-speaking models.
2. The encouragement of fluent and idiomatic use of the English language for both day-to-day and academic use.
3. Teach scaffolding techniques to help students comfortably express their opinions.
4. Provide maximum opportunities and pathways for teacher candidates to critically examine their own educational biographies (e.g., previous experiences as learners, beliefs, assumptions, and attitudes) in relation to the course content, and incorporate tools such as journal writing, peer observation, self-monitoring, and lesson video recording as suitable means to collect data that can be used as the basis for developing self-awareness and critical skills.
5. Develop and utilize decentralized textbooks with local teacher's own realities.
6. Incorporate an introductory course in teacher programs that focus on cross-cultural issues, concerns, and interests, and ensure that cross-cultural and multilingual perspectives are infused throughout the curricula.
7. Utilize teachers' narratives and literature by nonnative English speakers, who represent a range of English speakers from different cultures while also allowing for flexibility in course assignments to provide opportunities for developing contextually responsive content.
8. Rethink and possibly revise the English language standards to represent various other models of English competency.

Pedagogy and Methods

In view of recommended expansions of the curriculum, congruent changes should be made to the pedagogical and methodological experiences that

1. Facilitate distinguishing between teaching practices in non-Western and Western English-speaking countries and environments to encourage teachers to challenge and reflect on whether various methods and assumptions regarding language learning could be applied to their diverse teaching situations.
2. Promote diverse teaching methodologies based on SLA experiences other than in Western English-speaking countries to facilitate practical and effective teaching experiences for students while also educating teachers regarding the negative outcomes of deficit perspectives and discriminatory attitudes.
3. Facilitate nonnative English-speaking teacher candidates' adaptation of discovery-oriented and student-centered teaching practices found in Western English-speaking countries and practice in modifying methods and techniques to environments with larger classrooms that are under-resourced and less well equipped.
4. Provide experiences in environments that closely resemble teachers' own cultural environment in order to aid them in adopting new teaching methodologies developed in Western English-speaking environments.
5. Provide opportunities for practicum in environments that closely resemble the educational context in which teachers will teach.
6. Provide diverse teaching strategies under supervision of experienced teachers.

Research

Coupled with changes in curriculum and pedagogy are needed areas of continued and expanded research in the field of SLA, teacher education for ESOL/EFL candidates, as well as examining contextually relevant teaching placements that include

1. Action research in areas such as idioms, word collections, registers, and other areas in which English learners are generally weak.
2. Pairing native English speaking teachers with nonnative English-speaking teachers for research and projects to investigate concepts using real-life data, which highlights the differences between linguistic backgrounds and cultures.
3. SLA research in real classroom settings, where there may be many other influences on language learning from the larger society.
4. Decentralized action research in order to design decentered curriculum content in which students are exposed to the ways in which English relates to different communities.

Presently, no other language has the currency associated with English. Although, for example, there are far more native Chinese speakers than native English speakers, in terms of economy strength, that is, the measure of the economic worth of a language, Chinese ranks seventh, while English ranks first out of the "power" languages (Zughoul, 2002, 2003). With the globalization of English and recognition of world Englishes, the number of English learners around the world will continue to increase well into the future. Currently, demand for teachers of English has not kept pace with the need to prepare skilled teachers capable of utilizing sociopedagogic theory involving not only teaching content in a proficient manner but also developing contextual understanding of where and with whom teaching is carried out (Liu, 1998, 1999).

English language teaching has grown over the last half decade into one of the most flourishing areas of education stretching far beyond the British colonial empire to countries that have neither historical nor economic links to Great Britain or the United States. Increasing numbers and diversity among adult, children, and youth who are learning English require that education programs take care to prepare teachers who are not just sensitive but possess skills that enable them to address the needs of students from varied linguistic, cultural, and education backgrounds.

In this chapter, we addressed concern for preparing ESL/EFL teachers, nonnative English speakers, and native English speakers alike to teach in U.S. classroom contexts and where there exist tensions between the West and in countries where the demand for English is spreading. Over the past few years there has been increased interest in issues related to nonnative English speakers and their education. As a result, more attention has been given to the preparation and qualifications of teachers within and outside ESOL who work to increase the test performance and meet the academic needs of English learners.

We highlighted geohistoric stressors related to colonization, providing a historic context for understanding how the imposition of English affects real and socially constructed relations within countries that advantage English speakers, while creating disadvantage for those who are not English speakers. As well, we pointed out current tensions that result from geopolitics, globalization, and the quest for new economic markets and how these conditions give rise to concern about preservation of national identities, local languages, and religious/cultural/social traditions. A critical question raised here was how teacher education programs will prepare teachers to work with a student whose historical and educational circumstances differ sharply from the U.S. context. In closing, you are encouraged to remember that the educational contexts in which U.S.-trained teachers will work may differ significantly.

This is especially the case for teachers and students from particular parts of the world. It is our hope to develop a better understanding of the complexities involved in teaching and bridge differences toward a common goal, the teaching of English.

NOTES

1. For the purposes of this chapter Teachers of English to Speakers of Other Languages (ESOL) will be used to represent all teachers of English.
2. U.S. Census Bureau uses the term Asian when referring to people having origins in any of the original peoples of the Far East, Southeast Asia, or the Indian subcontinent (for example, Cambodia, China, India, Japan, Korea, Malaysia, Pakistan, the Philippine Islands, Thailand, and Vietnam.

REFERENCES

Al-Hazmi, S. (2003). EFL teacher preparation programs in Saudi Arabia: Trends and challenges. *TESOL Quarterly, 37*, 341–44.
Bailey, R. (1991). *Images of English: A cultural history of the language.* Cambridge, UK: CUP.
Baugh, J. (1999). *Out of the mouths of slaves.* Austin, TX: University of Texas Press.
Block, D., & Cameron, D. (Eds.). (2002). *English and globalization.* London: Routledge.
Bourdieu, P., & Passeron, J. (1977). *Reproduction in education, society, and culture.* London: Sage.
Braine, G. (Ed.). (1999). *Non-native educators in English language teaching.* Mahwah, NJ: Erlbaum.
———. (Ed.). (2010). *Nonnative speaker English teachers: Research, pedagogy, and professional growth.* New York: Routledge.
Carrier, K. A. (2003). NNS teacher trainees in Western-based TESOL programs. *ELT Journal, 57*(3), 242–50.
Council on American-Islamic Relations. (2006). *American Muslim voters: A demographic profile and survey.* Washington, DC: CARI.
Crystal, D. (2003). *English as a global language* (2nd ed.). Cambridge, UK: Cambridge University Press.
Edge, J. (2003). TEFL and international politics: A personal narrative. *IATEFL Issues, 175*, 10–11.
———. (Ed.). (2006). *(Re)locating TESOL in an age of empire.* New York: Palgrave.
Elyas, T., & Picard, M. (2010). Saudi Arabian educational history: Impacts on English language teaching. *Education Business and Society: Contemporary Middle East Issues, 3*, 136–45.

Eslami, Z. R., & Fatahi, A. (2008). Teachers' sense of self-efficacy, English proficiency, and instructional strategies: A study of nonnative EFL teachers in Iran. *TESL-EJ: The Electronic Journal for English as a Second Language, 11*(4).

Grant, R. A., & Lee, I. (2009). The ideal English speaker: A juxtaposition of globalization and language policy in South Korea and racialized language attitudes in the United States. In R. Kubota and A. Lin (Eds.), *Race, culture, and identities in second language education: Exploring critically engaged practice* (pp. 44–63). London: Routledge.

Haley, M. H., Grant, R. A., Ferro, M., & Steeley, S. (2010, Summer, In Press). New dimensions in language teacher preparation: Bridging divides in critical need languages. *US-China Foreign Language, 9*.

Holliday, A. (1994). The house of TESEP and communicative approach: The special needs of state English language education. *ELT Journal, 48*(10), 3–11.

———. (2008). Standards of English and politics of inclusion. *Language Teaching, 41*(1), 119–30.

Kachru, B. (1985). Discourse analysis, non-native English, and second language acquisition research. *World Englishes, 4*, 223–32.

———. (1991). Culture, style, and discourse: Expanding noetics in English. *South Asian Review, 1*, 11–25.

———. (Ed.). (1992). *The other tongue: English across cultures*. Chicago: University of Illinois Press.

Kamhi-Stein, L. D. (Ed.). (2004). *Learning and teaching from experience: Perspectives on nonnative English-speaking professionals*. Ann Arbor: University of Michigan Press.

Karmani, S. (2005a). Islam and English in the post-9/11 era: Introduction. *Journal of Identity, Language, and Education, 4*, 85–86.

Karmani, S. (2005b). Petro-linguistics: The emerging nexus between oil, English, and Islam. *Journal of Language, Identity, and Education, 4*, 87–102.

Liyanage, I., & Bartlett, B. J. (2008). Contextually responsive transfer: Perceptions of NNES on an ESL/EFL teacher training programme. *Teaching and Teacher Education, 24*, 1827–36.

Liu, D. (1998). Ethnocentrism in TESOL: Teacher education and the neglected needs of international TESOL students. *ELT Journal, 52*, 3–10.

———. (1999). Training non-native TESOL students: Challenges for TESOL teacher education in the west. In G. Braine (Ed.), *Non-native educators in English language teaching* (pp. 197–210). Mahwah, NJ: Erlbaum.

McArthur, T. (1998). *The English languages*. Cambridge, UK: Cambridge University Press.

Mesthrie, R., & Bhatt, R. (2008). *World Englishes: The study of new linguistic varieties*. Cambridge, UK: Cambridge University Press.

Mohd-Asraf, M. (2005). English and Islam: A clash of civilizations? *Journal of Language, Identity, and Education, 4*, 101–18.

Nunan, D. (2001). English as a global language. *TESOL Quarterly, 35*, 605–6.

Omar, Asmah Haji. (1992). Attitude in the learning of English. In A. H. Omar (Ed.), *The linguistic scenery in Malaysia* (pp. 117–42). Kuala Lumpur, Malaysia: Dewan Bahasa dan Pustaka.

Pennycook, A. (1994). *The cultural politics of English as an international language.* London: Longman.
Phillipson, R. (1996). Lingusitic imperialsim: African perspectives. *ELT Journal, 50,* 160–67.
Ramanathan, V., Davies, C. E., & Schleppegrell, M. J. (2001). A naturalistic inquiry into the cultures of two divergent MA-TESOL programs: Implications for TESOL. *TESOL Quarterly, 35,* 279–305.
Rahman, T. (1996). *Language and politics in Pakistan.* Karachi, Pakistan: Oxford University Press.
———. (2002). *Language, ideology, and power: Language-learning among Muslims of Pakistan and North India.* Karachi, Pakistan: Oxford University Press.
———. (2005). The Muslim response to English in South Asia: With special reference to inequality, intolerance, and militancy in Pakistan. *Journal of Language, Identity, and Education, 4,* 119–35.
Rao, Z. (2010). Chinese students' perceptions of native English-speaking teachers in EFL teaching. *Journal of Multilingual and Multicultural Development, 31,* 55–68.
Sarwar, Z. (2001) Innovations in large classes in Pakistan. *TESOL Quarterly, 35*(3), 497–500.
Sharifian, F. (Ed.). (2009). *English as an international language: Perspectives and pedagogical issues.* Bristol, UK: Multilingual Matters.
Shin, H. (2007). English language teaching in Korea: Toward globalization or glocalization. In J. Cummins and C. Davison (Eds.), *International handbook of English language teaching* (pp. 75–86). New York: Springer.
Simpson, S. T. (2008). Western EFL teachers and East-West classroom-culture conflicts. *RELC Journal, 39,* 381–94.
Velez-Rendon., G. (2002). Second language teacher education: A review of the literature. *Foreign Language Annals, 33*(4), 457–67.
Wang, Q. (2007). The national curriculum changes and their effects on English language teaching in the Peoples Republic of China. In J. Cummins and C. Davison (Eds.), *International handbook of English language teaching* (pp. 87–105). New York: Springer.
Wong, S. (2006). *Dialogic approaches to TESOL: Where the gingko tree grows.* Mahwah, NJ: Erlbaum.
Zughoul, M. R. (2001). The language of higher education in Jordan: Conflict, challenges, and innovative accommodations. In R. G. Sultana (Ed.), *Challenge and change in the Euro-Mediterranean region: Case studies in education innovation* (pp. 327–43). New York: Peter Lang, 327–43.
Zughoul, M. R. (2001). The language of power and the power of language in higher education in the Arab world: Conflict, dominance, and shift. *College of Islamic and Arabic Studies Journal, 23,* 21–30.
———. (2002). The power of language and the language of power in higher education in the Arab world: Conflict, dominance, and shift. *College of Islamic and Arabic Studies Journal, 23,* 45–52.
———. (2003). Globalization and EFL/ESL pedagogy in the Arab world. *Journal of Language and Learning, 1,* 106–46.

• 11 •

Expanding Horizons through Technology for Teachers and Students

Debra Sprague

In 2005, Thomas Friedman, the foreign affairs columnist for the *New York Times*, published a book in which he postulates that the world is flat. By this he meant that the world has become so interconnected and so interdependent that individuals can no longer view themselves as being isolated from others located across the world.

> Globalization 3.0 is shrinking the world from a size small to a size tiny and flattening the playing field at the same time. And while the dynamic force in Globalization 1.0 was countries globalizing and the dynamic force in Globalization 2.0 was companies globalizing, the dynamic force in Globalization 3.0—the thing that gives it its unique character—is the newfound power for *individuals* to collaborate and compete globally. (Friedman, 2005, p. 10, italics in original)

Friedman goes on to explain that one of the driving forces behind this flattening of the world is technology, specifically the software and the fiber optic networks that allow individuals to communicate across time and distance. The Internet is available to more than 20 percent of the world's population while more than two billion people use cell phones. Television is now available in 90 percent of the world's households, with news running twenty-four hours a day (Zhao, 2009). If technology has allowed the world to become flat, then technology can also be used to broaden global perspectives and contribute to teachers' international mindedness. This chapter explores ways to use technology in this capacity.

WATCHING, BUT NOT INTERACTING

Voyeurism carries many negative connotations in our country. However, it is the perfect word to explain one way of using technology . . . for the purpose of viewing other cultures from a distance. Like the term implies, voyeurism is the act of watching, but not interacting. There are several forms of technology that allow people to become voyeurs of other cultures.

One way to learn about a culture without interacting is through the use of video. Studying foreign films or watching foreign television shows can help students understand what a culture values and provide a glimpse into cultural norms and mores. However, one still views such films through one's own cultural lens. This can result in the meaning of the film and key events being misinterpreted.

Another way to view other cultures is through the use of video sharing websites, such as YouTube (2011) or FlipShare (2011). These sites allow people to upload videos they have created to the Internet. Other people can then access these videos and view them. At the time of this writing, a search for "Egypt" on YouTube resulted in 451,000 videos, while a search for "Greece" yielded 570,000 videos. Although most of these videos are snapshots of people's lives, some portray cultural or local events that can be used to understand what is happening in other countries (Glimps & Ford, 2008).

Digital stories are similar to video in that they can provide insight into other cultures. Digital stories are created using still images and voice-over narrative. Through this medium, people are able to create a story about their own experiences or perceptions. Having students view digital stories created by others is similar to having them view a video. However, having students create their own digital stories about their family and culture enables them to understand their own values at a deeper level. Having them create digital stories about another culture allows them to learn and reflect on that culture and enables them to challenge their own perceptions and stereotypes.

Another way to learn about a culture without direct interaction is through the use of virtual field trips. Virtual field trips involve the use of websites to "visit" other countries and other places that would be unattainable in real life. There are thousands of virtual field trips available on the Web. They allow students to visit museums, such as the Natural History Museum (2011) in London, or visit other countries, such as the communities of Ouelessebougou in Mali, Africa (Ouelessebougou and You, 2011). These virtual field trips usually contain text and pictures. In addition, some virtual field trips contain video and/or discussion boards where students can post questions to local experts. Teachers are also able to create their own virtual field trips, although this can be time consuming, as the images and websites need to be located and identified.

Virtual field trips have much in common with real field trips, in that they allow for active learning, allow for students to interact with each other, and transport students mentally to a different learning environment. However, with virtual field trips, students can move at their own pace, can access the site multiple times, and can visit places they might not be able to visit in real life (Bellan & Scheurman, 1998). Virtual field trips address many of the problems encountered with real field trips, especially when considering international travel. These problems include cost, equity (insofar as not everyone can afford to travel), difficulties faced by students with disabilities, and gender issues (female students may be hesitant to travel to areas perceived as dangerous for them) (Stainfield, Fisher, Ford, & Solem, 2000).

Similar to virtual field trips are WebQuests. WebQuests are inquiry-based lessons in which the majority of the information is obtained through the Web (Dodge, 1995). WebQuests involve the students completing a task to accomplish a goal. In the process, students learn and interact with the content being taught. For example, students can learn how to cope with cultural differences and cultural shock through one WebQuest (Yun, 2011). Another WebQuest has students planning a seven-day international vacation for a family of four in the country of their choice. In the process they learn important information about the country (Hunt & Taxman, 2011). Thousands of WebQuests have been created on various topics and are available on the Internet. Teachers may also create their own WebQuests.

Videos, digital stories, virtual field trips, and WebQuests can assist students in developing a critical social consciousness. "Critical social-consciousness skills develop through an intuitive process as a result of immersing oneself in situations in which one must constantly confront one's stereotypes and prejudices and learn from direct experience" (Glimps & Ford, 2008, p. 92). Viewing reenactments or actual footage of historical and current events can facilitate discussion and assist students in challenging their own perceptions and held stereotypes. Virtual field trips and WebQuests provide students with opportunities to view the world from different perspectives. This can also lead to new knowledge and perceptions and enable students to examine their own stereotypes. These tools are useful for developing knowledge of other cultures and are appropriate tools for teachers to use.

COLLABORATIVE PROJECTS

In order to broaden global perspectives and contribute to teachers' international mindedness, there is a need to move beyond observing cultures and begin interacting with the people who represent that culture. One way to do this is through collaborative projects. Collaborative projects can enable students to "overcome geographic barriers; to communicate and collaborate with their peers around the world; to publish findings and share words, images, and videos internationally; and even to talk to one another in real time" (Stewart, 2010/2011, p. 100).

Probably the best-known collaborative project website is ePals Global Community (2010). Active for the past fifteen years, ePals connects teachers from over two hundred countries and territories and enables them to engage in project-based, collaborative lessons. ePals has over twelve million registered students and teachers, speaking over 136 different languages. The projects allow students to conduct research and collect data on topics such as water quality or the incidence of violence in children's cartoons. ePals is also a place where students can practice their language skills while learning a second language (Choate, Arome, Oates, Lewis, & Choate, 2008).

The Asia Society, a nonprofit organization that focuses on educating the world about Asia, linked one hundred American schools with one hundred Chinese schools in classroom-to-classroom projects that promote cultural understanding and language learning (Stewart, 2010/2011). It also connects U.S. schools with Muslim schools in Indonesia and Pakistan. Students in this project create videos of their lives and then discuss them with their counterparts (Stewart).

The Tiger Eye Global Community links students from Fu-Hsing Private School in Taipei, Taiwan, with experts from the University of Missouri as a way to help the students improve their conversational English (Wedman & Wedman, 2008). This project emerged out of another project that connected students in Taiwan with students in Missouri. Technology for these projects included e-mail, video conferencing, and a secure virtual environment. What made these projects successful was the involvement of the University of Missouri. "Major universities have extraordinary resources that enable them to work at the International level, including faculty expertise, International students, and a worldwide alumni base" (Wedman & Wedman, 2008, p. 1378).

Teacher educators are also looking at ways to use technology to collaborate with colleagues in other countries in order to increase their preservice and in-service teachers' international mindedness. McPherson, Wang, Hsu, Tsuei, and Wood (2007) discuss a project in which preservice and in-service teachers in teacher education programs at universities in three countries (the United States, England, and Taiwan) used technology to facilitate knowledge exchange and communication. This project used a combination of blogs, wikis, Google tools, and digital storytelling. Their research revealed that the teachers gained new perspectives on global education, learned strategies for integrating global concepts into the curriculum, and developed technology skills for collaboration.

As another form of collaboration, Merryfield (2003) suggests hiring cultural consultants, educators from other countries who are trained in intercultural skills, to serve as co-instructors in teacher education courses. The cultural consultants interact with the teachers throughout the course and provide diverse knowledge and perspectives. They challenge the American mainstream assumptions and provide more global frames of reference. Merryfield examined the online interactions of ninety-two American teachers and twenty-two cultural consultants as they interacted within five graduate courses in order to determine the effectiveness of offering such courses online. The technology used for this project included a class listserv, chats, and threaded discussions. The research revealed that technology afforded people the opportunity to join the discussion from across the country or across the world. This enabled every course to have a cross-cultural learning aspect. The closed-threaded discussions provided participants with the chance to ask questions they might not feel comfortable asking in a face-to-face environment. "Closed online environments provide a secure place for people to take risks, share personal experiences, admit to the realities of prejudice and discrimination (a family member's racist acts, a colleague's bias against gays, one's own prejudices) or ask politically incorrect questions" (Merryfield, 2003, p. 158).

Ausband and Schultheis (2010) provided preservice elementary education teachers from the United States, Germany, Spain, and Bulgaria with an international experience. Preservice teachers from the four countries were placed into groups and utilized Web 2.0 tools to investigate a topic of their choice that related to curriculum, instruction, or lesson planning in elementary schools. Web 2.0 tools included blogs, wikis, discussion boards, Skype (2011) (a video conferencing tool that also allows free phone calls over the Internet), Doodle (2011) (an online scheduling tool), chat rooms, and online survey utilities. Their findings show that the preservice teachers realized that there were more similarities than differences in curriculum and instruction between the four countries. This enabled the teachers to realize they had more in common than they originally thought.

Although there are websites that can facilitate virtual collaborations, starting such a project takes planning and resources. Making connections to other faculty who would be interested in such projects can seem a daunting task. One way to accomplish this is to attend international professional conferences. Using contacts other professors may have, especially those that are foreign born, can also help to find like-minded collaborators (Ausband & Schultheis, 2010).

In looking for collaborators, it is useful to keep in mind that many American students are not fluent enough in a second language to be able to communicate well. Therefore, finding partners in whom the participants can speak English becomes important. Since many countries now require students to take English as a second language, and these projects allow students to practice their English skills, this may not be difficult (Ausband & Schultheis, 2010).

When beginning these types of projects, it is best to start small. Quick and easy success encourages students and keeps them motivated. Projects that take too long or are too complex lead to a loss of interest and nonresponsiveness from participants (Lu, Diggs, & Wedman, 2004).

These types of projects are only successful if they have a purpose. They must fit within the curriculum and derive multiple perspectives on topics and areas that lead to greater understanding among participants. Therefore, the context is crucial to the success of the project (Lu, Diggs, & Wedman, 2004).

Finally, the technology can be an asset to these types of projects, but it can also be a hindrance. It is important to know the technology limitations of the partner schools, especially if the collaboration involves those in developing countries. It is essential to make sure there is adequate equipment and reliable bandwidth for the project to be successful. It is also important to consider the level of technology competency held by the instructor at each location. If the students encounter difficulties, will this person be able to help, or is there some other form of support available? This should be addressed before starting such partnerships.

MULTIUSER VIRTUAL ENVIRONMENTS

Another technology that can be used for interaction is multiuser virtual environments, commonly referred to as MUVEs. MUVEs can take many forms, but they all allow multiple people to interact simultaneously. Some MUVEs, such as *Second Life* (Linden Research, 2011) and *Active World* (ActiveWorlds Inc., 2011), allow people to hold virtual meetings and serve as chat rooms where people interact and share ideas. Other MUVEs, such as *World of Warcraft* (Blizzard Entertainment, 2011) or *Runescape* (Jagex Games Studio, 2011), are gaming environments where people interact while completing quests or missions. There are even MUVEs designed for young children, such as *Webkinz* (Ganz, 2011), *Club Penguin* (Disney Online Studios, 2011), and *Build-a-Bearville* (Build-a-Bear Workshop, 2011), where children can play games and take care of virtual pets. Whichever type of MUVE one interacts with, they all have the same things in common (Book, 2006):

1. Shared space—many users are simultaneously sharing the same space.
2. Graphical user interface—focusing more on 3-D than on 2-D graphics.
3. Immediacy—interaction within the world takes place in real time.
4. Interactivity—participants can build, alter, and develop the world.
5. Persistence—the world is developed and changed internally, by the designers, even when there are no users interacting in it.
6. Socialization/community—the world allows and encourages the formation of in-world groups, such as teams, guilds, clubs, and neighborhoods.

In these virtual environments, people create representations of themselves, called avatars. Some people have their avatars represent what they look like in real life, some choose to create avatars that represent what they would like to look like, while others choose cartoon characters, thereby hiding their gender, race, and ethnicity. In the first category of MUVEs, the avatars can gather, communicate, and build worlds. Avatars are able to recreate specific locations, such as the Eiffel Tower in Paris or the Great Pyramids of Giza in Egypt, fantasy worlds containing castles and unicorns, or places based on literature, such as Hogwarts from the Harry Potter series (Lamb & Johnson, 2009). The worlds are created in 3-D, allowing for more interaction and a sense of presence. The sense of presence allows people to feel they are actually at a location, as opposed to seeing images of a location. This sense of presence is the defining experience for a good virtual environment (Di Blas & Poggi, 2007).

Although there is not much research published on the effectiveness of MUVEs for global understanding and international mindedness, there are projects being developed for school-age children that are designed to address these areas. One such project is *Skoolaborate*, a global project that uses virtual environments along with other forms of technology to connect young people from around the world in collaborative projects (Lamb & Johnson, 2009). According to their website, *Skoolaborate* currently has over forty schools and organizations from Australia, New Zealand, Taiwan, Japan, Singapore, Chile, Portugal, Canada, the United Kingdom, and the United States (Skoolaborate, 2011). *Kidz Connect* has students creating live shows with students from another country. "Guided by artists and educators from theatre and digital arts, students learned skills like playback theatre, digital storytelling, and 3D modeling" (Vega, Pereira, Carvalho, Raposo, & Fuks, 2009, p. 168). The students collaborate to write, create, and perform the show while learning more about each other's culture. They then meet in *Second Life* to create a virtual city that represents both countries. In this virtual space, they perform the show simultaneously live and online (Kidz Connect, 2011).

TappedIn is a virtual environment designed to provide professional development opportunities to teachers. Discussions on a variety of topics are held monthly. Much like a chat room, TappedIn allows teachers to meet and discuss topics relevant to the curriculum. It allows teachers to share ideas and best practices. Topics range from the Religious Educators Forum to Global Project-Based Learning (TappedIn, 2011). TappedIn brings together teachers from all over the world. The calendar on the website allows teachers to enter their time zone and see the local time when the discussions will take place. Although teachers can access the discussions as guests, those choosing membership (membership is free) are provided with a virtual office, a more private area that allows impromptu groups to meet.

The second type of MUVE is often referred to as massively multiplayer online games (MMOGs). In many of these MMOGs, players work to solve quests and earn money. Collaboration, role playing, and problem solving are necessary avenues to successfully move through the virtual game. These games create opportunities for situated learning by providing immersive and motivating contexts for players to engage in a variety of activities and to develop and practice the skills necessary to be successful in those contexts (Gee, 2003; Shaffer, 2006; Squire, 2003). They "encourage information sharing and collaboration both within and beyond game parameters" (Delwiche, 2006, p. 161).

MMOGs involve role playing, in which players take on an alternative personality through their avatars. Whether they project themselves into the role of a Roman politician or a pirate on the high seas, participants "are forced to shift perspective and imagine the world through different eyes" (Delwiche, 2006, p. 162). This shift in perspective can lead to understanding and empathy for others. Such understanding has the potential to overcome cultural differences and allow for international mindedness.

MMOGs are accessed by people from all walks of life. The stereotype of teenage boys engaged in online games is not an accurate portrayal of today's gamers. Lenhart, Kahne, Middaugh, MacGill, Evans, and Vitak (2008) report that "the demographic for gaming as a whole shows that the average age of a gamer is 35 and some three quarters of the gaming market is over 18," and "fully 99% of boys and 94% of girls play video games" (p. 1). Gamers are represented by multiple countries. It is not unusual for gamers to engage in a common virtual quest while the people behind the avatars are sitting in different countries. This provides an opportunity to get to know each other and to share similarities and differences.

RESEARCH ON MUVES

Although there has been much research conducted on the learning potential of MUVES, few of these studies have looked at the impact on cultural understanding. Di Blas & Poggi (2007) conducted a study that looked at the use of "Learning@Europe (L@E), a project developed by Politecnico di Milano in collaboration with Accenture International Foundation, and Stori@ Lombardia (S@L), a similar project funded by the Regional Government of Lombardy (Italy), both involving online learning communities based on a shared 3D virtual environment" (p. 129). Data collection involved over 1,800 students and teachers from all over Europe. Their findings show that the MUVE enabled students from different countries to meet, communicate in real time, collaborate, and even play together. Students being able to interact with foreign peers increased their interest in cultural themes. This turned out to be a major factor in their motivation to learn.

Kayler, Sprague, & Dede (2009) explored the development of cultural understandings that occur within MMOGs. Using a MMOG built around a military structure in which players joined an army and engaged in campaigns, Kayler and colleagues surveyed participants to see how they negotiated cultural differences while forming a group. Their findings showed that the participants first got to know each other as individuals, and only when they were comfortable with each other did they begin to discuss those aspects of group identity that tend to separate people (politics, religion, values). By the time these discussions emerged, the differences were irrelevant, for they had already formed a relationship within the game.

Kayler and Sprague (2011) conducted a study in which they explored sixty-one K–12 teachers' perceptions and experiences as they engaged in massively multiplayer online games of choice over a four-week period. In contrast to the findings of the other studies, Kayler and Sprague found that the teachers were fearful of interacting with strangers in the online environment. The teachers held stereotypes about gamers. These stereotypes led to fear and apprehension and prevented them from interacting with others. They found MMOGs to be lonely places. This is a concern, as MUVES of all types are generally safe environments. Although some precautions need to be taken (such as giving out real names or other personal information), Delwiche (2006) contends that human beings are never physically at risk while engaging in MUVES. In fact, in most MMOGs, even the person's avatar is not at risk. An avatar may lose experience points or turn into a "ghost" for a short period of time, but no permanent death occurs.

The teachers in Kayler and Sprague's (2011) study did not feel safe in the virtual environments. Delwiche (2006) states that this sense of safety was crucial as students who did not feel safe would shut down and not engage in the activity. In addition, Merryfield (2003) found that "when people feel safe and comfortable, they tackle topics that often lead to information that counters stereotypes, ignorance, or misunderstandings" (p. 158). Helping teachers to confront their stereotypes of online interactions and providing them with an environment that feels safe and secure is critical if one wishes to capitalize on the affordances of these technologies.

ADDITIONAL TECHNOLOGY TOOLS

Another technology that allows for interaction is video conferencing. One of the concerns expressed by the teachers in the Kayler and Sprague (2011) study was the inability of knowing who was behind the avatar. Video conferencing takes this concern away as it allows people to see and talk to each other.

Several of the collaborative projects discussed previously included the use of video conferencing as a means to connect students across distance. Currently, the most common video conferencing tool is Skype, a voice-over Internet protocol (VoIP) program that allows people to communicate for free over the Internet. If the parties have Web cameras (available for as little as twenty dollars), they can make video calls. Skype even allows for group video calls, connections between groups at multiple locations.

Social networking sites, such as Facebook, MySpace, LinkedIn, and VK.com (Russia's version of Facebook), allow people to share aspects of their lives through text, graphics, and videos. People choose who to "friend" on these sites. Once the person is a friend, he or she can see the postings made by that person. Although people can limit their virtual friends to people they know in real life, they also have the option of linking to friends of friends. This can create a network that has the potential of being worldwide.

This concept was recently experienced by this author. She logged in to her Facebook account one evening and scrolled through the posted messages. She encountered messages written in Arabic from her friends in Egypt discussing the revolution that was occurring at the time, messages in Greek from the Greek teachers she was working with, messages in Russian from the Russian teachers she worked with, and messages in Spanish from her sister-in-law and her friends in Mexico. Technology has allowed the world to be shared with anyone willing to engage.

There is concern about privacy issues on these social networking sites, and some teachers may react negatively to using sites like Facebook and MySpace for professional activities, given the reputation of these sites. If this is the case, LinkedIn might be an acceptable alternative. LinkedIn is a professional social networking site. Its purpose is to link professionals with other professionals. Although anyone can request to be in a person's network, they need to be approved by the person. Unlike Facebook, LinkedIn focuses on professional activities and can be used to connect teachers with other educators. Previous research has shown that such connections can help teachers realize that there are similarities in curriculum issues across countries (Ausband & Schultheis, 2010).

IMPLICATIONS FOR TEACHER EDUCATION

Technology allows people to connect with each other and flattens the world (Friedman, 2005). These connections can enable teachers and students to develop global awareness and international mindedness. However, for these connections to work, preservice and in-service teachers must have the opportunity to use these technologies in their teacher education programs. Research has shown that the most important factors for teachers to integrate technology into their classroom are an expectancy of success and the perceived value of the activity (Wozney, Venkatesh, & Abrami, 2006). If these two factors are high, a teacher was more likely to implement technology-based activities in the classroom. The way to develop an expectancy of success is through teachers having hands-on experience with the technologies and allowing them to interact with others across time and distance.

The majority of the teachers in the Kayler and Sprague (2011) study were not likely to use MUVEs in their classrooms. They did not see the value of the activity, nor did they achieve a sense of success due to their apprehensions caused by the stereotypes they held. If the goal is to have teachers such as these use MUVEs as a vehicle for collaboration with teachers and students in other countries, then the following needs to occur:

1. For teachers who hold stereotypes of online users, these stereotypes need to be confronted before any online activities can occur. The stereotypes lead to apprehension and a lack of understanding about online interactions. Without bringing these stereotypes into the open and acknowledging them, teachers will be reluctant to engage in online collaborative projects. This will reduce their understandings of other cultures to voyeurism . . . watching, but not interacting.
2. Teachers need opportunities to experience these technologies and explore their pedagogical implications. This needs to happen within teacher education programs. Although teachers may be familiar with YouTube (2011) and Skype (2011), they probably are not considering ways to use these to enrich students' understandings of other cultures. They also are not considering how MUVEs can be used to achieve this

goal. Without the guidance of teacher educators to help bridge their understandings of these various technologies, the perceived value of the activity and the expectancy of success will diminish.
3. Teacher educators need to arrange collaborative projects with their international counterparts. This will enable preservice and in-service teachers to experience the power of collaborative projects, enrich their understandings of other cultures, and enable them to move past their apprehension of using online technologies. Such projects can be arranged through ePals (ePals Global Community, 2010) or by communicating with others in various MUVEs, such as TappedIn (2011). Arranging such projects can also occur through interactions at conferences, especially those with a strong international presence.

By allowing teachers to experience the online technologies discussed in this chapter, teacher educators can help them see the perceived value of such tools. By engaging in the type of learning experiences we hope they will use with their students, teachers will develop international mindedness. This international mindedness, coupled with an expectation of success, will ensure that teachers will offer their K–12 students the same learning experiences, resulting in their development of international mindedness.

CONCLUSION

This chapter explored various technologies that can be used for online interactions. However, online interactions "can never substitute for face-to-face collaborative work and immersion experiences if teachers are to develop intercultural competence in working with others. Teachers need both vehicles for learning across cultures" (Merryfield, 2003, p. 162). Although face-to-face immersion experiences will be the best format for developing global awareness, for those who are unable to do so due to lack of opportunity, lack of finances, lack of mobility, or geographical isolation, using technology to engage in virtual interactions can be beneficial.

REFERENCES

ActiveWorlds Inc. (2011). *Active Worlds* [Online]. Accessed March 29, 2011, at http://activeworld.com.

Ausband, L. T., and Schultheis, K. (2010). Utilizing Web 2.0 to provide an international experience for pre-service elementary education teachers: The IPC Project. *Computers in the Schools, 27*(3), 266–87.

Bellan, J. M., & Scheurman, G. (1998). Actual and virtual reality: Making the most of field trips. *Social Education, 62*(1), 35–40.

Blizzard Entertainment. (2011). *World of Warcraft* [Online]. Accessed March 29, 2011, at http://us.battle.net/wow/en.

Book, B. (2006). *What is a virtual world?* [Online]. Accessed March 29, 2011, http://www.virtualworldsreview.com.

Build-a-Bear Workshop. (2011). *Build-a-Bearville* [Online]. Accessed March 29, 2011, http://www.buildabearville.com.

Choate, A., Arome, G., Oates, R., Lewis, S., & Choate, D. (2008). Infusion of global education through the use of technology. In K. McFerrin et al. (Eds.), *Proceedings of Society for Information Technology & Teacher Education International Conference 2008* (pp. 2535–38). Chesapeake, VA: AACE. Retrieved March 27, 2011, from http://www.editlib.org/p/27597.

Delwiche, A. (2006). Massively multiplayer online games (MMOs) in the new media classroom. *Educational Technology & Society, 9*(3), 160–72.

Di Blas, N., & Poggi, C. (2007). European virtual classrooms: Building effective "virtual" educational experiences. *Virtual Reality, 11*, 129–43. doi:10.1007/s10055-006-0060-4.

Disney Online Studios. (2011). *Club Penguin* [Online]. Accessed March 29, 2011, at http://www.clubpenguin.com.

Dodge, B. (1995). WebQuests: A technique for Internet-based learning. *Distance Educator, 1*(2), 10–13.

Doodle. (2011). *Doodle* [Online]. Accessed March 29, 2011, http://www.doodle.com.

ePals Global Community. (2010). *ePals global Community* [Online]. Accessed March 27, 2011, http://www.epals.com.

Facebook. (2011). *Facebook* [Online]. Accessed March 29, 2011, http://www.facebook.com.

FlipShare. (2011). *FlipShare* [Online]. Accessed February 16, 2011, https://www.flipshare.com.

Friedman, T. L. (2005). *The world is flat: A brief history of the twenty-first century.* New York: Farrar, Straus & Giroux.

Ganz. (2011). *Webkinz* [Online]. Accessed March 29, 2011, http://www.webkinz.com.

Gee, J. (2003). *What video games have to teach us about learning and literacy.* New York: Palgrave Macmillan.

Glimps, B. J., and Ford, T. (2008, November/December). Using Internet technology tools to teach about global diversity. *The Clearing House, 82*(2), 91–95.

Hunt, C., & Taxman, H. (2011). *Around the world in seven days* [Online]. Accessed March 29, 2011, http://questgarden.com/73/57/9/081118131557.

Jagex Games Studio. (2011). *Runescape* [Online]. Accessed March 29, 2011, http://www.runescape.com.

Kayler, M., & Sprague, D. (2011). *"You want us to do what?" K–12 teachers' experiences in virtual gaming environments.* Paper presented at the American Educational Research Association Annual Conference 2011, New Orleans, Louisiana.

Kayler, M., Sprague, D., & Dede, C. (2009). Online gaming: Building bridges that enhance cultural understandings. In C. Vrasidas, M. Zembylas, & G. Glass, *ICT for Education, Development & Social Justice* (pp. 183–200). Charlotte, NC: Information Age Publishing.

Kidz Connect. 2011. Kidz Connect: Connecting cultures through creative collaboration [Online]. Accessed March 29, 2011, at http://www.kidzconnect.org.

Lamb, A., & Johnson, L. (2009). The potential, the pitfalls, and the promise of multi-user virtual environments: Getting a second life. *Teacher Librarian, 36*(4), 68–72.

Lenhart, V., Kahne, J., Middaugh, E., MacGill, A., Evans, C., & Vitak, J. (2008). *Teens, video games, and civics.* Washington, DC: Pew Internet & American Life Project. Accessed March 29, 2011, at http://www.pewinternet.org/Reports/2008/Teens-Video-Games-and-Civics.aspx.

Linden Research. (2011). *Second Life* [Online]. Accessed March 29, 2011, http://secondlife.com.

LinkedIn Corporation. (2011). *LinkedIn* [Online]. Accessed March 29, 2011, http://www.linkedin.com.

Lu, W. H., Diggs, L., & Wedman, J. (2004). Building cross cultural partnerships through the Internet: What works and what doesn't. In L. Cantoni & C. McLoughlin (Eds.), *Proceedings of World Conference on Educational Multimedia, Hypermedia and Telecommunications 2004* (pp. 4782–86). Chesapeake, VA: AACE. Accessed March 27, 2011, at http://www.editlib.org/p/11754.

McPherson, S., Wang, S. K., Hsu, H. Y., Tsuei, M., & Wood, R. (2007). Using information and communication technologies (ICTs) in teacher education for increasing global awareness. In T. Bastiaens & S. Carliner (Eds.), *Proceedings of World Conference on E-Learning in Corporate, Government, Healthcare, and Higher Education 2007* (pp. 1112–16). Chesapeake, VA: AACE. Accessed March 27, 2011, http://www.editlib.org/p/26486.

Merryfield, M. (2003). Like a veil: Cross-cultural experiential learning online. *Contemporary Issues in Technology and Teacher Education, 3*(2), 146–71.

Myspace Inc. (2011). *Myspace* [Online]. Accessed March 29, 2011, http://www.myspace.com.

Natural History Museum. (2011). *Natural History Museum* [Online]. Accessed March 27, 2011, http://www.nhm.ac.uk/nature-online/art-nature-imaging/collections/index.html.

Ouelessebougou and You (2011). *Ouelessebougou and You* [Online]. Accessed March 29, 2011, http://www.uen.org/utahlink/tours/tourFames.cgi?tour_id=14693.

Shaffer, D. W. (2006). *How computer games help children learn.* New York: Palgrave MacMillan.

Skoolaborate. (2011). *Skoolaborate* [Online]. Accessed March 29, 2011, at http://www.skoolaborate.com/content/about.

Skype. (2011). *Skype* [Online]. Accessed March 29, 2011, http://www.skype.com.

Squire, K. (2003). Video games in education. *International Journal of Intelligent Simulations and Gaming, 2*(1), 10.

Stainfield, J., Fisher, P., Ford, B., & Solem, M. (2000). International virtual field trips: A new direction? *Journal of Geography in Higher Education, 24*(2), 255–62.

Stewart, V. (2010/2011). Education goes digital and global. *kappanmagazine.org*, *92*(4), 99–100. Retrieved February 16, 2011.

TappedIn. (2011). *TappedIn: A community of education professionals* [Online]. Accessed March 29, 2011, http://tappedin.org/tappedin.

Vega, K., Pereira, A., Carvalho, G., Raposo, A., & Fuks, H. (2009). Prototyping games for training and education in Second Life: Time2Play and TREG. In *SB-Games 2009, Seventh Brazilian Symposium on Digital Games and Entertainment*, pp. 167–75.

VK. (2011). *VK* [Online]. Accessed at http://vk.com.

Wedman, J., & Wedman, L. (2008). K–12 global partnerships: Uniting learners around the world. In C. Bonk et al. (Eds.), *Proceedings of World Conference on E-Learning in Corporate, Government, Healthcare, and Higher Education 2008* (pp. 1375–80). Chesapeake, VA: AACE. Accessed March 27, 2011, at http://www.editlib.org/p/29823.

Wozney, L., Venkatesh, V., & Abrami, P. (2006). Implementing computer technologies: Teachers' perceptions and practices. *Journal of Technology and Teacher Education*, *14*(1), 173–207.

YouTube. (2011). *YouTube* [Online]. Accessed February 16, 2011, at http://www.youtube.com.

Yun, J. (2011). *Culture shock? Culture shake!* [Online]. Accessed March 29, 2011, at http://questgarden.com/113/76/3/101206193756/index.htm.

Zhao, Y. (2009). *Catching up or leading the way: American education in the age of globalization*. Alexandria, VA: ASCD.

Section 3

CONCLUDING THOUGHTS

Developing Opportunities to Internationalize Teacher Education

Beverly D. Shaklee

This book has been devoted to the exploration of ways in which U.S. teacher education could become more internationally oriented and why we need to consider this evolution in our teacher education programs. We have reviewed conceptual frameworks from multicultural and international education; examined the disciplines and standards, family and child experiences as international citizens, professional development opportunities for U.S. teacher educators and teachers; as well as prompted thinking (we hope) about the notion of U.S. teacher education developing an international focus.

Cushner reminds us in his earlier chapter that even though many U.S. students in teacher education programs would welcome international experiences and study abroad opportunities, fewer than 3 percent of U.S. teacher education students actually have that opportunity. James and Davis (2010) note that "despite teachers' desire to prepare students for global citizenship, they feel unprepared to do so" (p. 41). Lack of clarity of terms, global or international or both; international resources across content domains and age groups; congruent pedagogy; and international clinical experiences are cited as major obstacles keeping teachers from engaging in this work.

Levine (2010) calls for rethinking of teacher education programs to address a "world being transformed by profound demographic, economic, technological and global changes" (p. 19–20). These changes, he maintains, are significantly influencing PK–12 education, and teacher education programs need to change to keep up. Zeichner (2010) commented that it is not the lack of willingness of the candidates in teacher education programs or even the teacher educators themselves, but that it is, in part, our national standards in teacher education that keep us from moving toward the internationalization of the curriculum. A longtime advocate of international perspectives in U.S. teacher education programs, he noted, "Without better integrating the work into the standards and assessments in teacher education programs, this important work will continue to remain out of the mainstream of American teacher education" (p. 16). Zhao (2010) notes that most teachers are "monolingual, with limited experiences learning a foreign language or experiencing a foreign culture" (p. 427). Therefore they need significant experiences to shift their thinking from local to global and to understand that we are preparing teachers for the world.

Calls for reform of teacher education programs have been long and loud. Recommendations have included separating teacher education from universities, establishing alternative tracks to licensure, or even relying on alternative models such as Teach for America. Further, recommendations have included recruiting higher-performing students to teacher education, insisting that teacher candidates have more knowledge of the content disciplines, more time in apprenticeship or clinical experiences, supportive mentoring into their first years of teaching, partnerships between schools and teacher education programs, use of social media in teaching, and other models for improvement (Ball & Forzani, 2010; Darling-Hammond, 2010; Ewbank, Foulger, & Carter, 2010; Fallon, 2010; Futrell, 2010; Gimbert, Desai, Kerka, 2010; Levine, 2010; Starnes, Sanderholm, & Webb, 2010). Some call for the removal of teacher education from university settings, and some say "teacher education stands on the threshold of a golden age" (Fallon, 2010, p. 34). What is surprisingly absent in the continued calls for reform, beyond "we need to prepare students for the twenty-first century," is the notion that among the calls for reforms we do not address issues of global importance, international topics, intercultural competence, clinical experiences beyond our borders, or world language skills for the teachers in practice or the teachers being prepared for the future. And yet our students, the ones being prepared for the twenty-first century, are often demonstrating stronger social media skills, language skills, and interest in global issues and international perspectives from their personal histories, and come from transnational, mobile families—a clear misfit with the teachers they have and the ones we are preparing to serve them who know they are underprepared for the challenge (James & Davis, 2010).

A number of credible organizations have spent time and effort and provided funding to support U.S. teacher educators in redesigning the curriculum for a more internationalized focus. Among those most active in teacher education has been the Asia Society along with the Council of Chief

State School Officers (CCSSO) and others such as the Longview Foundation (2009). In a recent joint publication, Mansilla and Jackson (2011) note, "No matter how deep their passion for developing globally competent students, teachers cannot teach what they do not know. Teachers need ongoing opportunities to develop their own global competence as well as the pedagogical capacities to foster global competence in their students" (p. 85).

While many teacher education programs are situated in international, global universities, the effort to internationalize campus life and course work seldom influences the teacher education program at large. In fact at a recent conference attended by the author, the vice provost of a major global university commented that although the college of education had exemplary programs, he doubted seriously that they even knew where Malaysia was, much less did they do any work in the region. Colleges of education are seen as entrenched, outdated, and out of touch with the real world. "By almost any standard, many if not most of the nation's 1,450 schools, colleges, and departments of education are doing a mediocre job of preparing teachers for the realities of the 21st century classroom," Arne Duncan, U.S. secretary of education, said in a major speech at Teachers College, Columbia University; he continued, noting, "America's university-based teacher preparation programs need revolutionary change—not evolutionary tinkering. Colleges of education need to make dramatic changes to prepare today's children to compete in the global economy" (U.S. Department of Education, 2010). Levine counters, but in part agrees with Duncan, when he writes, "The best of teacher education programs are being lumped with the worst. . . . The nation's teacher education programs, particularly those located at universities, need to adapt to a world transformed" (p. 22).

Noting the seeming disinterest on the part of colleges of education, Mansilla and Jackson (2011) further assert:

> States can utilize their teacher certification mechanisms to outline goals for teachers' own global competence in order to *drive change* in teacher preparation programs. Such needed changes in teacher preparation programs include better linkages between arts and sciences departments and colleges of education, expansion of study and teaching abroad opportunities for prospective teachers, and systematic training in how to integrate international content and perspectives into required education courses. (p. 92, author's emphasis)

If colleges of education and teacher preparation programs are driven by national and state systems of accreditation and licensure, it makes sense to look at aspects of licensure and accreditation to determine to what extent teacher education programs are required to ensure the development and delivery of global competency and to what degree the agencies reviewing teacher education programs espouse internationalization. Have we moved beyond historic notions of multicultural education, as noted by Kolar? Would core national standards (Engel & Olden, this volume) bring us into broader more representative concepts embedded in internationalization?

Approximately 650 institutions of teacher education in the United States are accredited by the National Council for the Accreditation of Teacher Education (NCATE, 2010), which over the past several years has undergone its own transformation in the process of accreditation. Space prohibits an extensive review of NCATE policies and procedures; however, we can look briefly at the NCATE standards for evidence related to global competency and/or international mindedness in the preparation of our nation's teachers. To provide some clarity, NCATE does not accredit individual courses or field experiences in teacher education programs; it accredits the unit (e.g., the teacher education unit and subsequent programs), which must show acceptable evidence in reaching the identified standard (NCATE, 2008). In looking for language that may reflect a disposition toward international or global competency, standard 4, "Diversity," comes closest to our discussion.

> The unit designs, implements, and evaluates curriculum and provides experiences for candidates to acquire and demonstrate the knowledge, skills, and professional dispositions necessary to help all students learn. Assessments indicate that candidates can demonstrate and apply proficiencies related to diversity. Experiences provided for candidates include working with diverse populations, including higher education and P–12 school faculty, candidates, and students in P–12 schools. (NCATE, 2008)

Standard 4, "Diversity," includes elements that address planning, curriculum, assessment, clinical experiences, and engagement with diverse faculty members in order to "develop proficiencies for working effectively with students and families from diverse populations and with exceptionalities to ensure that all students learn. Regardless of whether they live in areas with great diversity, candidates must develop knowledge of *diversity in the United States and the world*, professional dispositions that respect and value differences, and skills for working with diverse populations" (NCATE, 2008, author's emphasis).

The standard for diversity does include "the world"; however, it is questionable that teacher education candidates ever get past the notion of "diversity in the United States" and the historic definitions linked to this statement. If diversity in the United States continues to be defined by historical references to race and class, then perhaps we are missing a very large part of the current and future U.S. population. Narrowing our scope, we can look into specific association standards that participate in the accreditation process under the umbrella of NCATE (e.g., the National Association of Teachers of Mathematics [NCTM], the American Association of Childhood International [ACEI], the National Association for the Education of Young Children [NAEYC], and so forth). The specialized professional associations (SPAs) are linked to NCATE and are usually the first step in the accreditation process. (See NCATE for a list of associations and standards.) Although we cannot look at all of the SPA standards required of teacher education programs, a brief look at one can help us look at the issues of internationalization, diversity, and multicultural education.

The ACEI standards focused on K–6 teacher education encompass six areas: learning, motivation and development, curriculum (specifically content disciplines), instruction, assessment, and professionalism. In only one of the subsets of the broader standards is there language that would be related to diversity, internationalism, or multicultural education. "Standard 3.2: Adaptation to diverse students—Candidates understand how elementary students differ in their development and approaches to learning, and create instructional opportunities that are adapted to diverse students" (2007, p. 2) is clearly and directly related to diversity. However, within the explanation of each major standard one can find specific information that could be related to international perspectives, including "Candidates for elementary teaching understand that the ways in which cultures and social groups differ are important and affect learning" or "They consider diversity an asset and respond positively to it" (p. 4). Though these elements and expectations are provided in supporting explanatory materials, they are neither easily visible nor part of the major statements made by an association with "international" as part of its title. Again, international or global expectations are neither visible nor readily associated with the field of elementary education, and the definitions of diversity are not clearly apparent, leaving teacher educators to anchor these experiences in their personal notions of diversity. The clear exception to the associations is the National Council for Social Studies (NCSS), which has long been an advocate of preparing teachers and students as citizens of the world: "The primary purpose of social studies is to help young people make informed and reasoned decisions for the public good as citizens of a culturally diverse, democratic society in an interdependent world" (2010). However, social studies cannot shoulder the full responsibility for internationalization of the curriculum, and in our U.S. world of standardized testing, too often social studies teaching has moved from a living, vibrant, creative opportunity to engage students in learning about the world to a series of multiple-choice, memorized facts in order to pass the required test (Brodie, 2010).

In 2007, the American Council on Education published *At Home in the World: Bridging the Gap between Internationalization and Multicultural Education* (Olson, Evans, & Shoenberg, 2007) to explore the "conceptual frameworks underlying internationalization and multicultural education and the relationship between these two frameworks" (p. iv). The authors note that these terms are not clearly defined and often can overlap; however, they also note that multicultural education is typically used to address domestic diversity inside the United States, and international education is used to address diversity outside of the United States, along with global trends, issues, and cross-cultural concerns. However, if we rely on data provided throughout this book, it appears that the lines of "domestic" diversity in the United States have become blurred with the notions of diversity outside of U.S. borders, while our current definitions used in teacher education programs have failed to stretch and grow to encompass the families and children in our nation's schools. James Banks, well-known scholar in multicultural education, has provided a means by which to stretch historic views to be inclusive of global dimensions in teacher education. Banks contends that multicultural education is a conceptual foundation employing a process which transforms the learner (i.e., teacher educator, teacher, and student), helping to create, among other elements, school culture and social structure that "empowers all students from diverse racial, ethnic and cultural groups" (2004, p. 5), and we would add linguistic diversity.

Models of international education abound as well, although often not as well grounded or as well researched (Hayden, Thompson, & Levy, 2009). International Baccalaureate (IB), established as a curriculum model in 1962, has recently developed and launched a model for the preparation of international baccalaureate teachers known as the teacher award. Working in conjunction with recognized universities, IB has authorized universities worldwide to deliver graduate teacher education programs based on the IB approved standards (2008) for teacher preparation. The standards for the IB teacher education program include four required areas of inquiry and study: curriculum processes, teaching and learning, assessment and learning, and professional learning. Embedded within the overarching standards are systematic study and recognition of the nature and determinants of culture, cultural identity and its significance in developing intercultural understanding, and international mindedness of teachers as well as alternative strategies for developing intercultural awareness and international mindedness among the students. Further, teachers prepared in these programs use specific criteria for selection and evaluation of appropriate teaching and learning materials and resources to ensure cultural diversity, relevance, and sensitivity. Finally, they study current innovations in practice in international education and ways to extend collaborations between schools and between countries as a typical part of practice. While the pedagogical focus in the IB curriculum is on inquiry, the overarching theme is connecting to the world for teachers as well as students. For instance, the FAST TRAIN Advanced IB program at George Mason University, the first authorized program in North America, recruits cohorts of teachers from the United States and abroad, utilizes technology to establish international partnerships, and has created an innovative inquiry-based graduate program that fosters meaningful relationships across the world. Hill (2007) wrote that the "acquisition of knowledge and the development of skills, as cognitive elements only, [are] not a complete measure of success for an IB programme. The affective domain must also be stimulated so that attitudes of responsible world citizenship are cultivated" (p. 27). Perhaps it is intentionality that is the key.

U.S. teacher education programs that do promote internationalization do so with intention; they consciously integrate global, international content into all aspects of the program, from course work to clinical experiences. Their faculty model international perspectives in their teaching, scholarship, and fieldwork. Teacher education students not only have opportunity for international teaching experiences; they are conscientiously recruited and supported in their efforts to teach internationally (Cushner & Brennan, 2007). Merryfield, a U.S.-based teacher educator and lifelong advocate of preparing globally competent teachers, has continually espoused integrated and systematic models of teacher education that include global content, intercultural learning, and pedagogy for global perspectives as key elements in the conceptual framework for preparing global educators (1995, 2000). Colleagues James and Davis (2010) described their experience at Kent State University weaving international perspectives into teacher education. Kent State University, College of Education, Health and Human Services (EHHS), has a well-known international intercultural program based in the Gerald H. Read Center for International and Intercultural Education; however, as the authors noted, there was more that could be done to integrate international content and internationalization of the curriculum throughout teacher education (p. 40). Beginning with a self-study of what it means to be internationally minded, the early childhood faculty took on a yearlong study that included defining international mindedness, identifying what they had in place that fostered international mindedness in teacher candidates, what barriers they perceived, how candidate growth toward international mindedness could be assessed, and what next steps could be taken to internationalize the early childhood teacher education program. EHHS at Kent continues its exploration of global competency and international mindedness through participation in the Longview Foundation–funded project, *Internationalizing*

Perspectives and Practices in Teacher Education: Developing a Collaborative Model for Ohio (2011). Bringing together three major institutions, Kent State University, the University of Akron, and Miami University, the teams of global scholars (e.g., faculty) are dedicating time and effort to internationalizing their curriculum across multiple disciplines and creating a "specialized certificate in International Perspective and Practice" in the College of Education at each university (2011). There are other institutions, colleges of education, and program-specific examples of internationalization within U.S. teacher education; the point is that it only happens throughout a program when there is a critical mass of faculty, commitment, and intentionality in the design and delivery of internationalized U.S. teacher education programs.

Mansilla and Jackson (2011) identified several major initiatives in the United States that have influenced the development and delivery of internationalized teacher education programs. Among their major recommendations was to "retool teacher preparation programs to integrate international learning opportunities and substantially strengthen requirements and support for developing the capacity among prospective teachers to teach for global competence" (p. 99). In her chapter on the development of internationally minded teachers in Australia in this volume, Tudball echoes this sentiment, noting that while many Australian academics in teacher education have moved beyond a parochial view of teacher education, merely preparing teachers for careers in their home nations, "there is room for more widespread thinking and action to plan future directions in internationalization, and particularly to decide what should happen in program delivery and content" (Tudball, this volume). Even in programs that have moved toward internationalization of teacher education at the national and state levels, there is still considerable debate about what constitutes appropriate curricula, clinical experiences, and culturally appropriate pedagogy, and how both faculty and teaching candidates are prepared to deliver such programs.

Internationalized U.S. Teacher Education

Gardner (2004), writing about educational change in a time of globalization, notes that the youth of today are being prepared for a fundamentally different world and that there is little being done in education determining how this world should impact education. In this work he also recommends seven areas that should be integral to education in the K–12 system:

1. Understanding the global system;
2. Capacity to think analytically and creatively within the disciplines;

3. Ability to tackle problems and issues that do not respect disciplinary boundaries;
4. Knowledge of and ability to interact civilly and productively with individuals from quite different cultural backgrounds, both within one's own society and across the planet;
5. Knowledge of and respect for one's own cultural traditions;
6. Fostering of hybrid or blended identities; and
7. Fostering of tolerance (p. 253–55).

If we applied Gardner's recommendations to a U.S. teacher education program, what would such a program look like?

The Faculty

We begin with ourselves, faculty in teacher education programs. If we are to internationalize U.S. teacher education, then we need to ensure that the faculty we hire have had the opportunity and exhibit the willingness to be international citizens themselves. What have they done in their educational programs or extracurricular experiences that indicates they are people of the world? Are they multilingual? Have they studied or worked abroad? Have they done research in international settings? Have they done research or had sustained experiences in settings with students of significantly different cultural backgrounds? Do they exhibit knowledge of world research related to their areas of expertise (e.g., literacy, mathematics, foundations, history, science)? Do they have ideas, resources, or experiences that would engage teacher education candidates in international venues whether online or face to face? Do they demonstrate well-developed intercultural communication skills?

There are many other questions that could be asked of all teacher education faculty, those currently employed and those to be hired in the future. Awareness and intentionality, looking specifically for those attributes of international mindedness across faculty, including those from historically underrepresented populations and those from abroad, will not ensure the development of an internationalized U.S. teacher education program, but it will allow for beginning and sustained conversations about what it means to prepare U.S. teacher candidates to teach students of the world. Teacher education faculty who can think analytically and creatively, who can tackle problems and issues beyond disciplinary boundaries (e.g., content specific assignments such as elementary education or in secondary education the disciplines of science, English, and so forth), could create model, innovative, and internationally oriented U.S. teacher education programs.

The Standards

It may well be true, as Zeichner (2010) noted, that if the standards do not change then international perspectives will never be an important part of teacher education in the United States, but who writes the standards? In the case of NCATE, a coalition of more than thirty national associations representing the education profession at large "appoints representatives to NCATE's policy boards, which develop NCATE standards, policies, and procedures. Membership on policy boards includes representatives from organizations of (1) teacher educators, (2) teachers, (3) state and local policy-makers, and (4) professional specialists" (2001, p. 5). The persons writing the national standards come from the ranks of our own profession; we can and should influence their perspective on the accreditation of U.S.-based teacher education programs to include aspects of internationalization and international mindedness. We need to expand the definitions of diversity to include broader aspects of multicultural and international education. We need to continue to advocate at state and national levels for this shift in perspective in order to prepare teachers to better serve the students of the twenty-first century in the United States. An old adage comes to mind: "If you always do what you've always done; you'll always get what you always got." The same is true in teacher education. We need to couple what we have learned from research in teacher preparation with a vision of what we need teachers to know and be able to do to prepare students for a global present and future.

Teacher Education Candidates

No one would argue with holding teacher education candidates to high academic standards in their studies; nor would most argue against breadth and depth of content knowledge in their preparation. The question is how do we determine that candidates have accomplished these goals prior to becoming teachers? Some argue for more testing, and others know that passing a test does not mean that one can teach the content to a ten year old. Some argue for more time in the classroom (apprenticeship or professional development school models), while others note that spending more time in schools that do not support high-quality challenging and culturally appropriate teaching just magnifies the problem as teacher candidates replicate poor practice. Some current teacher education programs include experience with diverse student populations, multicultural education, and in some instances international experiences, courses, or extracurricular activities. However, as noted by Cushner and Brennan (2007), "Although these efforts undoubtedly offer some benefit in terms of increasing cultural awareness, they are not sufficiently linked to practice to influence the professional lives of participating candidates in a lasting way" (p. 5).

If we are to prepare U.S. teacher candidates to include international perspectives and to affect their professional lives in a lasting way, then we may need to rethink our U.S. teacher education programs. If our conceptual framework included knowledge of our own cultural heritage; intercultural competence and communication skills; immersion in a significantly different cultural community; understanding of global systems; as well as the ability to think analytically, creatively, and beyond disciplinary boundaries, what course work and clinical experiences would we provide to teacher candidates?

Rethinking Clinical Experiences

Clinical experiences for teacher education candidates would require experiences in significantly different cultural communities, including experiences in international settings. Cushner and Brennan's (2007) volume on intercultural student teaching not only gives specific models for how this can be accomplished (and is being done in some colleges of education) but also documents the value of such experience on the lives of teacher candidates. Romano and Cushner (2007) and Cushner and Mahon (2007) note changes in cultural identity, openness, self-reflection, cross-cultural communication skills, tolerance for ambiguity, and increased ability to work with English language learners as being among other areas which create cultural capital that a new teacher can bring back to U.S. classrooms. This is not just a brief excursion into another culture as we see too often in teacher education programs. This is full immersion in another culture in order to create profound changes in thinking about one's self and the world. A critical aspect of successful intercultural teaching is to have consistent guidance and scaffolding to promote an understanding and appreciation for difference while expanding worldviews. Working with immigrant populations, on Native American reservations, with displaced refugee families, or international school placements all provide an opportunity to question what it means to be a teacher in the United States. Given that the teaching profession is still primarily made up of white middle-class females, this opportunity to question self, worldviews, notions of social justice, fairness, and privilege is an imperative.

This also means having knowledgeable experienced teacher education faculty who can facilitate and support candidates' development in these settings. Providing sustained contact and exploratory experiences via technology as Sprague (this volume) points out is also a means to expand clinical experiences beyond borders and beyond local placements for all teacher candidates. Faculty should be actively involved in the development of clinical experiences

248   Beverly D. Shaklee

using technology to establish global partnerships and on-site placements that move candidates beyond levels of comfort and cultural borders.

World Language Skills

Fox along with Grant and Salahshoor argue successfully (this volume) the need to tailor teacher preparation programs with appropriate teaching content in the areas of second language acquisition, culturally appropriate pedagogy, and effective practices for intercultural competence in our international classrooms. The importance of understanding second (or third or fourth) language acquisition begins with teacher education candidates who have acquired second language proficiency. The process of learning a second language develops cognitive skills, creative and problem-solving skills, cultural awareness, and competency among other areas (NEA, 2007). We should seriously consider requiring second language competency for all teacher education candidates. Further, as part of course work, all teachers should learn and apply language acquisition research in their teaching. As we have noted, the increasing number of students coming to school as learners of English need teachers who are skilled in language acquisition and create classroom environments that foster English language learning. Although the field of ESOL is growing rapidly, due to demands of the current student population, there will never be enough teachers of ESOL to serve our growing population; all teachers should be capable of being teachers of English to speakers of other languages.

Intercultural Competence

A number of authors comment on the need for teachers who demonstrate intercultural competence in the classroom, school, and community with whom they work. Intercultural competence like international education has suffered from multiple definitions and lack of clear guidelines on the development of those skills associated with intercultural competence. For the purposes of this volume, we situate our thinking with Deardorff's (2009) synthesis of critical elements. Foremost in the discussion of intercultural competence is that it is a lifelong process of developing understanding of cultural values, communication styles, and worldviews to "better understand others' behaviors to interact effectively and appropriately with others and, ultimately to become more interculturally competent" (p. xiii). For teacher education and teacher candidates, the one course, one experience, one "shot" opportunity can, at best, begin the conversation and at worst entrench stereotypes and generalizations about others and their worldview. Having an immersed clinical experience in a different culture is not sufficient to become interculturally competent; it must be coupled with reflective guidance from teacher education faculty to question personal perspectives, promote identity development, develop understanding of culture, build relationships, and start the process of becoming interculturally competent. Day's chapter (this volume) on building relationships with international families through the cultural reciprocity process is a good example of how to begin with teacher candidates to develop intercultural competency. Assessing intercultural competence could also be addressed in teacher education programs; demonstrating competency in content and pedagogy through examinations such as Praxis I and II is important, but the ability to transmit and engage students cross-culturally is equally important.

Course Work

In many ways this could be the easiest and first line of internationalization of teacher education programs in the United States. Historically, as we once reviewed curricula for a multicultural perspective, culturally relevant resources, and pedagogical styles, we should continue to review course work in light of international perspectives, global systems, and global problems and foster problem-based learning that engages candidates in creative and analytical thinking. A wide variety of materials and resources are available online for teacher education programs to utilize in the expansion of perspectives into international areas. For example, the Peace Corps contributes a number of lessons, plans, and resources through their World Wise Schools website. The Global Issues Network supports ways to engage students in worldwide problems though empowering them to work internationally with their peers to develop solutions for global issues. The Student News Action Network allows students to take the concept of the "school newspaper beyond school walls and the confines of print media, allowing students to work collaboratively on a global level to create an interactive, multimedia-rich student-driven online newspaper" (Student News Action Network, 2011). How are we developing these same skills and dispositions in our teacher candidates through their course work and clinical experiences in teacher education? Where are the international, global resources and experiences (beyond social studies) in our literacy courses, science, mathematics, and other content disciplines? How do we involve through our university courses our candidates with other teachers across the world teaching English? How do we demonstrate the value of the "mother tongue" for U.S. students? Where do we examine differences in pedagogical approaches that influence what students bring to the classroom and how they engage in learning?

There are a multitude of resources available to teacher educators that are beyond the scope of this chapter; the question goes back to intentionality—do we intentionally review and include international perspectives in our teacher education course work? Do we engage our candidates in experiences, connections, and activities with others who are significantly different from them? Do we bring a worldview to teacher education at the university?

In Closing

Secretary Duncan might be right; it is not a case of simply retooling teacher education. It is a case of conceptually reframing teacher education at the university to include international-intercultural experiences, designing course work that reflects international perspectives and engages candidates in creative thinking and problem solving about global issues, ensuring that candidates are multilingual, and coming to the realization that we are an international community of teachers and learners in the United States. A number of well-respected authors represented in this book and others have called for the development of international teacher education curricula, clinical experiences, and intercultural competence for U.S. teacher candidates. Our attempt in this book has been to create a foundation from which we can move forward from discussion to action, from the sidelines to center stage.

REFERENCES

American Association for Childhood Education International (ACEI). (2007). *Elementary education standards and supporting explanation*. Retrieved from http://acei.org/education/ncate.

Arhar, J., Milam, J., Shively, J., & Chase, M. (2010). Internationalizing perspectives and practices in teacher education: Developing a collaborative model for Ohio. Grant funded by the Longview Foundation, Falls Church, VA.

Ball, D., & Forzani, F. (2010). What does it take to make a teacher? *Phi Delta Kappan, 92*(2), 8–13.

Banks, J. A. (2004). Multicultural education: Historical development, dimensions, and practice. In J. A. Banks & C. A. McGee Banks (Eds.), *Handbook of research on multicultural education* (2nd ed., pp. 3–29). San Francisco: Jossey-Bass.

Brodie, L. (2010, May, 21). Are standardized tests ruining social studies? Retrieved from http://www.psychologytoday.com/blog/love-in-time-homeschooling/201005/standardized-testing-what-happens-history-0.

Cushner, K., & Brennan, S. (2007). The value of learning to teach in another culture. In K. Cushner & S. Brennan (Eds.), *Intercultural student teaching: A bridge to global competence* (pp. 1–12). Lanham, MD: Rowman & Littlefield Education.

Cushner, K., & Mahon, J. (2007). The impact of overseas student teaching on personal and professional development. In K. Cushner & S. Brennan (Eds.), *Inter-

cultural student teaching: A bridge to global competence (pp. 57–87). Lanham, MD: Rowman & Littlefield Education.
Darling-Hammond, L. (2010). Teacher education and the American future. *Journal of Teacher Education, 62*(1–2), 35–47.
Deardorff, D. (2009). Preface. In D. Deardorff (Ed.), *The Sage handbook of intercultural competence* (pp. xi–xiv). Washington, DC: Sage.
Ewbank, A., Foulger, T., & Carter, H. (2010). Red Bull, Starbucks, and the changing face of teacher education. *Phi Delta Kappan, 92*(2), 25–28.
Fallon, D. (2010). A golden age for teacher ed. *Phi Delta Kappan, 92*(2), 33–35.
Futrell, M. H. (2010). Transforming teacher education to reform America's P–20 education system. *Journal of Teacher Education, 61*(15), 432–40.
Gardner, H. (2004). How education changes: Considerations of history, science, and values. In M. Suárez-Orozco & D. Qin-Hilliard (Eds.), *Globalization: Culture and education in the new millennium* (pp. 235–58). Los Angeles: University of California Press.
Gimbert, B., Desai, S., & Kerka, S. (2010). The big picture: Focusing urban teacher education on the community. *Phi Delta Kappan, 92*(2), 36–39.
Hill, I. (2007). International education as developed by the International Baccalaureate Organization. In M. Hayden, J. Levy, & J. Thompson (Eds.), *The Sage handbook of research in international education* (pp. 25–37). London: Sage.
James, J., & Davis, G. (2010). Striving for international-mindedness in teacher education: One program's journey. *Ohio Social Studies Review, 46*(1), 39–47.
Levine, A. (2010). Teacher education must respond to changes in America. *Phi Delta Kappan, 9*(2), 19–24.
Longview Report. (2009). Teacher preparation for the global age: The imperative for change. Falls Church, VA: Longview Foundation.
Mansilla, V., & Jackson, A. (2011). Educating for global competence: Preparing our youth to engage the world. New York: Council of Chief State School Officers and the Asia Society Partnership for Global Learning.
Merryfield, M. (1995). Teacher education in global and international education. *ERIC Digest*, ED384601, 1–6.
———. (2000). Why aren't teachers being prepared to teach for diversity, equity, and global interconnectedness? A study of lived experiences in making of multicultural and global educators. *Teaching and Teacher Education, 16*(4), 429–43.
National Council for Social Studies. (2010). *National curriculum standards for social studies*. Retrieved from http://www.socialstudies.org/standards.
NCATE. (2001). *Professional standards for the accreditation of schools, colleges, and departments of education*. Washington, DC: NCATE.
———. (2008). *Unit standards in effect 2008*. Retrieved from http://www.ncate.org/Standards/NCATEUnitStandards/UnitStandardsinEffect2008/tabid/476/Default.aspx.
———. (2010). *Professional education unit*. Retrieved from http://www.ncate.org/Accreditation/ScopeoftheNCATEReview/ProfessionalEducationUnit/tabid/293/Default.aspx.

———. (2011). *About NCATE*. Retrieved from http://www.ncate.org/Public/About/NCATE/tabid/179/Default.aspx.
NEA. (2007). *The benefits of second language study*. Retrieved from www.sde.ct.gov.
Olson, C., Evans, R., & Shoenberg, R. (2007). *At home in the world: Bridging the gap between internationalization and multicultural education*. Washington, DC: American Council on Education.
Romano, R., and Cushner, K. (2007). Reflections on the importance and value of the overseas student teaching experience. In K. Cushner & S. Brennan (Eds.), *Intercultural student teaching: A bridge to global competence* (pp. 215–26). Lanham, MD: Rowman & Littlefield Education.
Starnes, B., Saderholm, J., & Webb, A. (2010). A community of teachers. *Phi Delta Kappan, 92*(2), 14–19.
Student News Action Network. (2011). *About us*. Retrieved from http://newsaction.tigweb.org/about.
U.S. Department of Education. (2009). *Teacher preparation: Reforming the uncertain profession—remarks of Secretary Arne Duncan at Teacher's College, Columbia University*. Retrieved from http://www2.ed.gov/news/speeches/2009/10/10222009/html.
Zeichner, K. (2010, June). *Preparing globally competent teachers: A U.S. perspective*. Keynote address presented at the Colloquium on Internationalizing Teacher Education Curriculum, NAFSA: Association of International Educators, Kansas City.
Zhao, Y. (2010). Preparing globally competent teachers: A new imperative for teacher education. *Journal of Teacher Education, 61*(15), 422–31.

Index

ACEI, 241
ACEI Standard 32, 241
achievement gap, 20, 26
accountability, 77, 80, 81
action research, 181, 185, 188–91, 194–96, 199–200
adequate yearly progress (AYP), 26
Advanced Placement Program (AP Program), 155–63
American Council on Education, 242
AP audit, 157–58, 171
AP electronic discussion boards, 159, 163
AP International Diploma, 161–62, 171
Asia Society, 24, 25, 27, 32
Australia, 93–109
authentic realia, 187

Bethel University, 169
bilingual/bilingualism, 60, 62

Cambridge International Teacher Certificate, 169
capitalism, 29, 30, 79, 90
citizenship, 106
civil rights, 18, 19, 31
classroom culture, 17, 34
CLCC (cognitively and linguistically complex classrooms), 59

clinical experiences, 247
collaboration with families, 129
collaborative projects, 223–26; The Asia Society, 224; ePals Global Community, 224, 232; The Tiger Eye Global Community, 224
college admissions, 155, 160, 170
college board, 156–58, 160, 171
Common Core Standards, 77, 81, 85, 89, 90
competence, language, 74; actional, 69; communicative, 63, 68, 69, 74; discourse, 69; linguistic, 69; psycholinguistic, 68; socio-cultural, 74; socio-linguistic, 69, 70; strategic, 69
competencies, 24, 27, 30, 34
competencies, twenty-first century, 22, 24, 25, 26, 31, 34, 36, 40, 87
community of practice, 181, 196–97, 201
conflict, 139, 141, 152
contextually relevant teaching/instruction, 215
contextually responsive teaching/instruction, 205, 213
Cooke Islands, 95
cosmopolitanism, 30, 78, 88, 89
coursework, 249

254 Index

critical friend, 181, 184–85
critical multicultural education, 20, 21, 25, 26, 29, 34
critical pedagogy, 21, 26, 28, 29, 31, 133
critical-thinking skills, 87
cross-cultural, definition of, 42
cross-cultural diplomacy, 25
cross cultural learning, 65, 73
cross-cultural sensitivity, 25, 27
cross-disciplinary, 61, 74
culture, 60, 65, 67, 68, 71, 72, 73
cultural consultants, 225
cultural deprivation hypothesis, 20
cultural dissonance, 116
cultural reciprocity, 118
culturally diverse, 96
Cummins, 69, 70
curriculum, 94

decentralization, 80
demographics, 18, 19, 34, 35
Developmental Model of Intercultural Sensitivity (DMSI), 43–45, 48
digital stories, 222
diversity, 18, 19, 20, 21, 22, 26, 27, 31, 32, 86

educational change, 244
English: English as a Foreign Language (EFL), 64, 66; English as a Global Language, 66; English as a Second Language (ESL), 64; English for Speakers of other Languages (ESOL), 62, 68; English as an International Language (EIL), 66; English as a Lingua Franca (ELF), 66; English as a World Language (EWL), 66; English language learners (ELLs), 62, 63
ethnocentrism, 25, 27

family functions, 115
FAST TRAIN, 243

foreign language. *See* language, foreign
Friedman, Thomas, 221
Fulbright Teacher Exchange Program, 33

George Mason University, 169
global citizenship, 22, 23, 87
global competency, 27
global consciousness, 22, 23, 24, 29
global dimension of learning, 84, 88, 89
global economy, 24, 25
Global Financial Crisis, 79, 85
global marketplace, 29, 34
global mindedness, 17
Global Nomads, 54
global studies, 27
global warming, 23
Global Workshop Architecture, 166–68, 170, 172
globalism, 27
globalization, 29, 30, 77, 78, 79, 84, 87
Goals 2000: Educate America Act, 83, 85

Harvard's Project Zero, 29
Head Start program, 20
heritage language, 63
Hidden Curriculum, 17
Human rights, 18, 23, 28, 29

IB Diploma, 165, 170
IB teacher awards, 167, 169, 172
identity, 26, 27, 28, 29, 32, 33, 39, 60, 148, 149
immigrant, 139, 141, 146–48, 150, 152
immigration, 18, 19, 20
intercultural, 42, 61, 74
intercultural competence, 42–54, 248; defined, 42–43; measurement of, 43–47; of U.S. students, 46; of U.S. teachers, 45–46; role of experience in, 48–54; role of technology in, 53–54
Intercultural Development Inventory (IDI), 43–47, 48

International Baccalaureate, 97, 164–70, 242
International Baccalaureate Diploma Programme, 155, 163–70, 172
International Education and Resource Network (iEARN), 54
international mindedness, 6, 61, 78, 88, 150, 164, 167–70
international student, 141, 147, 148, 150
internationally minded faculty, 245
internationalization, 22, 26, 30, 39, 78, 93, 94, 95
international education, 17, 22, 23, 24, 25, 26, 27, 30, 32, 33, 34, 35
Italy, 95

Kent State University, 243
Kenyon Plan of 1950, 156-57
Krashen, 68, 69

language, 59–74; across the curriculum, 62; education, 68; first/home, 72, 74; foreign/world, 61, 62, 63, 67; heritage, 59, 60, 61, 63; language teaching/language teachers, 61; proficiency, 5; second language acquisition transfer, 69; world, 60, 63. *See also* second language acquisition/SLA research
linguistic, 67, 69, 70, 73; imperialism, 206. *See also* psycholinguistic; sociolinguistic
Literacy Education in Diverse Settings (LEADS), 33
Longview Foundation, 243

Malaysia, 95
metalinguistic awareness, 73
Mezirow's theory of transformative learning, 48–49
Montessori, 23, 24
migration, 2, 3, 96
multicultural, definition of, 42

multicultural education, 17, 18, 19, 21, 22, 25, 26, 27, 30, 31, 32, 34
multicultural international education, 32
multiculturalism, 18, 26, 27, 29, 31, 32, 34, 38, 78, 84, 87, 89
multiuser virtual environments, 226–30, 231–32; massively multiplayer online games, 228; research on, 228–30; Skoolaborate, 227; TappedIn, 227–28, 232

A Nation at Risk, 24, 38, 81, 85
National Association of Multicultural Education (NAME), 19, 31, 38
National Collaboration on Diversity in the Teaching Force, 21, 38
National Council of Teacher of Mathematics, 82-83
National Education Summits (1989 & 1994), 83
national security, 23, 24, 25, 27, 38
national standards, 238, 246
nationalism, 22, 26, 27, 30, 78
NCATE, 240
NCATE Standard 4, 240
neoliberalism, 29
New Public Management, 80
No Child Left Behind Act (NCLB), 26, 81, 84
North American Free Trade Association (NAFTA), 29

Oakland University, 169
Ohio International Education Advisory Committee, 22, 24, 25, 29, 38
Online Curriculum Centre, 168–69, 172
Organization for Economic Co-operation and Development (OECD), 79, 80
Oxfam, 88

parents: involvement, 118, 129; role, 117

Paolo Friere, 21
Partnership for 21st Century Skills, 24, 31
Peace Corps, 54
peace education, 22, 37, 39
pedagogy, 97
A People's History of the United States of America, 31, 40
preschool, 20, 29, 34, 37
problem-based learning, 186, 193, 249
professional development, 17, 28, 35
Professional Learning Communities, 17, 35
professional portfolio, 178–79, 184–85, 189, 191, 195, 197, 199–200,
professional standards in Russia, 181–82
professional standards in United States: science, technology, engineering, and mathematics, 180; foreign language (world language), 180–81
Programme for International Student Assessment (PISA), 80, 86, 97
psycholinguistic, 68, 69

Race to the Top, 84, 85
reflective practice, 183–85, 190, 200
reform of teacher education, 238
refugee, 139–52; children, 140, 143–52; defined, 141; families, 146–49; movement, 142, 143, 145, 149
revolutionary multiculturalism, 29

School and College Study of Admission with Advanced Standing, 156
schools, heritage language, 63
second language acquisition, 67–73
second language acquisition research, 66, 67–73; common underlying proficiency, 69; Krashen's monitor model, 69; Krashen's input hypothesis, 69; thresholds hypothesis, 69
segregation, 18, 38

Singapore, 95
sister school, 32
SLA. *See* second language acquisition
SLA research. *See* second language acquisition research
social justice, 18, 27, 28, 29, 34
social networking, 230–31
sociolinguistics, 70
South Africa, 90, 95
South Korea, 95
Stages of Cultural Identity, 27, 32
standardization, 26, 31, 77, 80, 81
student beliefs, 107
study abroad, 33, 47, 49

teachers and teacher education, 140; candidates, 246; formation, 89, 90; future, 105; implications, 231–32; in-service, 67, 71, 150; pre-service, 60, 67; preparation, 19, 20, 21, 35, 60, 67, 150; professional development, 60
teacher education, 21, 22, 28, 32, 33, 34, 37, 38, 39, 40
technology, 25, 32, 36, 37
technology integration, 184
The State of State Standards, 84
Toyota International Teacher Program, 33, 34
trauma, 139–41, 144, 146, 147, 150, 151
Trends in International Mathematics and Science Study (TIMSS), 80, 86

United Nations Millenium Development Goals, 29
U.S. Department of State, 33, 142, 175, 177

video, 222
video conferencing, 230
video sharing websites, 222
Virtual Field Trips, 222–23
voyeurism, 222, 231

war, 139, 140, 142, 145
WebQuests, 223
World Bank, The, 79
World Council for Curriculum, 108–109
world Englishes, 65, 66, 67

world language skills, 248
world languages, 68

YouTube, 222

Zhao, Yong, 221

About the Contributors

COEDITORS

Beverly D. Shaklee is professor and director of the Center for International Education, College of Education and Human Development, at George Mason University. She serves as a member of the Board of Trustees for the Alliance for International Education. Her areas of research and scholarship include international teacher education, peace education for teachers, and international mindedness in U.S. teachers.

Supriya Baily, assistant professor at George Mason University, works with practicing teachers through the Initiatives in Educational Transformation master's program and teaches in the International Education PhD Program. Her research interests address issues of power and nonformal education among rural women, the challenges facing secondary education in India, and the role of internationalism in teacher preparation.

CONTRIBUTORS

Kenneth Cushner is professor of Intercultural Teacher Education at Kent State University. He writes extensively in the areas of international and intercultural education and training. A former Fulbright scholar and founding fellow of the International Academy for Intercultural Research, he is current director of the Consortium for Overseas Student Teaching.

About the Contributors

Kimberley Daly, doctoral candidate at George Mason University, works with the Mid-Atlantic Association of IB World Schools as their college partnership consultant. Her research interests include university recognition of International Baccalaureate Programmes in the United States and abroad, policy in higher education, the Advanced Placement program, and teacher professional development.

Monimalika Day was an assistant professor at George Mason University, now returned to India. Her research focuses on collaboration between educators and families, inclusion of children with special needs, and preparing educators to develop inclusive classrooms. She is currently working as a consultant with Ambedkar University in Delhi.

Laura C. Engel, assistant professor of International Education and International Affairs, teaches in the International Education Program at George Washington University in Washington, D.C. Her research interests include international education policy, international large-scale assessment, and issues of citizenship and governance in Europe.

Rebecca K. Fox, associate professor of Education and Coordinator of the Advanced Studies in Teaching and Learning Program at George Mason University. Her research focuses on teacher professional development, portfolios, and reflective practice. In 2010 she was both the recipient of the Mason Teaching Excellence Award and named *Chevalier dans l'Ordre des Palmes Académiques* by the French government.

Wendy Frazier, associate professor of science education at George Mason University, is associate director of Mason's Center for Restructuring Education in Science and Technology. Her research interests include factors influencing K–12 teachers' efficacy for utilizing problem-based learning grounded in community issues as an instructional approach to STEM teaching.

Rachel Grant, associate professor of multilingual/multicultural education and director of the Center for Language and Culture at George Mason University. Her research interests include application of critical pedagogies focusing on intersections of race, class, and gender in first and second language literacies, literacy teacher education, and urban education.

Margret Hjalmarson is associate professor of mathematics education at George Mason University. Her research interests include engineering education, mathematics specialists' knowledge and development, and classroom-based assessment of students' learning of mathematics. She earned her PhD in mathematics education and an MS in mathematics from Purdue University.

Natasha G. Kolar, content analyst at Hanover Research, works on strategic research briefings for clients covering a wide variety of topics ranging from campus internationalization to adolescent literacy interventions. A recent graduate of the International Education Program at George Washington University, Natasha previously worked as a primary and middle school teacher both in the United States and in Malawi, Africa.

Kate Olden, an early childhood educator in Washington, D.C., works with English language learners and their families. Her research focuses on the transition to first grade and the incorporation of alternative instructional methods into formal education. She holds a master's degree in international education from George Washington University.

Maryam Salahshoor, doctoral student in multicultural/multilingual at George Mason University, works as a graduate research assistant. Her research interests address issues of multilingual education and exceptionality, and the challenges facing multilingual education in identifying and serving students with disabilities.

Debra Sprague, associate professor, works with teachers in the Elementary Education and the Advanced Studies for Teaching and Learning (ASTL) programs. Her research interest addresses the affordances of technology for teaching and learning. She served for ten years as the editor for the *Journal of Technology and Teacher Education*.

Libby Tudball is a senior lecturer in education and director of professional placements and partnerships in the Faculty of Education, Monash University, Australia. She supervises higher-degree research students, and her research interests include teacher professional learning, internationalization of education, Asian studies, social education, civics and citizenship, and values education.